Development A

MW01120361

Development Administration

S.A. PALEKAR

Professor & Chairman
Department of Studies and Research in Political Science
Gulbarga University
Gulbarga, Karnataka

PHI Learning Private Limited

New Delhi-110001
2012

₹ 250.00

DEVELOPMENT ADMINISTRATION
S.A. Palekar

© 2012 by PHI Learning Private Limited, New Delhi. All rights reserved. No part of this book may be reproduced in any form, by mimeograph or any other means, without permission in writing from the publisher.

ISBN-978-81-203-4582-9

The export rights of this book are vested solely with the publisher.

Published by Asoke K. Ghosh, PHI Learning Private Limited, M-97, Connaught Circus, New Delhi-110001 and Printed by Raj Press, New Delhi-110012.

Contents

Preface

Development is the keyword for the countries who have been moving from traditional towards the modern type, what Riggs calls from Agraria towards Industria, i.e., from agricultural-based-society to an industrialized society. The major tool for development in these societies is the administration. It is, however, unfortunate that people have distrust in administration due to former colonial legacy. They are also not sure of the capability of the administration to cope up with the new and growing tasks of development. In order to overcome this, there is a need for a democratic administration at various levels where the administrators and the public may approach each other without much barriers. There is a need to replace the traditional regulatory type of administration with the one with progressive orientation. This administration, with a new orientation to look after the social-economic change, is known as Development Administration.

In this book an attempt has been made to present an integrated picture of the Development Administration. The issues chosen to examine are the theoretical constructs in the concepts of Development and Development Administration; features of administration in developed and developing countries; the programme and project management; the planning machinery in India; the public sector; and a range of social and welfare services in India. The book argues that the state has a critical role to play in socio-economic development and it has to face new challenges resulting from liberalization and globalization. It also analyses the impact of economic reforms on the social sectors in India. It highlights the development issues, approaches and strategies which should be considered under different national, social, economic and administrative settings. The book is useful to the policy makers, practitioners, teachers and students of Public Administration and Political Science.

I thank the editorial and production teams of publishers PHI Learning for their careful processing of the manuscript and continuous co-operation and publishing of the book.

S.A. Palekar

Chapter

1

Development Administration
An Overview

DEVELOPMENT ADMINISTRATION: MEANING

Development administration as a concept is, for the large part, a by-product of public administration. To be more precise, development administration is a by-product of the comparative study of public administration and has a distinctive identity in relation to developing countries, which strive to attain self-generated economic growth. The explanation for such a trend is that conventional public administration does not offer an adequate response to some of the primary organizational needs of development. The expansion of concerns beyond conventional 'public administration' towards 'development administration' neither denies the many valuable contributions of the applied discipline of public administration, nor does it ignore the enormous and enlarging needs for competence in administrative performance that are inherent in development. The basic assumption behind the shift to development administration is simply that something more was also needed.

Before making a further distinction between general administration and development administration, it is necessary to understand the meaning and nature of the term development administration.

Development administration which continues to hold the stage, in spite of its fragile nature was first coined by U.L. Goswami, in 1955, but formal recognition was given to it when Comparative Administration Group of the American Society for Public Administration, and Committee on Comparative Politics of the Social Science Research Council of the USA laid its intellectual foundation.[1] Since then, there have been a number of definitions and interpretations of development administration.

Development administration is used in two interrelated senses. First, it refers to the administration of development programmes, to the methods used by large-scale organizations, notably governments, to implement policies and plans, designed to meet their developmental objective. Secondly, it involves the strengthening of administrative capabilities. These two aspects of development administration, i.e. the administration of development and development of administration are intertwined.

1

Viewed from any angle, the fact remains that development administration is essentially a concept of administration which is action-oriented rather than structure-oriented. In a broader sense, Weidner views development administration as "the process of guiding an organization towards the achievement of progressive, political, economic and social objectives that authoritatively is determined in one manner or another."[2] Following the initial attempt made by Weidner, several prominent scholars, notably Riggs, Heady, Montgomery, Esman and Pye have made substantial contributions to articulate the concept and its implications, chiefly as a by-product of their comparative studies of administrations in the developing countries of Asia and Latin America.[3] To Montgomery, development administration connotes "carrying planned change in the economy or capital infrastructure and to a lesser extent in the social services especially health and education".[4] For Merle Fainsod, "it embraces the array of new functions assumed by developing countries, embarking on the path of modernization and industrialization. Development administration ordinarily involves the establishment of machinery for planning, economic growth and mobilization and allocating resources to expand national income.[5]

Donald Stone has analyzed the development administration in terms of plans, policies, programmes and projects towards the achievement of developmental goals. He regards development as the dynamic change of a society from one state of being to another, regardless of the objectives of the country or the scope and character of plans and programmes. An essential to development in administration, broadly development administration is concerned with achieving national development. The goals, values and strategies of change may vary, but there always are generic processes through which the agreement on goals is reached, and plans, policies, programmes and projects (the four Ps) are formulated and implemented. Development administration, therefore, is concerned primarily with the tasks and processes of formulating and implementing the four P's in respect to whatever mixture of goals and objectives may be politically determined.[6]

To sum up, development administration covers both the administration of development (i.e. public administration as an instrument of national development) and the development of administration (i.e. measures to enhance the administrative capacity for development). It is an action-oriented and goal-oriented administrative system[2] which not only involves the study of a traditional and routine type of administrative system, but also is more directed towards the dynamics of an administrative system with a view to judging its capacity as an instrument of programme planning and execution.

DISTINCTION BETWEEN DEVELOPMENT ADMINISTRATION AND CONVENTIONAL ADMINISTRATION

The given definitions of development administration do not clearly distinguish it from conventional administration. It is only the word development that distinguishes it from the subject of conventional public administration. The basic problem arises from the limitations of the traditional theory of administration. The theory was propounded mostly on the basis of western experience, which was, by and large confined to highly definable and discrete organizational activities. Consequently, it was, relatively easy to develop an administrative theory capable of analyzing various organizational situations.[7] And it was good as far as it went. But the theories of organization management and human relations were found unable to suggest a system capable of integrating the confusing welter of social, economic, political and administrative parameters which dominate and characterize the development situation. In most of the key areas of development administration, it is difficult to observe any uniform pattern either in the activities or in the behaviour of the various elements. In the diffused sectors such as agriculture, education, community development, health, family planning and many areas of social welfare, it is virtually impossible to establish clear cut roles for social economic political and administrative institutions in development administration. As a result, the various institutions and processes working in the developmental context criss-cross each other causing considerable confusion in their working while the existing administrative theory remains in the side lines.[8] To pin-point the areas where the two types of administration do not meet, the following points are raised:

(a) Public administration as a discipline and as a field of applied technologies is generally concerned with making things better. Efficiency, rationality optimization and control are its catch phrases. 'System improvement' is the name of its most common game. Decision-making is an important element, but the focus is on implementation of decisions, and it is customarily assumed that the important underlying goals are given. Development administration claims an important share in policy making and in the choice of ends not the most basic aims of State, but important pragmatic goals or purposes.[9]

(b) Public administration is concerned with problem-solving. Development administration puts emphasis on problem finding, rejecting the policy administration dichotomy, development administration also rejects the problem defining/problem solving dichotomy[10]:

(c) Development administration does not limit its concern to the design and building of systems. It does not exclude a concern with "making things work better: but it embraces a more basic concern determine what kinds of things are likely to work as well as how to make them work."[11]

Tarlock Singh distinguishes development and conventional administration in the following manner.[12]

(a) In all branches of administration there is an element of hierarchy and levels of responsibility. But if the lines of authority as they operate in revenue administration or police administration were to prevail in the field of development, it would be extremely difficult to draw the potential knowledge and creative capacities of individuals working at different levels into the general scheme of development. In other words, the very process of development demands a system of open exchange and communication between various levels, so that in a real sense, the gaps caused by hierarchy may be overcome. However, it is not so easy to achieve because many public servants are not well-trained in taking along those functioning at the lower levels of responsibility, as their colleagues and partners in a common enterprise.

(b) The second distinction between general and development administration is that when there is so much to be done and development embraces a very wide range of activities, the only way to get the work done is to divide it between a number of agencies. Therefore, various ways have to be searched for achieving coordination between many agencies engaged in allied and complementary tasks. This is the reason why it becomes more difficult to escape boards and committees, and more essential to undertake pre-planning, to have in view a clear scheme for enmeshing diverse activities into a common design, and to define responsibilities with a great care. Thus, we are brought back once again to the basic approach of a plan of action and of eliminating at the stage of planning as much of guess work as may be possible.

(c) The third special feature of development administration is that during development, many agencies and institutions which do not belong to the structure of the administration have a vital role to fill. Examples of this are cooperative movements, voluntary organizations, institutions for research and teaching, and trade unions. These represent an aspect of administration where only the first step has yet been taken, but there is little doubt that the entire scheme of development in India would fan out and strike deeper roots if we could ensure in real life an organic and continuous role at key points for institutions and groups outside the government. This is, in fact, to emphasize that for more than the physical targets of the investment undertaken development implies a process of change at the level of the community in skills and practices, and in ways of thinking.

Nature of Development Administration

A fairly good idea about the nature of development administration can be made on the basis of the above-discussed distinction from traditional administration and on the basis of the definitions of development administration given earlier. The peculiar features that emerge, indicate development administration as an action-oriented and goal-oriented administration. It is an innovative administration acquiring new skills and ideas and involving a lot of experimentation. It indicates a willingness to take risks in order to encourage change and growth. It emphasizes group performance and inter-group collaboration rather than individual performance. Along with this, individual roles are continuously changing under development administration as structures are shaped and re-shaped according to goal requirements. It involves employing of trained manpower and improving the existing staff using sophisticated aids for decision-making and adopting empirical approach to problem-solving as well as emphasizing problem finding. Development administration functions in a rapidly changing environment, and also strives to contribute to change the environment itself. Thus, it involves an interdisciplinary campaign looking for the new functions and new dimensions having flexibility, innovativeness, dynamism, participation and goal orientation as its basic elements. The nature of development administration may also be elaborated in enunciating section.

Structural and Functional Differentiation

In order to perform more and more diverse developmental functions, within the development administration system as a whole as well as within each organization comprising it, a high degree of division of labour or differentiation takes place to attempt to cope with such functions efficiently and effectively. This trend is further accentuated by the use of modern technologies. This means classification of functions into specialized types. This process is accompanied by structural specialization. The administrative structure tends to split up into specialized organizations with defined objectives and functions. New organizations with specific functions are also created. Generally for undertaking many types of economic and social functions, the existing departmental organization may be modified and more flexible, and autonomous organizations such as companies, commissions, corporations and boards may be set up as the need may arise.

Goal Orientation and Innovation

As defined by Jagannadham, development administration is a process of action motivated by and oriented to the achievement of certain pre-determined goals. Development administration in a way is concerned with the will to develop, mobilization of existing and new resources, and cultivation of appropriate skills to achieve development goals. The clustering of innovative ideas and activities involves a lot of risks. In fact, introduction of administrative and other innovations calls for "an earnest willingness to experiment and to take reasonable risks a willingness to question accepted practices in every aspect of administration and development, the ability and willingness to re-examine values which have hardened into dogma and apply to dogma pragmatic tests of its utility."[13]

Flexibility and Adaptability

Innovations and change call for flexibility and adaptability to the changing environment. The structure and functions of development administration are shaped by the requirement of goals. The system of development administration is required to have the capacity to adapt itself to changing general or contextual environment, and develop meaningful relations with its task environment which comprises other systems or organizations with which it has input–output relations or transactions. Administrative capability, thus, means the flexibility of the system (or set up) to adjust to both types of environment.

New Techniques and New Attitudes

While developing countries have taken up several new developmental responsibilities, they have for the most part still to adapt and modernize their administrative tools, techniques, organizational structures and staffing patterns to the requirements of development. This is not totally a new aspect of development administration, but in terms of urgency and magnitude of needs it is one of the core problems. Here, there is a wide scope for the adoption of advanced techniques of project planning and management programming and evaluation of results etc.[14]

Citizen's Participation

No development programme can be successful without the involvement and participation of its beneficiaries. One of the important dimensions of development administration is therefore, participation of citizens in the development process. Such participation in view of the wide scope and the large scale developmental functions and responsibilities of the government in the developing countries is a *sine qua non* for the success of development plans. Development administration pays increasing attention to programmes of community development, plans for recognition and reorientation of institutions of urban local government and mobilization of peoples' support. Citizen's participation is also required for accelerating social change in areas such as family planning, community development, etc.

Attitudinal Changes

Besides sharpening the skills of the personnel right, type of administration for development requires changes in the attitude of manpower. There is a growing recognition that the attitudes of the civil service are ridden with procedural rigidities of the law and order of the state and have not changed to meet the demands of new developmental responsibilities. Development administration does call for some new attitudes and values such as initiative, drive a sense of responsibility to make decisions, a shift in the emphasis from procedures to end results, a concern for the citizens comforts and needs, etc. This also requires a change in the individuals and group values and norms and attitude of the political executive.[15]

Need for Development Administration

As discussed above, conventional public administration does not offer an adequate response to some of the primary organizational needs of development. The emerging problem is how to combine skills which now exist in the developing countries and bring them to bear more effectively in action programmes which will accelerate economic growth, expand social well-being and improve public services. This is the essence of development administration.[16] Though conventional public administration made many valuable contributions to the applied side, yet it is a new oriented and development type of administration with a prime concern for change and innovation needed to carry out developmental tasks. The following reasons may be mentioned for the need of such an administration:

(a) To carry out development strategies, certain kinds of knowledge are to be mobilized and put to use. It requires enmeshing together economic, social, political and administrative elements.

(b) The organizational structure in the conventional administration is not to conduct the rapid socio-economic transformation. It has 'primary maintenance functions to perform, and lacks dynamics and innovative spirit for development.

(c) The role of government in the developing countries, which endeavour to accelerate their socio-economic development, differs from that in the developed counties.

(d) Public administration being the main instrument of socio-economic change in the developing countries is expected to play a vital role in building institutions such as co-operative societies, limited companies, public corporations, departmental organizations, etc., for sustaining and promoting industrial revolution to carry out industrial business and other public utility services for the people. It plays a vital role for the regulation and equitable distribution of essential commodities, trade unions and other interest political groups and other organizations based on national as against racial or regional loyalties, etc.,

(e) The task of translating policies and plans into accomplishments and deeds is difficult and arduous. Attention is not paid to fixing specific individual responsibility for producing results within agreed time schedules.

(f) To quicken the pace of development, the administration is expected to play an important role in human resource planning and development, which requires cultivation of technical, professional and managerial skills for running new industries and governmental organizations.

(g) Lack of appropriate attitudes and temperaments impedes many programmes of socio-economic development. It is the administration that needs to play the role of human resource development which involves changing the very attitude and temperament of people so that they may adjust to the needs and circumstances of technological civilization.

(h) There is a paucity of trained administrators with developmental skills. Also the long drawn procedures and methods are not in pace with the requirements of bringing about development.

(i) Public administration in the new and developing countries is conditioned by their colonial past, and is not suitable for carrying out developmental task, because it possesses the inherited features of centralization, impersonality, urban orientation, and lacks developmental orientation.

(f) Lack of participatory spirit fails many major programmes of societal transformation. Development administration has to be increasingly involved in securing the support, collaboration and participation of the people in the development efforts.

It cannot be stated exactly whether an administration is a non-development or a development administration. But certain essential features should be associated with administration to carry out effective developmental programmes. Some scholars have identified development administration with a high degree of innovation in the administrative system, which, in turn, is expected to encourage innovations in non-administrative areas. Weidner has stressed that "...the problem of how to maximize the effectiveness of a bureaucracy so that it contributes to growth in the direction of modernity or nation building and socio-economic progress is a problem of how to strengthen the innovational force in the bureaucracy.[17]

Scope of Development Administration

Take into consideration both aspects of development administration, i.e. administration of development and development of administration. The two aspects cover all the areas of governmental activities initiated to accelerate national development, touching all the dimensions of development viz., economic, social political and administrative. For *Riggs*[18] the scope of development administration extends to all those areas in which a government makes efforts to carry out programmes designed to reshape its physical, human and cultural environment, and also to the struggle to enlarge a government's capacity to engage in such programmes.

Tarlock Singh[19] divided the "field of study and action represented by development administration" into the following areas.

(a) Extension and community services

(b) Programme planning

(c) Project management

(d) Area development

(e) Urban administration

(f) Personnel development and administration

This is by no means a complete list and leaves out, for instance, areas such as the role of administration in guiding and regulating private activity, labour administration, financial administration, and others. A few words may be said here to draw attention to some significant features in each of these areas although frequently many different elements have to be seen together.

Extension and community services

Extension and community services are best seen as a form of partnership between government agencies, which provide technical, institutional or financial services, and the people. Their significance comes from the fact that they are a substitute for a system based on government action alone and are rooted in the belief that it is the community at the local level which receives the services, responds to them and in the process itself grows the initiative and responsibility. They imply community organizations of one kind or another at the base. The most difficult problem met within the extension is that, within the limits of the resources available, benefits do not easily reach the sections of the population who are in a situation of weakness, unable to contribute their own share or to claim what is due to them. Therefore, there is a need both for first-hand investigation of social situations, for better devices and instruments for dealing with social disabilities, psychological handicaps and other lacks, and for more comprehensive social, economic policies.

Programme planning

Problems of programme management run right through the entire range of development in various sectors of the economy. They include questions on organization of personnel delegation and attitudes in administration, but if one issue should be identified more sharply than any other, it is the critical role in programme management of planning for supplies and inputs. Invariably though, facts will assert themselves soon enough, plans err in accepting commitments and targets, in excess of supplies and inputs and other material resources which are in fact likely to be available. This failure in planning itself is a cause of much failure in implementation, which may occur partly due to lack of measurement and systematic estimation, and partly due to pressures have a way of persuading and planners may be tempted to leave difficult choices to others.

Project management

Project management, more especially management of public enterprises, has become an altogether crucial area, because major projects account for a high preparation of new investment and make demands on resources in men, materials and organization which are frequently underestimated. They call for decisions and procedures at the policy level which would facilitate their preparation and execution, and at the same time, there must be efficiency, initiative and compactness in the organizations responsible for them. They are undoubtedly a major challenge to administrative and technical capacity to achieve development. From the various management studies which have been undertaken, it can be said that whatever may have been the difficulties in the early stage, success and failure in the management of enterprises are not a matter of chance or only of favourable circumstances. It is proper to ask for complete accountability at every point and to judge by results as it is essential also to be ruthless against failure.

The life cycle of a project from inception to operation contains well-marked stages such as project definition and pre-construction, phase construction management and operation management. The techniques and methods required in each phase as a matter of sound planning and execution have now been sufficiently established in terms of India's own experience and the analysis to which this has been subjected. In presenting this view, it is also important to recognize that project authorities face several problems beyond their power, which can only be resolved by the agencies concerned at the level of government. The responsibilities of these agencies should therefore be equally stressed. For instance, it is for the agencies to ensure that such an enterprise has the requisite organization, competent top-level personnel and boards of directors with the necessary authority. They have to secure effective communication with the project and evolve a system of management information and control which will help anticipate problems and provide for them in advance.

Area development

Area development is an extremely difficult field of administration and one for which we do not yet have sufficient successful experience. It was perhaps too readily assumed in the past that the problems which arise at the area level would be adequately dealt with by men and institutions on the spot. It was not realized that area development requires a clear frame of delegations and procedures within which, both at the state level and all the districts and blocks level, each agency could act on its own as well as identification of the points at which its activities should be complementary to those of other agencies. At the district level, there are three sets of institutions which have to work together. The institutions are Panchayati Raj in the rural area, district officials functioning with the Collector outside the scheme of the Panchayati Raj and local self-governing institutions in towns and cities. The role of cooperative organizations and voluntary agencies at the area level should also be noted. Before we can make a success of area development, far more knowledge and understanding will have to be brought to bear on the problems at the local level. Local problems are best regarded as facts of difficult national problems, looked at in terms of given areas and communities. They demand no less expertise and knowledge from the higher levels of administration and from universities and research institutions than problems at the state and national level.

Urban administration

Municipal institutions in the urban areas first came into existence towards the end of the 19th century, but they have not yet become effective means of involving urban communities in the solution of their own problems or of the efficient administration of social services. To secure their effective working in relation to civic life and development, there is a need as much for a changed outlook towards urban problems and allocations of larger resources as for more intensive and systematic training.

Personnel development and administration

Over the past decade, training facilities have expanded at a rapid pace. To a large extent, the problem of numbers has been taken care of but not that of quality and motivation. There are still important areas requiring attention, specially where links between different sectors of activity and system of planning are involved. The organization of training programmes, availability of personnel at each level of receiving training, effective use of trained personnel, and adoption of improved methods of planning and management should form a composite scheme of development. In such a scheme, it would be necessary to impart, to each individual, a wider understanding of the objectives for which he is working, a greater commitment towards them, a capacity to cooperate and lead, and the courage to work for what may be right and to dissociate from what may be wrong along with the technical skills. In other words, in all personnel development, what has to be achieved is a combination of skills, character and motivation.

ADMINISTRATION FOR DEVELOPMENT

The administration system is considered to be the major instrument of socio-economic change, and it is precisely for this reason that a large number of administrative theorists accord primacy to the process of administrative development. It is held that only through an effective administrative system can the goals of nation building and socio-economic development be achieved. Developing countries frequently find that their public administration systems, (generally the product of the accretion of organizations and procedures over time) are inadequate or inappropriate for the purposes of national developmental tasks. The implementation gap, a common occurrence in many developing countries is to some extent a manifestation of the weakness and orientation of public administration systems.[20]

By and large, however, the public administration system tends to lag behind national development needs. A number of factors contribute towards this lag. The newly independent states among the developing countries give first priority to administrative requirements associated with the transfer of power and related urgency of nationalizing public services. It is only after building the minimal administrative infrastructure and staffing it with local personnel that these countries are able to give attention to the public administration requirements for economic and social development. Public administration also tends to lag behind development requirements in some developing countries which are in the process of articulating and revising their constitutional systems and political philosophies. Pending the finalization of basic laws and political institutions of a country, public administration becomes a difficult exercise. In other cases, changes in the form of government and political institutions may bring about a divergence between new national governments and orientation of the prevailing public administrative systems. Over and above, there are forces which impinge on all developing countries. These include the tempo of change and the rapidity with which new pre-occupations come to dominate public affairs. This is illustrated by the issues such as international monetary disturbances, inflation, food energy to name only a few.[21]

With the growing multi-functional character of administration, it is being increasingly recognized that the traditional approaches to structural change alone may not be adequate. The traditional and obsolete method of administration not only create barriers to open communication but also tends to lower the morale and initiative of experts and specialists whose role should be central to the process of administrative change. A faithful adherence to rules and procedures becomes an end in itself, and the resultant inflexibility in the administrative process brings down the capacity of the administrative system to effectively respond to the demands of the changing environment. Joseph La Palombara rightly cautioned, "the time is evidently past when public officials were expected to sit on the developmental sidelines limiting their roles to the fixing of general rules and to providing certain basic services and incentives for those private entrepreneurs who are the major players in the complicated and exciting game of fashioning profound changes in economic and social system."[22] A system of public administration must have a sound base of rules and regulations, division of responsibilities and an efficient system of coordination for its smooth functioning. There must also be something much more than this. But the bureaucracy, except for minor and ad hoc changes, has confined its role to fixing up the legal framework. It has remained more or less bound by hierarchy functioning in accordance with predetermined laws, rules and procedures.

To make the administration conducive to successfully take up the developmental task, the entire structure of the governmental machinery needs an overhauling. It is argued that it would be desirable to create new structures to perform new functions relating to social transformations. An environment of innovation and experimentation with newer organizational models can help enhance the vitality of the administrative system. The development bureaucracy should be concerned with promoting creativity and, therefore, it should build up an ethos which rewards creativity and innovation.[23] Bureaucracy does not concern itself with all segments of society, and is often confronted with pressures and counter, pressures, of differing priorities conflicting tactics and a conglomeration of demands. It has to function in a social milieu and is acted on by other social institutions.[24] An important duty of a civil servant today is to canvass support for government policy. He also has to seek public participation in the execution of such a policy. He has to not merely remain responsive to popular needs and demands but also be responsible for fulfilling them. Development administration requires committed public officials who possess a sense of emotional integration with the policies and programmes, and identification with the interests of the common man. So to cope with the future challenges, there must be co-existence of administrative integration and innovative spirit.

EXERCISES

1. Discuss the meaning and nature of development administration.
2. Examine scope and need of development administration.
3. Write short notes on the following:
   (a) Conventional administration
   (b) Administration for development

REFERENCES

[1] Goswami, U.L., "The Structure of Development Administration", *Indian Journal of Public Administration*, Vol. I, 1955, pp. 110–18, quoted in Verma, S.P. and Sharma, S.K. (Eds.) *Development Administration*, IIPA, New Delhi, 1984, pp. x–xi.

[2] Weidner, Edward, "Development Administration: A New Focus for Research", in Ferrel Head and Sybll Stokes (Eds.), Papers on Comparative Public Administration, *Institute of Public Administration*, University of Michigan, Ann Arbor, 1962, p. 98.

[3] Khosla, J.N., Development Administration: New Dimensions, *Indian Journal of Public Administration*, Vol. XIII, No. 1, 1967, p. 16.

[4] Montgomery, John, "A Royal Invitation Variations on Three Classical Themes", in Montgomery and William J. Siffin (Eds.), *Approaches to Development: Politics, Administration and Change*, McGraw Hill, New York, 1966, p. 259.

[5] Fairisod, Merle, "The Structure of Development Administration", in Irving Swerdlow (Ed.), *Development Administration: Concepts and Problems,* Syracuse University Press, Syracuse, N.Y., Syracuse, 1963, p. 2.

[6] Stone, Donald C., *Introduction to Education for Development*, Brussels, 1966.

[7] Pai Panandiker, V.A., Introduction, in Pai Panandiker (Ed.), *Development Administration in India*, Macmillian, New Delhi, 1974, p. xi.

[8]　*Ibid.,* p. 103.

[9]　William J. Siffin. "Development Administration as a Strategic Perspective". in United Nations, Interregional Seminar on Major Administrative Reforms in Developing Countries, Vol. II, Technical Papers, Pt. 2 Falmer, Bringhton, United Kingdom, 25th October–2nd November 1971, New York, 1973, p. 153.

[10]　*Ibid.,* pp. 118–119.

[11]　*Ibid.,* p. 126.

[12]　Tarlok Singh, "Administration for Development", in Pal Panandiker, (Ed.), *Development Administration in India*, Macmillan, New Delhi, 1974, p. 7.

[13]　Kieloch, Edward A., "Innovation in Administration and Economic Development", *Indian Journal of Public Administration*, Vol. XII, No. 3, 1966, p. 610.

[14]　Khosla, J.N., "Development Administration: New Dimensions", *Indian Journal of Public Administration*, Vol. XIII, No. 1, 1967, p. 28.

[15]　Weidner, "Development Administration: A New Focus for Research", *op. cit.,* pp. 28–29.

[16]　Esman, Milton J. and Montgomery, John D., "Systems Approach to Technical Cooperation; the Role of Development Administration", *Public Administration Review*, Vol. XXIX, Sept–Oct. 1969, Washington D.C., pp. 508–9.

[17]　Weidner, Edward (Ed.), *Development Administration in Asia*, Duke University Press, Durham, N.C., 1970, p. 421.

[18]　Riggs. "The Context of Development Administration", in Riggs (Ed.), *Frontiers of Development Administration*, Duke University Press, Durham, 1970, p. 75.

[19]　Tarlok Singh, "Administration for Development", *op. cit.,* pp. 8–11.

[20]　United Nations, Department of Economic and Social Affairs, Public Administration and Finance for Development, New York, 1975, p. 41.

[21]　*Ibid.,* pp. 41–42.

[22]　La Polombara, Joseph, "An Overview of Bureaucracy and Political Development", in La Polombara (Ed.), *Bureaucracy and Political Development*, Princeton University Press, Princeton, New Jersey, 1967, p. 4.

[23]　Arora, Ramesh K., "Bureaucracy and Development—Themes and Variations", in A. Avasthi and Ramesh K. Arora, *Bureaucracy and Development: Indian Perspective*, Associated Publishing House, New Delhi, 1978, p. 225.

[24]　Jones, H. Moris, in C.H. Phillips (Ed.), Politics and Society in India, London, George Allen and Unwin, 1963, quoted in S.K. Sharma, *Development Administration in India*, p. 21.

2

Developed and Developing Countries

INTRODUCTION

Most countries in the world are either developed or developing. The nations of Western Europe, North America and English speaking dominions of the British Commonwealth are usually recognized as the developed societies. The newly independent poor countries of Asia, Africa and Latin America are called developing countries. We talk about and discuss developed and developing countries, but to explain exactly what we mean by these countries is not so simple, as it seems. Generally, the terms underdeveloped, backward, 'undeveloped' or poor has been used as synonymous and interchangeable terms till recently. However, in the current literature on the subject, the use of the term developing as it sounds more respectable in comparable terms, is preferred to underdeveloped, poor or backward. Different scholars have attempted to define developed, developing and undeveloped countries differently.

According to Prof. Jocob Viner, "A developing country is one, which has good potential prospects for using more capital, or more labour, or more available natural resources, or all of these to support its present population on a higher level of living".[1] Gunnar Myrdal has termed developing countries as soft states.[2] Coupled with these economic features, developing countries are run through traditional administration, based on outdated processes and procedures, corrupt practices and ill-equipped politico-administrative leadership.

Since development is a multi-dimensional concept or phenomenon, our study of the characteristics of developed and developing countries would be incomplete if we lay emphasis only on the economic features of these countries. Thus, we will have to understand the political, administrative, social and cultural aspects also. But the major difficulty is how to draw a common sketch of an underdeveloped country and a still more difficult task is to locate a typical country on the world map possessing the representative characteristics of an underdeveloped system. Some of the scholars have categorized all the underdeveloped or developing countries as:

(a) High income countries

(b) Middle income countries

(c) Low Income countries

This classification indicates that there are wide differences in the rate of economic growth of these countries and at the same time, these countries differ in various other aspects too. Some countries have developed faster than the others. The major points of difference amongst developing countries are:

1. They differ widely in advancements of technologies

2. Some of the developing countries are over-populated while others are under-populated

3. Some have communal land tenures while the others continue to follow the old individual tenure system

4. The developing countries also differ politically, socially, culturally and institutionally

5. Attitudes and aptitudes of their people differ widely

All these points of difference within the less developed world cause variations in their pattern and rate of economic development. But in spite of this diversity, there is a fundamental uniformity in the developing world. Although it is extremely difficult to locate a representative developing country, yet it is possible to trace some common characteristics of many developing countries. These common characteristics may not be found to be of the same degree in all the developing countries, nor are these the only features of a developing country. However, these characteristics do present in combination a typical picture of the poor world.

CHARACTERISTICS

For the sake of simplicity, we would discuss the characteristics of developing and developed countries under the following heads:

(a) Political characteristics

(b) Social characteristics

(c) Economic characteristics

(d) Administrative characteristics

It must be mentioned here that it is not possible to isolate political characteristics from social characteristics and so on. Thus, an element of overlapping while discussing these features cannot be ruled out. For instance, the social aspect of a country represents the macro-environment and all other systems are sub-systems of the social system. Similarly, the administrative system is directly or indirectly influenced by the prevailing system in a country.

Political Characteristics

Political stability

Most of the developing countries of the world suffer from incipient or actual instability. The instability may be a carry over of the patterns that were developed within the native movements against a colonial power. There is widespread frustration due to the unmet goals of development. Whatever political institutions exist in these countries they do not provide adequate representation to all communities. The feelings of discrimination among the members of diverse tribal, linguistic or ethnic groups have taken strong roots. Under these conditions, the developing countries cannot remain politically stable. For instance in a country like India, political instability is all pervasive. Feeling of discrimination amongst the Muslims, the Sikhs, the scheduled castes and scheduled tribes are increasing. At the same time the stimuli for violence are also present. All these factors make these countries politically unstable.

In the developed countries, political stability is the major requirement. At any cost, they want to keep their country politically stable. With this objective in view, these countries have developed political institutions which provide not only adequate representation to all communities, but have set strong traditions. The possibility of discrimination is very remote. Political parties play an important role in the national integration of the country. The governments come and go without any hue and cry. True democratic norms are followed.

Commitment to development amongst the political elite

Among the political elite of the developing countries, there is a lack of commitment. They are interested in achieving their personal goals rather than looking at the aspirations of the people. Their main aim is to retain power by all means. The recent happenings in various parts of India are indicative of this notion of acquiring power at the gun point. If such a situation prevails in the developing world, commitment to development among the political elite is a remote possibility. An interesting feature is that bad elements which have been discarded by the society are trying to enter politics for selfish ends. Smugglers, murderers and terrorists are trying to take the reign of these countries in their hands.

The situation in the developed world is altogether different. Among the political elite, there is a widely shared commitment to development, the commitment in the developed countries often takes on ideological trappings common goals are to increase agricultural or industrial production, living standards, improved programmes for public health, education and individual pensions, changes in the traditional roles of women or the lower castes; and change of one's loyalties from a tribe to the newly conceived nation".[3]

It does not mean that the developing countries are not willing eyeing these goals. However, the goals are never achieved, due to lack of commitment on the part of the political elite. Their first priority is to retain power. Some of the sincere leaders are willing to introduce drastic changes and are committed to nation building, but their actions are thwarted by those who are interested in their personal goals but a few sincere leaders are eliminated physically or politically by foul means.

Modernizing and the traditional elite

In underdeveloped countries, a lot of gap exists between modernizing and the traditional elite. The modernizing elite tend to be urban, oriented towards the West, well-educated and committed to political social and economic change. On the other side, the traditional elite tend to be oriented towards the rural world and local customs. They are bent towards the indigenous religion, and at the same time opposed to change. They consider this change a threat to the values.[4] The new elite may control the technological skills that are vital to the nation's development, but the older elite may retain the intense loyalties of the people in the country side and the urban slums. In fact, these two contrasting models of the elite in the underdeveloped countries generate internal conflicts. Under these circumstances and conflicts the energies for modernization and change cannot be channelised in the true sense.

Legitimacy of political power

The political system in underdeveloped countries is not always legitimate. In a number of countries, power is acquired through illegitimate means. The political systems in the underdeveloped countries can be divided into[5] the following:

(a) Traditional autocratic systems

(b) Autocratic elite systems

(c) Polyarchal competitive systems

(d) Dominant party semi-competitive systems

(e) Dominant party mobilization systems

(f) Communist systems

In the traditional autocratic systems, the political elite owe their power position to a long established social system which usually emphasizes inherited monarchy or aristocratic social status. Some of the examples of this system are Yemen, Saudi Arabia, Afghanistan, Ethiopia, Libya, Morocco and Iran. In some of the countries like Iran, major changes have taken place.

However, in autocratic elite systems, military professionals and sometimes civilians are the rulers, for example are South Korea, Thailand, Burma, Indonesia and Iraq.

In Polyarchal competitive systems, states like Philippines, Chile, Israel, Argentina, Brazil, Turkey and Nigeria have political systems that conform most closely to the models of western Europe and the United States of America. However, in dominant party semi-competitive systems, there is a dominant political party which holds the monopoly of actual political power, but other parties are legal though they do not have much control. Political power in this sense is not legitimate. Similarly in Communist Systems, the commitment is to the Marxist and Leninist ideology. Examples are North Korea, Vietnam and Cuba, In dominant party mobilization systems, the dominant party is usually the only legal party. Other parties, if permitted are surrounded by restrictive controls. Examples are Algeria, Bolivia, Egypt, Ghana and Mali.

According to Heady, in all these systems political power is not as legitimate as it is in the democratic systems of Western Europe and North America, which are the most developed countries of the world. To be more specific, political power in the developed world tends to be more legitimate and acceptable to the masses.

Range of political activity

The volume and range of political activity in various underdeveloped countries is less because of the absence of political consciousness amongst the masses. Whatever institutions exist are dormant. Since power is not legitimate in these countries, political activity too is in a restricted form.

On the other side, such a situation does not prevail in the developed world. In fact, these societies tend to have a welfare state. The welfare state arose to deal with the problems of industrialization, urbanization and rising populations which were a part of the process of development. Modern industry polluted the atmosphere and resulted in bad living conditions for the workers. The magnitude of problems increased so rapidly that it got beyond the control of the individuals and voluntary agencies. Hence, the state was more and more depended on protecting the helpless citizens. Thereby, there was a tremendous increase in legislative activity. This process naturally resulted in an extension of the functions of the political administrative systems.

Participation of the people in the political system

In developing countries, the interest and involvement of the people in the political system is not encouraging. Most of the people do not understand the importance of political activity because of illiteracy. However, in some countries like India, people do involve themselves and take interest in the political system of their country, but this participation is negligible in comparison with the developed world. In fact, in developed societies, people take a lot of interest and are usefully involved in the political system, although this does not necessarily mean active participation by the citizenry in political decision making. People in these countries are organized politically, and have strong pressure groups and play an important role in forming the policy of the government. The political party in power in developed countries cannot ignore the view point of the pressure groups in formulating the policy.

Rationality in political decisions

In our preceding discussion of the political elite, we indicated that underdeveloped societies are characterized by a strengthening tendency of the traditional elite. However, in the developed countries, there is a weakening tendency of the traditional elite. Under these circumstances, where traditional elite continue to have a lot of power and influence, it is difficult to make decisions on the basis of reason and also on secular lines. Political decisions are taken after passing all the norms of justice and reasoning in favour of one particular community or another. For instance, it is difficult to enforce monogamy among the Muslims by law in India today, because of political reasons. Similarly, the caste system still prevails among the Hindus, and many high caste Hindus continue to practise untouchability in parts of rural India. Even elections are fought on religions or caste basis. All these conditions clearly indicate that political decisions in the developing countries can never be on rational and secular basis unless some drastic changes take place and good sense prevails amongst the people in these countries. All these countries will have to be pragmatic in their approach if they intend to cope with the developed world.

Political features and development

There is an imbalance in the development of various political features. The former colonies within the developing world still try to retain some features of the legislative, executive and administrative forms of the former colonist power, resulting in a wide gulf between the formal procedures and actual practices. Because the legislatures and the executive departments are not sufficiently manned by experienced men. The combination of weak legislatures and inefficacious chief executive plus an ambitious military elite have led occasionally to coup or take overs by the army. Such a state of political uncertainty is a serious impediment to development in underdeveloped countries. However, such a situation does not exist in developed countries. These countries have created their own systems of Government in accordance with the wishes and requirements of the people. No such imbalance exists in these countries. If at all some tendencies crop up, the same are set right through democratic methods and procedures without ignoring the wishes of the masses. The possibility of coups or military take over is remote.

Political parties

Political parties have come to occupy an important position in the political system of both developed and underdeveloped countries. But it is rather unfortunate that the political parties in the underdeveloped countries have not delivered the goods to make the country politically stable. For instance, in a country like India, we have failed to develop a strong party system for providing clear alternatives to the people because of its multi-party character. There are various parties which are based on language, religion and caste. Again the political parties in India are characterized by laxity of discipline. This laxity of discipline among the members has been reflected in the ever-growing practice of defections which has greatly contributed to the instability of governments in the states. Further, the political parties in the underdeveloped countries have shown a tendency to foster narrow party interests, quite often at the cost of national interests. However, such a situation does not prevail in the developed countries. The political parties have clear programmes and the word defection does not exist in the political dictionary of the developed world. At the same time they provide clear alternatives to the masses. Caste considerations do exist in the developed world but are not that rigid, and at the same time, national interest are the upper most to the well-organized political parties in these countries.

Social Characteristics

In the developing countries, the allocation of roles is by ascription rather than by achievement. However, it is quite opposite so far as developed countries are concerned. Both, the developed and the developing or underdeveloped societies have social stratification. To be more specific, there are strata of classes and castes, but the chief difference between the developing and developed societies is that while in an underdeveloped society, the allocation of status is mainly by ascription or birth in the developed countries, it is determined by achievement rather than by ascription.

Caste structure

Even in developing countries, caste structure is rigid. In India, in lot of places people practice caste system, and intercaste marriages are sin. For it is interesting to note that the administrative system in our country bears resemblance to the system of stratification. Thus, we have in the administration classes I, II, III and IV. It is unthinkable and impossible for a member of class IV to be promoted to class I. Hence these classes partake of the characteristics of the castes. In the developed countries like the USA, there are no such rigid classes and promotion is from position to position according to the qualification.

Social conflicts

In the developed countries, the magnitude of social conflicts is less but in the developing countries such conflicts take the form of communal riots, regionalism and so on. For instance, in India, communal riots happened at many instances. It does not mean that such a situation does not prevail in the developed world. In these countries too, propagation of myths like racial superiority, colour discrimination and absolute nationalism etc., have resulted in communal riots, strikes, threats to peace, deaths or destruction. But the situation in these countries cannot be said to be that alarming. These are occasional outbursts. Because of these social conflicts, some powerful developed countries are trying to control the underdeveloped countries and want to keep them under their grip.

Economic Characteristics

Underdeveloped countries do not have a homogeneous nature or uniform problems. But still, it is possible to bring out some basic economic characteristics which are common to the underdeveloped economies.

Per capita income

Poverty is a paramount fact in the underdeveloped countries. In fact, a country is regarded as underdeveloped or poor when it has a very low per capita income and low standard of living as compared to the advanced countries like the USA, the UK, Australia, etc. An underdeveloped country is characterized as a poverty ridden area of the world. In this regard, it has been very rightly opined that underdeveloped economies are the slums of the world economy.

In comparison with the developed countries of the world, poverty is so acute in the underdeveloped countries that the gaps in per capita income are quite visible. The intense poverty in developing countries is apparent from the fact that in these countries 70 per cent of the income is spent on fixed items in comparison with 20 per cent in developed countries.

Primary producers

One of the basic features of an underdeveloped country is that it is a primary producer. In fact, the structure of production in an underdeveloped country is dominated by food stuffs and raw materials. A typical underdeveloped country is primarily agricultural. For instance, in a country like India, more than 70 per cent of the people depend on agriculture for their livelihood. However, in the developed countries it is negligible. In the USA and the UK only 4 per cent and 3 per cent of the population depend on agriculture, respectively. A well-known economist, J.K. Galbraith has rightly opined that too much dependence on agriculture can hinder the growth. In other words, a purely agricultural country is likely to be unprogressive even in its agriculture. Similarly, underdeveloped countries possess a small industrial sector. Since the underdeveloped economies have a predominantly agrarian character, the system of land tenure plays a significant role. Land is often fragmented into small holdings. For instance, in India the average farm size is below 2 hectares. However, in the USA it is over 125 hectares, and in the UK it is over 45 hectares.

Besides, lower productivity is another feature of agricultural production. The level of output per acre is very low in comparison with the developed world. For instance, the productivity of rice in Japan is more than three times than in India. A similar situation pertains to other crops also.

Natural resources

In the developing countries natural resources are there but they have not been fully exploited because of the lack of technical know-how. The general impression is that underdeveloped and developing countries are poor because they are in scarcity of natural resources. This is not true. However, one thing is certain. All the underdeveloped countries are not rich in all the natural resources. They have some resources in plenty and in some they are deficient. Even in the developed world the natural resources, in spite of their full exploitation, cannot satisfy the requirements of their masses. That is why it is generally said that India is rich, but the Indians are poor. This means we have rich resources, but they have not been fully explored or utilized as per our requirements.

It is quite interesting to point out here that nature has endowed underdeveloped and developing countries with plenty of water resources. Thus, we can say that underdeveloped countries are poor, because they have not succeeded in overcoming the problem of underutilization of natural resources.

Nature of economy

In almost all the developing countries there is economic dualism. That is to say they are composed into two sectors—market and subsistence.

But this situation in the developed countries is almost negligible or it is altogether absent. The market sector is in the urban areas. However, the subsistence sector is found in the rural areas. Both the sectors are completely opposite to each other. The former is modern and developed in terms of scientific advancements (as is the case in the developed world), and the later is primitive and underdeveloped. For instance modern transport and communication facilities like—cars, buses, trains, aeroplanes, palatial residential buildings equipped with all the modern gadgets, telephones, radios and televisions are all available in the cities. But on the other side, the subsistence sector is backward and primitive with subsistence farming as its main stay. Such a heterogeneous economy is rarely to be found in developed countries.

Level of technology

The level of technology in the developing countries is low. In the agricultural and manufacturing sectors, the techniques being followed in these countries are mostly backward and primitive. The technology which becomes outdated in the developed countries is borrowed by the underdeveloped world. Similarly, technological dual is also a very prominent feature of developing countries. For instance, in India, we find the most modern techniques side by side with the most primitive ones, which are prevalent in the production process. An example of this kind pertains to the textiles. The handicrafts are producing coarse cloth using crude and obsolete techniques on the one hand, and the textile mills are producing fine cloth with the most modern techniques on the other. This is a glaring case of technological dualism. To be more specific, we can say that in comparison with the developed countries, where modern technology is of utmost importance the underdeveloped countries do not make much use of modern technologies for production process. Such a situation is interlinked with so many other factors. According to Prof. Kurihara, "Deficiency of capital hinders the process of scrapping off the old techniques and the installation of the modern techniques. Similarly, illiteracy and absence of skilled labour force are the other major hurdles in the spread of techniques in the backward economies. Thus, it can be opined that technological backwardness is not only the cause of backwardness, but it is also the result of it".

Population pressure

Increasing population in the underdeveloped and developing countries is another striking feature. In India, for instance, population is growing at the rate of 2.5 per cent per annum. This population pressure is due to two major factors working simultaneously, i.e., high birth rates and declining death rates. On this count, the situation in the developed countries is not that alarming. The birth rate is generally low. Another interesting feature of the demographic pattern in the developing countries is that a large portion of the total population is in the younger age group. For instance the percentage of population below 15 years is over 45 per cent in Asia, Africa and Latin America, but in the USA it is only 25 per cent.

In terms of life expectancy, the developing and underdeveloped countries lag behind. For instance in India, it is 56 years, whereas in the USA and the UK it is 70 and 71 years respectively. From these figures, it is quite evident that in the underdeveloped countries, the number of persons dying at a younger age is larger and at the same time the span of productive years for the survivors is shorter in these countries. The result is the larger proportion of non-producers to producers, and the consequent heavy burden on the national economy on account of birth, bringing up, education, etc., of the unproductive age group, Prof. Harvey Leibeistein gives the demographic characteristics of the underdeveloped countries as follows:

(a) High fertility rate, usually above 40 per thousand;

(b) High mortality rate and low expectation of life at birth;

(c) Inadequate nutrition and dietary deficiencies;

(d) Lack of rudimentary hygiene, public health and nutrition and

(e) Rural overcrowding.

However, all these observations are partly applicable to all the developing countries.

Employment opportunities

In the developing countries, lack of employment opportunities keeps most of the people engaged in agriculture. But this is not the case in the developed world. However, it does not mean there is no problem of unemployment in these countries. In fact the technological revolution has simplified work procedures but several other problems including unemployment have come into the forefront. Still, the situation is not that alarming. However, in the developing countries, it is going from bad to worst. Apart from unemployment, there is the problem of disguised unemployment. Much of the labour force working in the farm sector can be removed without reducing agricultural output. For instance, it is often observed in India, that the whole family of the peasant farmer works on the family farm which may be very small in size. Disguised unemployment creates a situation in which it is difficult to identify any particular person as unemployed or underemployed in the family. It may be added that in a country like India, disguised unemployment is no more confined to the rural sector. It is gradually spreading to industry also. This new trend in our urban sector is providing a big drag on the economic progress of the country.

Quality of human resources

Human resources play an important role in the economy of every country. It is rather unfortunate that most of the developing countries lack quality in population. There is a high degree of illiteracy and the people possess a conservative outlook. They are after traditional and stick to old values of life and religious beliefs. The backwardness of the human resources is visible in many forms. According to W.A. Lewis, "Many people/workers do not want to work for wages regularly five or six days a week all the year round. They prefer to have a lower standard of living and more leisure. Thus, apathy towards hard work is generally a common feature in these countries." However, this situation does not exist in the developed countries because of the high level of education. People are willing to work day and night for material gains and at the same time to raise their standard of living. More importance is given to the individual well-being. It is this notion, which motivates them to work. On the other hand, more importance is given to the family, caste or class to which one belongs in an underdeveloped country. Prof. Aldwin very rightly opines that in the underdeveloped world, an individual's status is ascribed in terms of who he is rather than being achieved by his own efforts. To be more specific, people are evaluated not according to what they can do, but according to their position in a system of social classification by age, skin, kin, clan, caste, etc.,

Economic organizations

Another prominent feature of underdeveloped countries pertains to poor economic organizations. Various studies clearly indicate that economic institutions vital for economic development in these countries are not adequately developed. The banks and other credit agencies are not well-developed. For instance, in India, in spite of the vast infrastructure of banks and other institutions, both in the cities and the countryside, money lenders continue to play an important role. The illiterates and the poor lend money from them to fulfill their daily requirements. In fact, the poor economic organization of an underdeveloped country is directly related to its inefficient and unskilled administrative set up. On the other hand, banks and financial institutions are very common and well-developed in the advanced countries.

Entrepreneurial ability

We find that most of the underdeveloped countries do not possess dynamic entrepreneurial ability. In fact, lack of initiative and modern enterprise is one of the major reasons for underdevelopment. In the developed world, there is no dearth of entrepreneurship and people are ready to take risks and possess tremendous initiative for a new venture. However, people in the underdeveloped world are found wanting in entrepreneurial leadership. The social system with its caste rigidities, the forces of indigenous philosophy traditions and customs, distrust of new ideas, and lack of intellectual curiosity to discover new paths are some of the factors, which inhibit the emergence of dynamic entrepreneurial ability.

Availability of capital

Most of the developing countries are generally characterized as capital poor or low saving or low investing economies. The rate of capital formation in these countries is between 5 to 8 per cent which is regarded as the lowest rate. In contrast, in a country like Japan, it is over 45 per cent; and in Finland, it is over 35 per cent. In India, capital formation has touched 20 per cent. In spite of this, it has failed to deliver the goods to the people.

The problem of capital deficiency in an underdeveloped country appears to be quite serious when we interpret in term of capital in the broader perspective. In fact, capital deficiency in the underdeveloped countries is reflected in the techniques of production which these countries have adopted. Productivity in these countries is low. Low productivity causes shortage of capital which in turn results in low productivity. This is how the vicious circle of poverty operates in an underdeveloped country.

Reliance on the public sector

There is a high degree of reliance on the public sector for leadership. Many developing countries have evolved structures that have a socialist or Marxist orientation. The leadership comes from the public sector. At the same time there is heavy reliance on the bureaucracy for the management of the public sector.

Although the scenario is changing and the private sector is strongly coming up still in a number of areas, the public sector is dominant. This is generally not the case in the developed countries.

Administrative Characteristics

Degree of task specialization

Low degree of task specialization is a major characteristic of the administrative system in the developing countries. On the other side all advanced countries of the world have organized their administrative systems on the principle of task specialization. On this count, the differentiation or high degree of division of labour in the administrative system in a developed society has been greatly emphasized by Fred Riggs. To him, the developed societies are comparable to the diffracted multi-coloured light coming through a prism. The white or fused light is comparable to the medieval society. In the middle is the prismatic society. He compares the developing or prismatic societies to what happens within the prism where the light is being transformed into the multi-coloured spectrum. This is the prismatic model of Fred Riggs. In this model, the emphasis is on the degree of differentiation of functions in a developing society. In medieval India, an emperor like Aurangzeb was the executive, the legislature and the judiciary of his government, as he made the law, implemented it and also used to decide whether it had been justly enforced or not.

In a modern society, however, we have separate organizations to perform all these functions. This is what Riggs means by diffraction. It is interesting to point out that during the days of early British administration, the Indian Civil Service performed the functions or legislation, execution and also of adjudication. Infact, the members of the Indian Civil Service used to be nominated by Councils under the Indian Councils Acts, and thus, participated in legislation. At the same time, they were civil servants, and therefore, were the members of the executive. They also performed judicial functions. Now of course in India, the legislature, the executive and the judiciary are distinct from each other although in some states, the executive authorities at the district level continue to administer criminal justice. The district magistrate combines in himself responsibilities for the maintenance of law and order revenue collection planning and development, and for this, he has to maintain coordination and control over all the developments. The office of the district magistrate is thus still a good example of an undifferentiated structure. Such instances are rarely to be found in the advanced administrative structures of the developed countries.

Expansion and extension of administrative activities

In the developing countries, the magnitude of administrative activities is quite low because industrialization is not taking place rapidly. Most of the population is living in the country side. Although urbanization is taking place in the developing countries yet it is partial. In contrast, there is widespread expansion and extension of administration in the developed world. It is due to the large scale of industrialization and urbanization that the spread of scientific research in almost every field is quite fast. Information revolution has made the government work in the most simplified manner. Simple methods of administering are being evolved in these countries. Every effort is being made to minimize the widening gap between complexities and administrative procedures. But such a situation exists to a very extent in the developing countries.

Pattern of public administration

The pattern of public administration in the underdeveloped countries to a large extent imitates the West. It often imitates the administrative system of an erstwhile ruling power. The administrative system is often not an indigenous growth, but is borrowed largely from the developed countries. The developed countries, over a period of time have developed their own administrative structure according to the requirements of their society. They have evolved their own administrative models which are best-suited to them alone. Unfortunately, these administrative patterns have been adopted and incorporated by a number of erstwhile colonies in their own systems without much pre-thinking. The patterns borrowed from the west or from the ruling countries have shown disastrous results.

Professional level of bureaucracies

Bureaucracies in the underdeveloped societies tend to be deficient in skilled manpower. For these countries in order to accelerate the pace of their development such manpower is not suitable. In fact, the problem is generally not of employable manpower. There is almost universal overstaffing in the lower ranks such as those of assistants, clerks, typists and peons. The shortage is that of trained administrators. In India also with so much unemployment among the educated youth there is still a paucity of trained managers. However, such a situation does not prevail in the developed countries. The administrative system in those countries is considered to be professional and advanced. In these countries professionalization is a sign of specialization among the bureaucrats.

Bureaucratic interests

An interesting feature of the administrative system of the underdeveloped countries is that bureaucracies tend to serve their personal interests to a greater extent than to fulfill organizational objectives. It does not mean that the developed societies do not exhibit such desire. They do exhibit such desire but at the same time, they give the priority to the organizational objectives. In India and other developing countries, corruption is deep rooted amongst government officials. This means that they are often prepared to overlook the public interest for personal gains. Further, they tend to protect not only their individual interests but the interests of their social communities and administrative cadres such as IAS or PCS. This is called nepotism and favouritism. In the nutshell, we can say that favouritism and nepotism are a part of the administrative system in the developing and underdeveloped world, and have gone to the very roots of our society. To get rid of such negative developments seems to be a remote possibility.

Discrepancy in form and reality

There is a widespread discrepancy in form and reality in the administration of the underdeveloped countries. Riggs calls this phenomenon as formalism.[6] It reflects the urge to make things look somewhat more as they ought to be rather than what they really are. For instance, in educational institutions, when the head of the district or any other officer goes on an inspection tour all the institutions under the jurisdiction of the district collector or district education officer try to set their houses in order with a view to present a rosy picture of the institutions to the top level functionaries. This process continues upon the top level. Further, the gap between expectations and actualities can hardly be filled. What is done is to adopt a set of rules and regulations which are acceptable to all. Later, these rules and regulations are quietly by-passed. For instance, a rule may be interpreted so as to favour the people of a certain religion, caste, region or political affiliation. Inefficiencies in administration caused by formalism cannot be dealt with by introducing modern techniques of management. In contrast, in the developed countries generally the discrepancy between form and reality does not exist. Most of the organizations are actually performing the tasks for which they have been created and follow strictly the prescribed procedures and rules.

Operational autonomy and power of bureaucracy

The bureaucracy in a developing country is apt to have a generous measure of operational autonomy and power. Colonialism was essentially the rule of the Bureaucracy with policy guidance from remote sources and this pattern persists even after the freedom of these countries. It is interesting to note that in spite of the democratic masters the administrative system headed by the civil servants has almost a monopoly of technical expertise and has the prestige of the professional expert. As already discussed, in these countries political parties are weak and are not as representative of the vast masses as in a developed country. The result is that the Bureaucracy becomes very powerful and comes to have a greater control over policy making than is desirable from the democratic view point. Riggs calls it negative development. However, such a situation does not prevail in the developed countries. It is because of well-organized political parties. Political institutions and the capability of the political system that bureaucracy in these countries tends to serve the society rather than striving for more powers and prestige. Their professional expertise is well-accepted by the political elite who do not interfere in the day to day working of the administration.

Administrative coherence

The administrative system of the developing countries suffers from the lack of administrative coherence, whereas in the development countries there is no lack of coherent relations between numerous services and regulatory agencies. Administrative coherence in a federal country like India is quite important for its smooth functioning. In fact state policies and their implementation cannot be achieved without effective coordination. Coordination is a process which implies unity of action on the part of all field agencies, units and departments, which are spread throughout a vast country. The developed countries like the USA have been able to achieve it with the help of executive chiefs at all levels of the hierarchy. Coherence implies similarity in tone or speech, i.e., all the field units work act and behave in the same fashion and use the same language.[7] All field units and agencies perform activities and functions on the same wavelength. But in the developing and underdeveloped world administrative coherence seems to be a remote possibility. Although it is an important ingredient of an administrative system yet it is not considered seriously by these countries.

Overlapping

Overlapping refers to a situation in which the economic, political, social and administrative systems cannot be differentiated from one another. The traditional society may be said to be fused because in such a society very little differentiation takes place. That is to say, economic, political, social and administrative systems cannot be distinguished fully. However, in a developed society complete differentiation exists. Social, economic, political and administrative functions which differ clearly are not performed by a single individual. In a developing society, overlapping does exist. There is a combination of political and administrative functions. Political functions consist in representing the various interests in the society and formulating policy so as to provide for the fulfillment of these interests. This is known as a function of interest aggregation. However, in the underdeveloped countries political parties are weak as already mentioned. They do not have experts, finances, scientific material, etc. Hence, the function of formulation is also done to a large extent by the bureaucracy. It is rather at which level it has been implemented. Riggs calls all this as interference complex. Whereas the bureaucracy has a large hand in political functions, the ministers have to perform some administrative functions.

Towards the end, it can be said that the political, social, economic and administrative systems of the underdeveloped and developing countries are characterized by many features distinct from the developed or advanced countries. Moreover, as quoted by Ira Sharkansky, "more differences in their systems are observed among the less developed nations than among the relatively few societies that qualify as more developed".[8]

What the advanced countries had earlier experienced (during the stages of growth and development), the underdeveloped countries are trying to over jump, particularly the advent of industries, urban growth, use of technology in agriculture and industries and so on. There is no alternative available with the developing countries but to depend on an ambitious programme of the development of science and technology. No agrarian economy can come near take off stage without indulging in large scale industrialization. The highly advanced countries too had shared the historical legacy of transition from feudalism to democracy and ultimately to capitalism. The centuries old traditional traits of behaviour are still highly discouraging factors to transform these societies from underdevelopment state to the state of modernization.[9] However, the developing countries are now caught up in the process of development. They are fast acquiring the advanced techniques and technology to meet the challenges thrown by the western world. They are also shedding their retarding traits and are already on the path of development. Now some of the countries even share a few features with the developed countries.

The preceding discussion clearly shows that public administration is not the same thing in the developed and developing societies. The specific roles played by it in different countries are greatly influenced by their respective environmental conditions. Hence, the study of public administration should not ignore the specific and concrete context of administration.

Some writers maintain that the main distinction between administration in developed, developing and underdeveloped countries lie in differences in their respective economic environments. Although economic environment plays an important role in influencing the functioning of administration, socio-cultural and political environment also influences its role in any society, in which it functions. As Riggs points out, administrative systems evolve in accordance with their social, economic, cultural and political contexts.

EXERCISES

1. Examine political and social characteristics of developing and developed countries.
2. Explain economic characteristics of developed and developing countries.
3. Discuss the pattern of public administration in developed and developing countries.

REFERENCES

[1] Viner Jocob, 'The Economics of Development', in *Approaches to Underdevelopment*, 1985, R.N. Aggarwal and S.P. Singh (Eds.), Oxford University Press, New Delhi, p. 17.

[2] Myrdal, Gunnar, *The Challenge of World Poverty*, Pantheon, New York, pp. 208–52.

[3] Sharkansky, Ira, *Public Administration*, Rand Manally College, Chicago, 1978, pp. 38–40.

[4] *Ibid.,* p. 39.

[5] Heady, Forrel, *Public Administration: A Comparative Perspective*, Prentice Hall, Englewood Cliffs, 1966, p. 16.

[6] Riggs, F.W., *Administration in Developing Countries: The Theory of Prismatic Society*, Houghton Miffin, Boston, 1964, p. 10.

[7] Chester, D.N. (Ed.), *The Organization of British Central Government*, George Allen and Unwin Ltd., London, 1968, p. 1.

[8] Sharkansky, Ira, *op. cit.,* pp. 38–40.

[9] Sharkansky, Ira, *Public Administration*, Rand Manally College, Chicago, 1978, p. 40.

Chapter
3
Development Programmes
Their Planning and Implementation

Most of the developing countries have launched a number of development programmes in various fields. Since the advent of planning, India has also started a large number of new programmes in fields like agriculture, community development, irrigation and industry. The principle aim and objective of all these programmes have been to bring upon change in the existing structure of socio-economic and industrial institutions and to achieve certain clear goals and targets in these fields.[1]

WHAT IS A PROGRAMME?

The word programme has been used in many different ways. The dictionary meaning of programme is a plan or schedule to be followed or a coordinated group of things to be done or performed. Moving from management to scientific viewpoint, *Neal* [2] defines a programme as "a set of activities a social enterprise with certain inputs of resources and conditions certain ways of organizing and certain outputs with standards for evaluating them".

Deniston and others[3] have given the following formal definition of a programme, "an organized response to eliminate or reduce one or more problems where the response includes one or more objectives, performance of one or more activities and expenditure of resources". In a U.N. Publication. *Professor Egbert de Vries* defines programme as a form of organized social activity with a specific objective, limited in space and time. It often consists of an inter-related group of projects and is usually limited to one or more organizations and activities[4]. From the problem solving viewpoint a programme is an organized response to reduce or eliminate one or more problems.

Programmes are often divided into projects so that the resources available are channeled in a definite direction. Moreover, innovation in organizational and administrative matters can be obtained without changing basic structures through the projects. An innovative project is more limited in approach and scope than a programme. If such projects are linked together and become mutually supportive, it will have a great effect. But it should be noted that a programme is more than the sum of a number of projects. The enumeration and adding up of the totality of development projects in a country is not equivalent to a developmental programme. [5]

Programme Planning

Programme planning involves the specification of objectives activities and resources for a particular geographical area or section of society and for a fixed period of time. For a better understanding of the process of programme planning the above terms need some elaboration.

Objective

An objective is a situation or condition of people or of the environment which responsible programme personnel consider desirable to attain. To permit subsequent evaluation the statement of an objective must specify:

(a) the nature of the situation or condition to be attained

(b) the quantity or amount of the situation or condition to be attained

(c) the particular group of people or portion of the environment in which attainment is desired

(d) the geographic area of the programme, and

(e) the time at or by which the desired situation or condition is intended to exist.

Ultimate objective

A condition which is desired in and of itself according to the value system of those responsible for the programme. Reductions in morbidity and mortality are examples of the conditions that are typically regarded as inherently desirable.

Programme objective

A statement of that particular situation or condition which is intended to result from the sum of programme efforts. It may or may not be considered inherently desirable, that is an ultimate objective.

Sub-objective

A subordinate or sub-objective is an objective which must be attained before the programme objective may be obtained. A sub-objective is seldom inherently desirable.

Most programmes have several sub-objectives. All sub-objectives are related in time to each other and to the programme objective: that is, the programme planner believes that they must be accomplished in a particular order. Frequently, two or more sub-objectives must be attained simultaneously. In some programmes, sub-objective must be accomplished before sub-objectives 2, 3 and 4 are to be accomplished; and 2, 3 and 4 may have to be accomplished simultaneously in order that sub-objective 5 may be obtained and so on. Some writers have used such terms as intermediate objectives or activity goals to describe sub-objectives.

There is a commonly used distinction between long-range and short-range objectives. The phrases are not recommended because they can be ambiguous as the following examples illustrate:

Example 1: In some circumstances long range refers to a programme objective and short range to a sub-objective. Thus, the long-range (programme) objective might be a 90 per cent reduction in the prevalence of tuberculosis after five years and one short-range (sub) objective might be that all people with tuberculosis know how to follow a prescribed chemotherapeutic regimen.

Example 2: In other instances long range and short range refer to amounts of the programme objective that can be expected to be achieved at any given stage. The long-range objective might be a 90 per cent reduction in the prevalence of tuberculosis after five years and the short-range objective might be its reduction by 20 per cent after one year.

The meanings of the concepts are different in these two examples. In Example 1, the short-term objective is actually a sub-objective which might be wholly attained and still not imply any attainment of the programme objective. In Example 2, the short-range objective represents partial attainment of the programme objective. The distinctions used in this paper make it possible to describe plans and outcomes without differentiating between long-range and short-range objectives.

Activity

Activity is the work performed by the programme personnel and equipment in the service of an objective. Activity as we use it does not imply any fixed amount or scope of work. It may be applied with equal validity to such diverse efforts as writing a letter or providing comprehensive healthcare. An activity can usually be subdivided into more specific activities. Providing comprehensive healthcare, for example, could be subdivided into providing curative healthcare and providing preventive healthcare. These in turn are capable of further subdivision and specification.

Distinction between an activity and an objective

James has made the distinction in terms of an analogy to a bird—the activity is flapping the wings the objective is being at some desired place. Activities consume programme time and resources, whereas objectives do not.

The distinction between and activities may be further clarified by an analogy between the logic of an experiment and the logic of a programme plan. In an experiment, the investigator asks whether a cause effect relationship can be demonstrated. He performs some procedures on a group of subjects (cause) and predicts that a specific result will or will not occur (effect). The experimental procedure is linked to the expected outcome by a hypothesis. The hypothesis can be stated in an "if....then" form, that is, if treatment A is provided then effect B will result, programme planning parallels the logic of an experiment. After the identification and analysis of needs or problems a programme objective is established and decisions are made about the activities to be undertaken. A programme objective is parallel to the experiments expected result or effect and the programme activities are parallel to the experimental procedure or cause. The planner hypothesized that a given method or set of activities will lead to the attainment of the objective. If a certain activity is performed then the desired objective will be achieved. The hypothesis can be tested only by evaluation.

Resources

Personnel funds, materials and facilities are available to support the performance of activity. Resources, like activities may be described with varying levels of specificity.

To start with, it includes an analysis of the historical trends of economic development and what may be called a diagnosis of the present situation. This analysis shows the changes which have taken place in the economy and their causes, and at the same time enables appreciation to be made of possible future development always assessing that the various factors continue to have the same effect. It will reveal the nature and extent of possible structural changes in the development, and will present a series of problems connected with the financing, the institutional framework, and the economic policy necessary for the achievement of the objectives.

Let us assume that programme objectives, as defined earlier, have been established (a statement has been formulated) that the programme is intended to attain a given situation or condition in a particular group of people or portion of the environment in a given geographic area, by a particular time and to a particular extent.

The next step is to identify alternative activities which might be effective in attaining the objectives. Anticipated costs and effectiveness of each alternative are thoroughly considered. Finally, the best alternative is selected in terms of the assessments of programme appropriateness adequacy effectiveness and efficacy. Current approaches selecting objectives and activities include planning, programming, budgeting, cost benefit analysis and operations research.

The final phase of planning is assignment of resources of support the activity selected.

As regards the programme management and its operation, a few questions arise These are where should the focus of management be centralized—regional, local, or interlocked? If it is to be interlocked, what are the ways? What are the steps in implementation?

The organizational plan, with indication of delegated or autonomous authority should be established including all participating groups. Management policies or guidelines for the authority and responsibility of top positions in the programme should be established. A detailed plan of operation based on programme priorities and resources available should be drawn up. Alternate plans of action for possible extenuating circumstances should be developed as should the procedures and working relationships with the legislative body, and/ or advisory groups.

The preparation and establishment of a programme thus, calls for a multi-dimensional complex decision-making process. Its operation entails continuous planning and re-planning. Being innovative in character in most of the programmes, the impact and costs cannot be

Development Administration

foreseen or the chances are that there will be unforeseen effects. The uncertainty often creates reluctance on the part of the government to commit its regulation to risk losses or disappointment and to spend large amounts of money. Many programmes therefore, begin small with hope and for those already conceived—expectations of wider applications.[6]

Characteristics of a Good Programme

A good programme usually has innovative elements a new initiative a new experimental approach and application of new insights. Administrators and social engineers tend to recommend and initiate a programme if the existing form of organization becomes an obstacle to efficient performance or changing functions.

The UN publication on programmes and projects[7] indicate the following characteristics of a good programme:

(a) A clear well-expressed goal

(b) Determination of the instrumentalities best to achieve that goal

(c) A set of consistent policies and/or interrelated projects to achieve the goal most effectively

(d) A measurement of the expected costs and of the benefits one hopes to derive from the programme

(e) Relationships with other on going activities and programmes

(f) Measures, including staffing and financing, needed to execute the programme

In many cases, there also exists the need for supporting policies and for measures outside the programme to assist in its successful operation and for an outlook on the consequences of wider geographical or functional expansion of the programme in case of success. Thus, a programme is seldom a self-contained isolated operation.

Types of Programmes

The programmes can be categorized into three main types[8]. These are as follows:

(a) Technical economic programmes: in which the objective is profit;

(b) Socially directed programmes, where the objective is service;

(c) Identity directed programmes, in which respect is the aim

In technical economic programmes, the innovative element in programme organization plays a major role. The programme is pushed at the most effective way of bringing agencies people and sources of income together. The ethos is rationality and profit: utmost efficiency in the execution is necessary. The choice of staff especially of the key team is of the utmost importance. Such programmes depend on the technical programmes. As long as this is effective or at least promising, the best people and ample funds flow to the programme.

In socially directed programmes, the services are frequently provided by the dedicated groups of staff, supported by volunteers and voluntary groups. They depend on the quality of their services and on the reciprocal relations with the benefited groups families and individuals. Cost-effectiveness is not the first measure of performance. There is however a high degree of cost consciousness as compared with the technical programmes, perhaps because there is less opportunity to express the results in economic and financial terms. It is difficult to measure benefits which are often intangible. Criteria for measuring performance are badly needed.

Among the identity directed programmes, distinction can be made between those stressing organization identity and those concerned with a political image. As to organizational self-identity most organizations and especially the voluntary one need activities to remain in existence to maintain the interest of the members and to attract new membership. The need may be discovered outside the organization, but self-identity is the main purpose.

In modern government, the image-building programme is more important than ever. The political influence of many politicians and party leaders depend upon surprise programmes. For instance, the well-known Point Four Programmes of the United States of America was based on comparatively limited technical properties and a high degree of intuition of President Truman.

If one considers this way of handling a programme rather irrational it should be remembered that most social decisions of great importance are motivated by irrational drives. Scientific programmes are often motivated by a search for identity or a desire to solidify identity.

Evaluation and Feedback

There must be proper evaluation and feedback of the development programmes. The quality of a programme should be assessed and compared with other programmes according to a certain scale of values in order to establish an order of priorities or to bring about improvement in the current programme. What is required is a systematic comprehensive approach to evaluate the effectiveness of programmes.

In evaluating the efficiency and effectiveness of programme specific measures for the accomplishment of each sub-objective and programme objectives are set up and data on the attainment of each are collected systematically following accepted principles of research design. In addition, data are collected on the extent to which resources are used as planned. For this it is necessary to set up internal data collection and evaluation and periodic reports for outside evaluation, if possible with a scientific institution or a constant.

Finding from the several sets of data are used to strengthen subsequent programme planning.

Problems of Programme Management

Past experience has highlighted certain problems which come in the way of efficient programme management. These are:

Inadequate administrative planning

It has been repeatedly observed that, both in the organized and the diffused sectors, there are at present no planning agencies which prepare administrative and operational plans for the programmes in all their aspects. If almost no programme is here today, a clear estimate of the type of organization and the various kinds of inputs are required to put the entire programme in operation. Nor is there a phased plan of operations worked out in terms of manpower, materials, money and organization required. Inevitably many of the programmes have run short of key personnel or suffered due to delays in supplies of critical materials and other inputs.

The problem was highlighted in the first Fourth Plan Draft Outline thus:

".....beyond the scheme embodied in an overall plan whether for the economy or for a sector, there is a great deal of detailed planning which must be done within an enterprise or in a department concerned with a specific development programme. Such planning greatly influences the quality of implementation and should receive the closest attention."[9]

Organizational and staffing problems

Secondly, several difficult problems have emerged with respect to the structure and staffing of such programmes. In most cases organizational systems and staffing practices in these programmes are carried over from the traditional governmental systems. Functional analysis of these practices has repeatedly shown that they are neither supportive nor conductive to the management of development programmes. Because of the orientation of development programmes towards achievement of certain specific goals and targets within a time period it has been found that the departmental type of organization for handling such activities tends to diffuse both authority and responsibility. Development programmes then get impeded by an organizational system, which cannot carry the qualitative load of work. Instead, it tends to be obstructive and often negative, thereby thwarting the general orientation of development programmes.

Similarly, the type of skills available within the present public personnel is, more often than not, insufficient to tackle the complex managerial tasks involved in developmental schemes. The general orientation of the existing personnel is towards executive type of work, fulfilling the legal requirements of a government job rather than moving towards the achievement of goals and targets within the prescribed time-cost parameters, which is the essence of development administration. The shift towards specialized types of governmental activities necessitates the support of professionally qualified and managerially competent personnel. In the absence of a suitable personnel policy and programme, the traditional type of personnel have continued to staff the new jobs with the result that not many have handled their assignments with even reasonable efficiency.

Procedural deficiencies

Thirdly, several difficulties have been experienced regarding the prevailing financial and administrative rules and regulations. In most cases it has been noticed that these rules and regulations have corroded initiative, discouraged boldness, and have cast a negative spell over the efficiency of the operation. Ordinarily, these rules and regulations should be designed so that they would assist managerial personnel in administering programmes efficiently, and according to the schedule. Instead, they have been geared to bring about greater administrative regimentation to exercise rigorous checks and counter, resulting in the negation of initiative and effective operation of programmes.

Operational Problems

Fourthly, many of the development programmes have had serious problems of coordination. These have been complicated by the fact that in our administrative system more than one agency is involved in the management of a programme. In a few cases there is a well-coordinated and properly conceived programme of action. As a result, many of these agencies have been pulling in different directions, and accountability for the poor performance has been virtually impossible to fix.

Fifthly, the existing pattern of direction and supervision of operations has proved to be haphazard desultory and ineffective. There is no regular inspection of the operation of the subordinate levels by the higher personnel, nor is there a good system of reporting and regular appraisal of performance. At every level where direction is expected to be provided there is a lack of purposefulness or a consciousness of achieving the development goals. Poor morale and indiscipline have therefore been the bugbear of these programmes.

Sixthly, development programmes have been noted for inadequate planning for the supplies and inputs necessary to put them into business. While some of the problems of supplies are outside the control of programme agencies, it has been often noted that they do not assess their supplies and input requirements in detail. Nor do they plan these supplies so that the programme can proceed according to the schedule.

Programmes, through their innovative component are a product of changing objectives and at the same time, a catalyst of change. They may lead the way to organization reforms and renewal. Initiating a programme may engender public attention and support may fill people with motivation, enthusiasm and initiative, and may facilitate financing. As a result of rapidly changing situation throughout the world, there is a rapid growth of programmes of all sorts. Indeed one may ask whether there are too many programmes and if the programme approach is a suitable solution to the manifold problems in modern and modernizing societies. The answer is rather difficult. Programmes in most cases are a transitory solution not serving adequately more permanent structural changes in society. They must at some time be absorbed into the composite system of societal relations. Hence, governments as well as non-governmental organizations must avoid an undue proliferation of programmes. On the other hand, against the hard-core conservatism and reluctance to accept structural changes prevalent in many societies, programmes are the only way to initiate possible changes.[10]

EXERCISES

1. What is a programme and explain programme planning?
2. Examine main types of programmes.
3. Discuss the problems of programme management.

REFERENCES

[1] Panandiker Pai, V.A., "Programme Planning and Management", In Pai Panandiker (Ed.), *Development Administration in India*, Macmillan, New Delhi, 1974, p. 69.

[2] Neal, F.W., "Doctors, dilemmas, data and decisions", Programme Evaluation in Mental Health Services, Training Institute Poruand Oregon, October 24, 1966.

[3] Derision OLIM, Rosen-stock, and Gatting, V.A., "Evaluation of Programme Effectiveness, *Public Health Reports*, April 83, pp. 323–35.

[4] *Vries, Egbert de*, "Programme Formulation and Implementation in United Nations", Administration of Development Programmes and Projects, New York, p. 25.

[5] *Ibid.*, p. 4.

[6] *Ibid.*, p. 54.

[7] *Ibid.*, p. 7.

[8] *Ibid.*, pp. 40–45.

[9] Panandiker, Pai. *Ibid.*, pp. 73–75.

[10] Planning Commission, Fourth Five Year Plan—A Draft Outline, New Delhi, 1966, p. 155, quoted in Pai Panandiker, *op. cit.*, pp. 73–74.

Chapter
4
The Riggsian Model and Development Administration

Development administration, which is focused on development activities also needs administrative development to suit the needs of development. The term development administration originated in 1955 with an India scholar, Goswami. But the conceptualization and elaboration of the concept were done by the western especially American scholars. The most important single contribution came from the Comparative Administration Group (CAG) in USA organised in 1960–61 under the aegis of the American Society for Public Administration. Disappointed with the results of the US Government's technical assistance programme for public administration in the developing countries, the members of the CAG— a small group of political scientists and students of public administration, undertook research and seminars on the administrative problems of some of the third world countries. As the long-time chairman of the CAG, Fred W. Riggs came to be regarded as the prime mover of academic interest in the field of development administration.

Development, according to Riggs, "is a process of increasing autonomy (discretion) of social systems, made possible by rising levels of diffraction." Discretion, according to him, "is the ability to choose among alternatives", while diffraction refers to the degree of differentiation and integration in a social system.

Riggs considered differentiation and integration as the two key elements in the process of development. Differentiation means existence of a situation in which every function has a corresponding specialized structure for its performance. Integration means a mechanism to tie together, to co-ordinate the various kinds of specialized roles. The necessity of integration arises in Development Administration because there are a variety of specialized roles which may lead to confusion and chaos unless they are carefully co-ordinated with each other.

According to Riggs, diffraction leads to development, and the higher the level of differentiation and integration, the greater the level of development. If the society is highly differentiated and poorly integrated, it is prismatic.

The level of differentiation in any country depends on the technological and non-technological factors. The more the development of technology, the higher the level of differentiation.

The integration depends on the two important factors—penetration and participation. Penetration is the ability of a government to make and carry out decisions throughout the country. Participation is the willingness to carry out the laws and the policies which government has formulated. The more the willingness and ability to participate on the part of the people, the higher the level of penetration and participation, which facilitate the integration of differentiated structures resulting in development.

Riggs, like Weidner, views development administration as a goal-oriented administration, an administration which is engaged in the task of achieving progressive political, economic and social goals. In this context, Riggs has presented the concept of administrative development, which refers to the increase in the capabilities of an administrative system to achieve the prescribed goals.[1]

F.W. Riggs has been primarily interested in conceptualizing the interactions between administrative systems and their environment. He maintains that an administrative system operates in the context of its socio-cultural, political and economic environment and there is a continuous interaction between the environment and the administrative system, both influencing mutually. This ecological model is the focal point of Riggsian analysis and has been one of the most creative models in analyzing the administration of developing countries. In presenting his concepts, he has taken the help of structural functional systems, and ecological approaches. The structural functional approach considers structures as patterns of behaviour which have become standard features of a social system. Functions represent the interrelationships among various structures or the consequences of one structure over the other structures. In Riggsian terms, the less number of functions a structure performs, the more diffracted it is, and conversely, the more functions a structure performs, the more fused it is. A combination of both creates prismatic structures.

A social system is a vast network of interrelated parts, each one of which can be understood in relation to other parts and to the whole system. Accordingly, Riggs suggested that administrative structure and behaviour being an integral and interacting part of the entire society, could be comprehended properly only in the context of the social system in which it is embedded. The environment influences the system in the form of inputs which are converted into outputs by the system. Through a process of feedback, the outputs cause the emergence of the new inputs. The interaction between a system and its environment is characterized as an ecological interaction. Using the ecological approach, Riggs considers public bureaucracies as one of the several basic institutions in a society that interact with other sub-systems in a society, viz., the political, the economic, the social and cultural systems. Riggs has particularly studied the differences in social, cultural, historical or political environment and their effect on administration. He has also studied as to how an administrative system affects the society of which it is a part. This interaction of the environment with administration has been termed by him as ecology of administration.

Development, according to Riggs, is a process of increasing autonomy (discretion) of social systems, made possible by rising levels of diffraction.[2] The development level of a society is reflected in its ability to make decisions in order to control its environment. This decision-making capability is based on the level of diffraction in a society. Diffraction in turn, is a function of differentiation and integration. A high level of differentiation coupled with a high level of integration makes a society or a system diffracted. However, a low level of differentiation with corresponding level of integration makes a system fused. Lastly, a high level of differentiation with a low level of integration makes a society prismatic.

Riggs views development administration as a goal-oriented administration—an administration which is engaged in the task of achieving progressive political, economic and social goals. In this context Riggs has presented the concept of administrative development, which refers to the increase in the capabilities of an administrative system to achieve the prescribed goals.

Riggs has been primarily interested in social change and in understanding the process of transition in developing societies. Here a reference will be made to two of his typologies, first the agraria-industria typology, and second the fused-prismatic-diffracted typology. In the first model, Riggs differentiated two types of societies—societies where agricultural institutions dominated, and societies where industrial institutions were predominant. Riggs has identified certain structural features of agrarian societies, such as [3]

(a) There is a dominance of ascriptive, particular and diffuse patterns

(b) The local groups are stable and there is very limited spatial mobility

(c) Occupational differences are very simple and stable

(d) There exists a differential stratification system of diffuse impact

The chief features of an industrial society are the following:

(a) There is a dominance of universal, specific and achievement norms

(b) The degree of social mobility is higher

(c) Occupational system is well-developed, and cut-off from other social structures

(d) There is an egalitarian class system based on generalized patterns of occupational achievement

(e) Associations are functionally specific and non-ascriptive in nature

The transition society represents a transitional stage of society between the agrarian and the industrial sector.

On the basis of empirical research, Riggs later came out with his second model which constructs two ideal polar types as follows:

(a) A refracted society, where every function has a corresponding structure that specializes in its performance

(b) A fused society which a single structure performs all functions

For example, in developed societies, the family performs certain social functions, the market performs the economic functions and the legislature and political parties perform political functions. In traditional societies, it is not unusual to see a few structures such as a family or a leader performing a whole allocation set of junctures like rule-making, rule adjudication, economic allocation, and even health administration. As society grows and develops, specialized structures increase in number, each one of which becomes engaged in specific functions. So, differentiation of structures is often viewed as the essence. So differentiation of structures is often viewed as the essence of development.

Riggs talked about the prismatic society as a mid-point between the two ideal types, combining the features of both, fused and refracted, that are characterized by heterogeneity (the simultaneous and viewpoints); formalism (the extent to which discrepancy exists between formal structures and actual modalities, between the prescriptive and the descriptive, between impressions and real practices); and overlapping (the extent to which is described as administrative behaviour is actually determined by non-administrative criteria).

In a prismatic society, pressure for change is external as well as internal. When it is external, it is termed as exogenous, and when internal, it is termed endogenous. Riggs is of the view that greater formalism, heterogeneity and overlapping are likely to exist in an exo-prismatic society in comparison with an endo-prismatic one. Problems of formalism, heterogeneity and overlapping are faced by prismatic or transitional societies in their bid to assimilate social change in the shortest possible time.

The Riggsian approach tries to provide an integrated perspective on public administration as he maintains that an administrative system operates in the context of its socio-cultural, political and economic environment and that the process of interaction between the environment, and the administrative system is a continuous one. Both interact with and influence each other. He makes it very clear that administration is different in different social settings. He thereby focuses on the obvious nexus between the administrative system and the society in which it is embedded.

Riggs has since changed his original views about the prismatic society. In his later publication entitled Prismatic Society Revisited (1975), he considers his earlier conceptualization as a mistaken 'one-dimensional approach and suggests a new definition of prismatic society based on a two-dimensional approach. The original dimension was degree of differentiation, and along this dimension, societies were classified into three types—fused, prismatic and diffracted.

In his new formulation, Riggs has introduced the second dimension of degree of integration among structures in a society that is differentiated (a fused society is, by definition undifferentiated and hence, integrated). The possibility of mal-integration or lack of coordination among social structures accompanies the process of differentiation.

According to Riggs, differentiated social systems can be ranked on a mal-integrated-integrated scale. The two basic social models of diffracted and prismatic (where differentiation can be found) are further subdivided into finer types on the basic societal models of diffracted and prismatic (where differentiation can be found) are further subdivided into finer types on the basis of degree of integration. Accordingly, diffracted societies are reconceptualised as eco-diffracted, ortho-diffracted, and neo-diffracted, Prismatic societies are similarly fine-grained into eco-prismatic, ortho-prismatic, and neo-prismatic.

This reformulation means that the prismatic model would include any society that is differentiated but mal-integrated. Also, a diffracted model refers to any society that is differentiated and integrated. Prefixes (eco-, ortho, neo) are attached to both the prismatic and diffracted types to suggest stages in the degree of differentiation.

The two-dimensional approach, as Riggs claims, has the advantage of conceding that prismatic conditions need not be confined to less developed countries only, but may occur in societies at any level of differentiation including those in developed nations.

In the three principal models, the bureaucracies are correspondingly unique. In the fused model, traditional bureaucracies were functionally diffused. Each official typically performed a wide range of functions, affecting political and economic as well range of functions, affecting political and economic as well as administrative functions. At the other end of the spectrum, the differentiated societies (especially well-integrated ones that are reconceptualised as neo-diffracted) have bureaucracies that are much more functionally specific as the chief—though by no means the only—agents for performing administrative tasks. In the transitional prismatic societies (the ortho-prismatic models), the bureaucracies are neither diffuse nor narrowly specific, but are intermediate as to the degree of functional specialization. They do not blend well with the other institutions within the political system, and thus, tend to fuel the forces of mal-integration. Prismatic societies thus suffer from a serious lack of balance between the rates of political and bureaucratic growth. Due to bureaucratic hegemony, the bureaucrats often encroach upon the jurisdiction of the politician and try deliberately to affect the political process.

While acknowledging the pioneering enterprise of Riggs, it needs to be admitted that the prismatic-sala model has lost its specificity, as Riggs himself has later conceded that it is into meant for exclusive, as Riggs himself has later conceded that it is not meant for exclusive application to the developing countries alone. The Riggsian model suffers from overgeneralization, as the so-called developing countries are not a homogeneous category. Any meaningful conceptualization has got to reckon with the subtle peculiarities of the new nations in terms of their culture, history, administrative tradition, economy and geography.

EXERCISES

1. Explain in brief Riggs views on Development Administration.
2. Analyse Riggs prismatic-sala model for Development Administration.

REFERENCES

[1] Nigro Felix A. and G. Lloyd Nigro, *Modern Public Administration,* 6th ed., Harper and Row, New York, 1984, p. 15.

[2] Riggs, F.W., *Administration in Development Countries,* Houghton Mifflin, Boston, 1964, and *The Ecology of Public Administration,* Asia Publishing House, Bombay, 1962.

[3] Sham Shun Nisa Ali, *Eminent Administrative Thinkers,* Associated Press, New Delhi, pp. 103–104.

Chapter
5

Ecological Dimensions of Development Administration

Changes in land use and use of resources associated with agriculture, industry and urban development in many European countries affected ecological stability in all times between nomadic cultures and modern industrialization. Until World War II, environmental problems were few, and the resource use implications of a mixed agricultural and industrial society was relatively modest. The post-war period has, however, witnessed scars of violence and assault done to the natural environment on a large scale.

ENVIRONMENTAL HAZARDS

Environmental problems have been persisting at local, regional and international levels. Today environmental pollution is, by far, the most serious and irrecoverable. Consequently, the deterioration of the quality of environment has become the subject of discussion and intensive research in both developed and developing nations. Halting and reversing ecological degradation, which has now assumed dangerous proportions, has been identified as a major priority in a growing volume of national and international studies and reports. No development (which does not find a solution to the cause of environmental impoverishment) is worthy of its name. The independent commission on international development issues (1983) made strong references to this concern by stating: "growing pressure on land, increasing use of chemicals, desertification and deforestation are reducing the productivity of soils in many parts of the world."[1]

In a similar vein, the United Nations group of governmental experts had stated in its report: their can no longer be the slightest doubt that resource scarcities and ecological stresses constitute real and imminent threats to the future well-being of all people and nations. These challenges are fundamentally non-military, and it is imperative that they be addressed accordingly."[2]

Likewise a citizens report' brought out by the centre for science and environment (New Delhi) reflects the belated recognition that man has been too cavalier in his relations with nature. The report states.''… the steady destruction of our natural forests, pasture lands and inland and coastal water bodies has not only meant increased economic poverty for millions of tribals, nomads and traditional fisher folk, but also a slow cultural and social death; a dismal change from rugged self-sufficient human beings to abjectly dependent landless labourers and squalor-stricken urban migrants.''[3]

These and other reports have brought this generation to a greater awareness and understanding of the interdependence between nature and man. Research findings in environmental monitoring and biological sciences, combined with harsh experiences in international economic development, have made the world community realise that its own health and well-being and the world community realise that its own health and well-being and the fate of future generations depend on action to avert environmental catastrophe. This new understanding has helped to bring into sharper focus the interrelatedness of environment and development. It emphasizes the importance of ensuring a healthy relationship between the man and his environment on which his survival depends. To quote P.V. Narasimha Rao at the recent earth summit: "Today it is clear, we cannot have conservation of the environment without the promise of development even as we cannot have sustained development without the preservation of the environment,''[4] consequently, environment and sustainable development have become a policy issue of major significance.

ENVIRONMENT AND DEVELOPMENT

Environment conservation and improvement and resource use have become guiding principles for development plans and projects. Indeed, there appears to be practically no development project or programme which does not have some detrimental impact on the environment. The 1972 Stockholm conference on the human environment pronounced "both aspects of man's environment, the natural and man-made, are essential to his well-being and to the enjoyment of basic human rights—even the right to life itself."

Environment

The concept environment can, therefore, best be understood as the totality of all components surrounding the man. The environment pollution panel of the United States President's science advisory committee (1965) referred to environment as "the sum of all social, biological and physical or chemical factors which compose the surroundings of man." Each component of these surroundings constitutes a resource on which man depends for his well-being and survival. Unlike all forms of life, man is capable of exerting great influence upon the environment, which in return, affects almost all the life process and form of organisms.

Sustainable Development

Given the global and local effects of environmental decay, it is no surprise that sustainable development has become a catch-phrase in development planning and resource management.

However, interpretation of this concept is still ambiguous. According to the Brundtland report,[5] the idea of sustainable development reaches far beyond environmental protection, as it means a process of change in which exploitation of resources, direction of investments, orientation of technological development, and institutional changes are made consistent with future as well as present needs. It is not a fixed state of harmony, but rather a balanced and adaptive process of change. Sustainability takes for granted "a balance between economic development—all quantitative and qualitative changes in the economy that offer positive contributions to welfare—and ecological sustainability—all quantitative and qualitative environmental strategies that serve to improve the quality of an ecosystem, and hence also have a positive impact on welfare". Both economic and environmental systems need a certain minimum threshold value to survive. Ciriacy–Wantrup[6] emphasized the use of safe minimum standards for conservation by avoiding over exploitation of critical zones of the environment by limiting human activities that make it uneconomical to halt or reverse environment degradation. Thus, the idea of sustainable development requires a careful consideration of sustainable threshold levels for the economic and environmental systems.

Environment Administration

The fact that environment is used to cover every activity of man, it becomes difficult to develop a practical yet comprehensive definition of the concept environment administration. To begin with, it is beyond the capability of any environment administrator to master the detailed functioning of each of the components of environment. Environment pollution, depletion of resources and socio-economic infrastructure, human population and cultural heritage constitute vast technical areas and are best left to the specialist concerned. The job of the administrator or manager is merely to study and exercise control over the process by which these factors interact with one another and the manner in which they finally contribute to his particular goals. Edmunds and Letey define environment administration as a concept of managing human affairs in such a way that biological health, diversity and ecological balance will be preserved.[7] Environment administration may be defined as the process of carrying out activities which are concerned with protection and enhancement of the quality of the environment. It seeks to achieve equilibrium between man and his environment, minimization of his assaults on the various eco-systems and maximization of the survival of all forms of life. Some aspects of environment administration lie in the premises of economics, sociology, management, politics, law, philosophy, etc. It concerns man and his environment. As such the field of environment administration concerns human decisions which affect and adapt the environment.

Relevance of Developmental Issues to the Environment

The purpose of this chapter is to engender a broader appreciation of the central role of environmental issues in the wider socio-economic context. It is meant to facilitate a more comprehensive approach by demonstrating that the economic problems cause environmental despoliation which, in turn, makes economic and structural reforms more difficult to achieve.

Breaking the vicious circle requires increasing attention by nations in their approach to international environmental co-operation. Following are some of the important developmental aspects of the present situation which have negative consequences on the environment.

Arms Race

One major cause of environmental destruction is the arms race. To indicate its magnitude, expenditure on arms by the developed countries rose from $312.4 in 1970 to about $1 trillion in 1990, compared with $69.9 billion to $200 billion in the corresponding period by the developing countries. In contrast, expenditure on health was about $60 billion for the developing countries and $600 billion for the developed countries in 1990. If expenditure on arms could be reduced, the resources thus released could then be used to deal with furthering human welfare.

Poverty

Poverty is an alarming environmental problem. At the Stockholm conference, the problem was seen largely as a problem of pollution, and Indira Gandhi, the late prime minister of India, summarized the viewpoint of the development countries when she asked, "are not poverty and need the worst polluters?" the implication was that taking care of poverty would solve the problems of pollution in these countries.

According to statistics made available by the commonwealth Secretariat, around 1 billion people, representing one-fifth live in absolute poverty; 800 million people are starved everyday; 150 million children under 5 years of age are malnourished; 14 million children die every year before they turn five. About two-thirds of the undernourished live in South Asia and one-fifth in sub-saharan Africa.[8] Further, the per capita gross national product of low-income economies averaged $520 in 1989 compared with $18,330 of the high-income economies corresponding to the same period.[9] In the case of India the GNP per capita in 1998 was $430 compared to $29.340 of United States in the same year. As for distribution of income, the richest fifth receives 82.7 per cent of total world income as compared to 1.4 per cent by the poorest fifth.

Poverty not only degrades the human environment but also obstructs development. Lack of potable drinking water for over 1,500 million people and of sanitation for over 2,000 million is by far the most important cause of environmental pollution resulting in 25,000 deaths a day and 80 per cent of world diseases. Further, inadequate shelter and slum dwellers in the rapidly growing urban areas of the developing world increase vulnerability to environmental crisis. Poverty also contributes to human population pressure. The poor and village dwellers have a major stake in the larger families. They see in the largest possible family a chance of security in old age. Although mortality rates have come down through the impact of technological innovation, birth rates have continued to follow a traditional pattern owing to lack of economic development. Growing pressure on land, removal of forest cover, incautious use of chemicals and fertilizers and soil erosion reduce the agricultural potential of scarce land resources causing further increase in poverty. The starting point must be to provide for the establishing of the economic means needed to deal with issues of water, nutrition and human settlements of the poor in the development world.

Population Growth and Agriculture-related Problems

Rapid population growth, agricultural stagnation, and environment degradation are closely interrelated and mutually reinforcing.

Agricultural development in the developing world provides food for human sustenance and employment for its growing population, but it does not maintain sustainable production. While the world as a whole produces enough food to meet the present needs of its population (5.6 billion), inequality in food distribution leave millions of people near the subsistence level. Inappropriate agricultural practices and varied land problems have not only produced less than optimal yields, but have also contributed to land exhaustion as well as to soil erosion, desertification and stalinization. Excessive use of fertilizers and pesticides combined with large-scale irrigation will, to a great extent, affect the agricultural potential of land.

Countries with low per capita arable land and high population growth, such as Ethiopia, Ghana, Kenya, Nigeria, India and Bangladesh, are experiencing an economic and environmental crisis of agricultural stagnation, deforestation, land degradation, and desertification. Agricultural stagnation and environmental degradation also affect population growth. High infant and child mortality rates caused by food shortages and malnutrition induce men and women to have more children, partly to ensure that some survive to support them in old age.

Debt Burden

The debt burden and regressive terms of trade are becoming major global issues. Developing countries are facing mounting difficulties in their efforts to find adequate and appropriate resources, particularly foreign exchange, to quicken their pace of socio-economic development. This has often forced them to pay attention to short-term aspects without giving serious thought to the long-term considerations. Thus, the effect of such international economic issues, has been to abridge the gap of co-operation. A one per cent raise in interest rates adds about 5 billion to the debt burden of the developing world, the total debt service payments for all developing countries in 1990 were $500 billion. The debt burden, therefore, places pressure not only on the economic surplus produced by the developing world, but also on resources which have to be over-exploited to ease this burden. For example, for one Latin American country it took 9.8 times as much beef to purchase a barrel of oil in 1981 as it did in 1973.

Patterns of Consumption

The scars of violence done to the environment are largely man's own affluence marked by resource wasteful lifestyles. Over-consumption and wasteful use of resources by the developed countries and the privileged strata in the developing world also contribute to the degradation of the human environment. The demands of the developed world for resources from the developing world add to the pressures on their environment. Increasing demands on fish resources and tropical forest cover provide two instances. Thus, the effect of increase in the size of population and people's patterns of consumption and production has been to create an imbalance between people and resources, causing further increasing environmental degradation.

People are forced to migrate to semi-arid areas and into tropical forests to establish new farms. Consequently, population pressure is causing not only soil degradation, but also deforestation and falling agricultural output.

Global Warming

The build-up of carbon dioxide in the atmosphere and industrial and transportation emissions are contributing to global warming. It is feared that carbon dioxide concentration would double from its current levels of about 350 parts per million (ppm) to 700 ppm from the year 2030–2075, causing an increase in global mean temperatures by between 1.5 and 4.0°C celsius and raise sea levels by 20 cm to 1 meter. Further, this doubling will increase the incidence of flooding, typhoons, hurricanes, and other climatic effects. There is great pressure from the developed world to cut down emissions, slow deforestation, and so on and to join a schemes for carbon taxes. The developing countries, on the other hand, have argued that they have not been the primary source of greenhouse emissions, and that their inclusion in schemes for carbon taxes will truncate their development.

Energy Dependence and Crisis

Energy, especially petroleum, is becoming a major global issue due to the growing reliance of the world economy on it. Today, the average manufactured commodity in the industrialized nations is being produced with 20 per cent less energy input than a decade ago.

Today in sub-saharan Africa, fuel wood accounts for about 80 per cent of energy needs, and it is in very short supply. As the situation worsens, farmers have to burn animal dung and crop residues instead of using them to increase soil productivity.

Now, there is an increased dependence on coal and on nuclear energy with potential impacts on the human environment. While the developed countries have devised several devices to assess the environmental impacts of energy, the developing countries have just started to give attention to this issue. Indeed, any energy transition must be achieved in full understanding of the environmental impacts of various forms of energy generation and use.

As part of co-operation among the development countries, the g-15 countries have adopted solar energy application as a key project for joint research and development.

Imprudent Technology

Environmental problems also occur because of the inappropriate application of technology. Examples of such problems are toxic wastes, threats to the ozone layer, possible climatic changes, etc. The economic effects of such problems could be disastrous, and the impact of technology on the environment is crucial. While in the developed countries, the capacity to evaluate its impact is growing, only a small percentage of the world scientific and research capacity is found in the developing countries. For the developing world to be tied to environmentally, imprudent environments and economies but also for the global environment. Increased transfer of technology to the developing world should be accompanied by the provision of data which would permit informed choice in the light of local conditions.

ENVIRONMENTAL PROBLEMS IN INDIA

Like other countries, India too faces a wide array of environmental problems which affect the well-being of its citizens. While for developed countries environmental problems are largely due to pollution caused by resource wasteful lifestyles, the stresses of India's environmental resources come mainly from the pressures for satisfying the basic needs of a large and growing population. The Secretary General of the Indian Environmental Society has observed that "physical growth cannot go on indefinitely on this finite earth, and the explosion of human population and its increasing indiscriminate encroachments on the biosphere poses a grave danger to man's own survival."[10] In another publication it has been stated that "Conservation and improvement of the environment are vital for the survival and well-being of the mankind. National resources of land, air and water have to be used wisely a trust to ensure a healthy environment for the present and future generation."[11]

According to the Sixth Plan, environmental problems in India can be grouped into two categories, "(a) those arising from conditions of poverty and underdevelopment; (b) those arising as negative effects of the process of development." The first category has to do with the impact on the health and integrity of our natural resources (land, soil, water, forest, wildlife, etc.) as a result of poverty and the inadequate availability for a large section of our population, of means to fulfil basic human needs (food, fuel, shelter, employment, etc.). The second category has to do with the unintended growth and development. The second category comprises "the distortion imposed on national resources from poorly planned development projects and programmes, lack of attention to long-term concerns by commercial and vested interests." Thus, it would be clear that environmental conservation is an integral part of the total development effort.

LEGISLATIVE MEASURES AND ADMINISTRATIVE ACTION

India is one of the few countries of the world that have made specific reference in their constitutions to the need for environmental protection and improvement. Article 48A (inserted after the 42nd Amendment Act in 1976) and Article 51A of the Indian Constitution lay down the following duties for the state and the citizen: "The state shall endeavour to protect and improve the environment and to safeguard the forests and wildlife of the country" (Article 48A). "It shall be duty of every citizen of India to protect and improve the natural environment including forests, lakes, rivers and wildlife, and to have compassion for living creatures"(Article 51A).

The United Nations Conference on Human Environment held in Stockholm in June 1972[12] provided an impetus for the centre to establish a National Committee on Environment Planning and Coordination (NCEPC) to act as a high level advisory body to government. On 23 January 1980, the President of India in his address to the first joint session of the 7th Parliament expressed the need for setting up a specialized machinery with adequate powers to maintain ecological balance.[13] Accordingly, the Government of India constituted a high-powered committee under the chairmanship of N.D. Tiwari (then Deputy Chairman of the Planning Commission) on 29 February 1980, to recommend legislative measures and administrative machinery for ensuring environmental protection.[14] The Committee in its report (15 September 1980) recommended that a Department of Environment (DOE) should be set up to provide explicit recognition to the pivotal role that environmental conservation must play sustainable national development. [15]

India's overriding concern for ecological balance has been emphasized in its National Polity for socio-economic development. *The Sixth Five Year Plan framework* document as approved by the National Development Council on 30 and 31 August states "It is imperative that we carefully husband our renewable resources of soil, water, plant and animal life to sustain our economic development." The document also mentions the following as on of the objectives of the plan:

"Bringing about harmony between the short- and long-term goals of development by promoting the protection and improvement of ecological and environmental assets."[16] Concern about deteriorating natural resources and human environment has also been expressed in the 7th and 8th Five Plan (1992–1997) documents.

Legislative Measures

The Directive Principles (Articles 48 and 51A) of the Indian Constitution and the Development Policy of the Government of India have provided a strong bases for enactment of legislative measures for the protection of environmental resources. Several laws have been enacted from time to time that directly or indirectly relate to environmental protection and improvement. Among the more recent ones are: (i) Insecticides Act, 1968; (ii) Wildlife (Protection) Act, 1972; (iii) Water (Prevention and Control of Pollution) Act, 1974; (iv) Air (Prevention and Control of Pollution) Act, 1981; (vii) Environment (Protection) Act, 1986; and, (viii) Public Liability Insurance Act, 1991. The Water Act, 1974, the Forest Act, 1980, and the Air Act, 1981, were amended in 1988.

Institutional Measures

Department of environment

The Government of India set up a Department of Environment on 1 November 1980. The functions of the department have been identified as:

(a) Nodal agency for environmental protection and eco-development in the country;

(b) Carrying out of environmental appraisal of development projects through other ministries/agencies as well as directly; and

(c) Administrative responsibility for:

   (i) pollution monitoring and regulation,
   (ii) conservation of critical eco-systems designated as biosphere reserves, and
   (iii) conservation of marine eco-system

This department was integrated into the Ministry of Environment and Forests in 1985 at the centre. Twenty-two states and Union Territories have set up separate department of environment.

Pollution control board

Besides the creation of department of environment. There are 21 State Pollution Control Boards and one Central Pollution Control Board in the Country.

National Wastelands Development Board and National Land Use and Wastelands Development Council

They were set up in 1985 to:

   (a) increase tree and other green cover on wastelands;

   (b) prevent good land from becoming wasteland; and

   (c) formulate perspective plans and programmes for the development of wasteland in country.

A Central Ganga Authority was constituted in 1985 to guide and oversee the implementation of a programme for restoring the quality of the river.

Indian Board for Wildlife

It was set up in 1952 with the objective of managing zoos. The board deliberates and takes decisions regarding several important issues, such as framing guidelines for control of visitors to wildlife reserves, formulating a national policy on management of zoos, posting competent, motivated and well-trained personnel in the protected areas, and curbing encroachments in them.

Environment Information System

An Environmental Information System (ENVIS) for the collection, processing and dissemination of environmental information to aid planners and decision-makers was set up in 1982 as a decentralised system. The ENVIS network with the Department of Environment as its focal point presently consists of 17 ENVIS centres in diverse areas of environment such as pollution control, toxic chemicals, environmentally sound and appropriate technologies, energy and environment, degradation of wastes, etc.

Environmental Impact Assessment (EIA)

With a view to ensuring that plans for development in all sectors are in harmony with the objective of maintaining the health of life-sustaining eco-systems and other environmental resources, a process of Environmental Impact Assessment (EIA) is essential. The ministry of environment and forests has been assigned the responsibility for appraisal of projects with regard to their environmental implications. Based on environmental impact assessment and issues arising thereto, decisions are taken by the competent authorities in respect of projects, including selection of sites. During 1992–93, out of 247 projects appraised, 101 projects were granted environmental clearance.

Pollution monitoring and control

The water and air acts are implemented through the central pollution control board and the state pollution control boards. Under the national water quality monitoring programme, 480 stations had been set up till 1992–93. These include 25 ground water stations and 27 stations under the ganga action plan.

In addition, 260 air quality monitoring stations and 173 coastal monitoring stations have been set up. Under the Environment (Protection) Act, 1986, 27 industries have been identified in respect of effluent standards. Moreover, used-based classification of 14 major rivers in the country has been completed.

Control of hazardous substances

The Environment (Protection) Act, 1986, provides for laying down procedures and safeguards for the handling of hazardous substances and prevention and control of accidents. The ministry of environment has prepared three sets of rules for this purpose: These are (a) rules for the manufacture, import and storage of hazardous and toxic chemicals. (b) rules for the transportation of hazardous and toxic chemicals by road; and (c) rules for the management of hazardous and toxic wastes.

Biosphere reserves programme

Biosphere reserves are intended to preserve genetic diversity in representative eco-systems and provide for conservation of plants, animals and micro-organisms. They also provide scope for research in natural eco-systems vis-à-vis man-modified eco-systems. Thirteen biogeographical zones in the country have been identified for establishing biosphere reserves. So far, 7 of them have been set up in the country—Nilgiri, Nanda Devi, Nokrek, Great Nicobar, Gulf of Mannar, Manas and Sunderbans.

In conclusion, it can be said that traditional economic and industrial approaches are often incompatible with sustainable environmental development. A basic question to consider today, is not whether to choose between industrialization and environment. It is how to select patterns of development that improve the quality of the environment. International economic co-operation is vital in this context. However, this cannot be achieved unless nations recognize the crucial relationship between sound environmental management and international economic development. What is required is a more integrated approach towards evolving an international environmental system which responds adequately to the development needs of developing countries in the context of growing environmental despoliation.

EXERCISES

1. Explain relevance of development issues to the environment.
2. Discuss in brief environmental problems in India.
3. Examine legislative and administrative measures for environmental protection.

REFERENCES

[1] *Second Report of the Independent Commission on International Development Issues (on) Common Crisis: North-South Co-operation for World Recovery,* Pan Books, London, 1983, p. 126.

[2] *Report of the Secretary General on the Study on the Relationship between Disarmament and Development,* United Nations, New York, 1981, para 72, p. 30.

[3] Centre for Science and Environment, *The State of India's Environment 1982: A Citizen's Report,* New Delhi, Centre for Science and Environment, India, 1982, p. 190.

[4] Speech of the Indian Prime Minister at the Earth Summit of the United Nations Conference on *Environment and Development*, Rio-de-Janeiro, June 12, 1992.

[5] World Commission on Environment and Development, *Our Common Future,* New York: Oxford University Press, 1987.

[6] Ciriacy-Wantrup, S.V., *Resource Conservation,* University of California Press, Berkeley, 1952.

[7] Edmunds Stahrl and Letey John, *Environmental Administration,* McGraw-Hill, New York, 1973, p. 3.

[8] Quoted from the *Commonwealth Current,* August/September 1992, p. 2.

[9] World Bank, *World Development Report 1991,* (Oxford University Press, New York: 1991).

[10] Chauhan Eklavya, "The Environmental Dilemma", in Desh Bandhu and Eklavya Chauhan (Eds.), *Current Trends in Indian Environment,* New Delhi, Today and Tomorrow, 1977, p. 13.

[11] DAVP, *Science and Technology Series* No. 6/13/80/p.v., Ministry of Information and Broadcasting, New Delhi, May 1981.

[12] U.N. *Conference on Human Environment, op. cit.*

[13] *The Hindustan Times,* January 24, 1980.

[14] Department of Science and Technology, India, Resolution No. 1/14/80 29 February 1980.

[15] *Tiwari Committee's Report,* New Delhi: Department of Science and Technology, 1980, p. 37

[16] *India's Sixth Five Year Plan,* 1980–85, p. 34.

Chapter

6

Project Management

Project as a part of development strategy plays a significant role in accelerating the race of socio-economic change in a country. The preparation of projects is the final phase in the formation of development programmes, and the connecting link with the practical stage of execution. National development and a better standard of living of the people depend on the optimum utilization of available resources, and timely completion of various projects.

PROJECT: DEFINITION

A project is a scheme of action, an undertaking prepared and carried out to achieve the desired ends. The end product of a project is a segment of broader developmental goals. Although they are more common in such fields as construction industry, transport and resource development they are used in practically every sector. A project may be large or small limited or comprehensive in scope capital or labour-intensive production or problem-oriented production. It may be limited to a specific sector or it may cut across a number of sectors.

A project approach to development means a diversion from the conventional, administrative system. It implies a special administrative and technical arrangement that cannot be dealt with in a routine manner. Projects are generally of innovative nature and involve a large degree of experimentation.

Stages of a Project

Broadly, a project has three main stages:

(a) Project formulation

(b) Project installation

(c) Project operation

These are not easily definable stages and may overlap one another 'Manual of Economic Development Projects', a U.N. publication has mentioned the stages of projects as follows:

(a) Selection of projects

(b) Preparation of preliminary projects, which will justify allocation of resources for further studies

(c) Preparation of preliminary projects to determine preferences between the various possibilities

(d) Allocation of priorities between the projects studied

(e) Preparation of final projects

(f) Installation of the new productive units

(g) Entry into operation and normal operation of the productive units

After selecting the kind of project and the determination of its objects, stages:

(a) Related to the preliminary studies stage

(b) Leads to economic evaluation of the problem stage

(c) Related to the formulation of the project and stages

(d) Cover the execution of the project[1]

As indicated earlier, projects are the final link in a country's development plans. The lack of well-conceived projects does not facilitate the carrying out of even the very well-conceived development plans. The impetus for one or the other project may arise from within the departments or organizations or it may come from outside sources. But the choice of new projects should be very selective and be made in the light of overall development plans and programmes. The impetus to set up a project can come from the political parties pressure groups interest groups or can emerge from the researches evaluations or studies conducted by the universities/training institutes etc.[2] Before a project takes birth it is necessary to ensure that the project is:

(a) According to the socio-economic policy of the country

(b) According to the priority needs of the people

(c) Linked properly with the objectives and goals of planning

(d) Fitted into the overall economic and social development of the country

(e) Properly linked with the projects in the allied area

(f) Able to achieve useful and permanent results[3]

Formulation of a Project

Project formulation is concerned with developing an optional or at least workable plan of activities that make up the project including specification of their inter-relationship. It is not a simple task, but it involves a complex process of decision-making. It is also one of the most important aspects of project management. Even the sincerest efforts may fail and the resources may remain idle or unavailable because of the lack of well-planned projects. It is also true that however carefully a project is prepared, it cannot fully cover all the factors which affect it, nor can it anticipate all the difficulties which will have to be overcome on the spot with respect to its organization initiation and operation. But an existing project of a similar nature does represent the rational basis for the decision to set up an enterprise, and hence, it must be studied as thoroughly as possible.[4] It must be supplemented by other studies such as market studies, project engineering or feasibility studies etc. Such preliminary studies should also be systematic and planned which, in fact, constitute a part of the project. The number of such studies should be within reasonable limits. The following tips may prove helpful in this regard[5]:

(a) To the extent that a country has developed information on its unable resources and environment usually through surveys it will save information on the major alternatives available for utilization in the context of its national ideals and aspirations.

(b) In an ongoing administrative system, experiences will have already indicated the important variables pertinent to development planning and the possible projects that can be prepared.

(c) Projects do not have to be prepared in detail at the preliminary stage.

Though the planners should be careful in regard to the costs involved in making preliminary studies, it should also be mentioned that a project idea on which preliminary work has been done, but which is not included in the plan or approved for implementation is not necessarily a waste of time and resources. If it is rejected, amended or postponed because of its unsuitability in terms of the criteria of national development it will have prevented the wrong allocation of resources.[6]

After the project idea is accepted and its objectives are laid down, a plan is to be made to carry out the idea. In other words, it is necessary to programme it in the manner in which the defined objectives can be achieved. Assessment of the necessary resources and their availability administrative potentials and an analysis of the internal and external environment is to be made. Possible obstacles should be identified and measures should be specified to check them.

Sound formulation of projects will automatically facilitate their effective implementation. It indicates not only the process of sub-dividing the project into its component activities and developing their sequential relationship but also to include for each of these activities the selection of methods the assignment of resources the estimating of time requirements and the establishment of scheduling data. Only persons having the deepest knowledge of the work should participate in the process.[7]

The manual of health project management lists nine steps required for the project formulation as shown in Figure 6.1[8].

It is advantageous to consider the overall job as consisting of a number of related but separate activities. It is not practical to attempt to work with the entire project control. Component activities should consist of logical subdivision of work.[9] In this regard network techniques have been developed for the planning scheduling and control of projects. The best

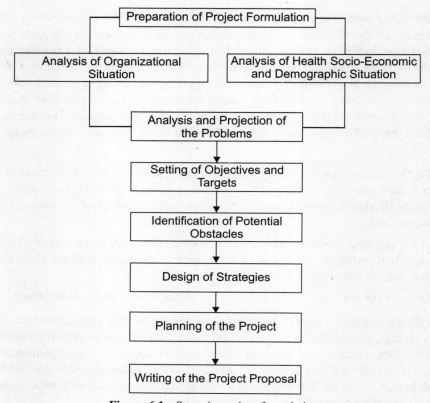

Figure 6.1   Steps in project formulation.

known of these network techniques are the Critical Path Method (CPM) and the Programme Evaluation and Review Technique (PERT). Although these two systems had been designed to tackle different types of problems, they had in common the use of network as a schematic model of the project. In both the approaches, the basic steps involved are more or less the same and consist of:

(a) Preparation of the list of individual jobs/activities

(b) Establishing the inter-relationships between the activities

(c) Estimation of the activity duration

(d) Development of the network

(e) Review of the network to check logic time estimates and resource availability

(f) Establishment of work schedules

(g) Following up the schedules

(h) Updating of networks.[10]

To illustrate the method of network diagramming a project with limited activities is assumed. The activities are inter-related or inter-dependent. Activities B_1 and X are dependent on Activity A. Activities B_1 and X must be completed before Activity C may commence. Activity B_2 may be performed concurrently with Activity C. Activity X signifies an external activity, such as the furnishing by others of an item of equipment to be installed, or the checking and approval of plant drawing. Finally Activity D can be started after the completion of Activity B_2 and Activity C.[11]

The subdivision of the project into activities and their sequential relationships are shown in Table 6.1

Table 6.1

Activity	Activity duration (days)	Must precede activity
A	1	B_1, X
B_1	4	B_2, C
B_2	6	D
X	2	C
C	2	D
D	1	—

Figure 6.2 shows the network diagram of the above subdivision of the project.

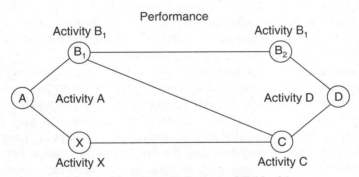

Figure 6.2 Network diagram of Table 6.1.

For effective project implementation, the management must work according to an implementation plan that indicates the chronological order of the various component activities or tasks. Such a plan must be completed before starting work on the project.

Project Installation

The installation of the project is one of the most complicated and significant aspects. It raises the basic question as to which agency or body is to undertake the installation job. A project may be undertaken by any of the following bodies:

(a) An existing or new organization without establishing a special unit to handle it

(b) A new special unit within an existing organization

(c) A new government

(d) A contractor

Sometimes, a project may have to be split up for implementation in parts by existing and/ or new government agencies, and in parts by contractors.[12] Certain problems relating to the fundamental engineering aspects of the project may be considered. Their relative importance will vary with the projects, but they will be under the following heads:[13]

(a) Preliminary research and testing

(b) Selection of the production process

(c) Specification of operation and assembly equipment

(d) Buildings and site layout

(e) Plant layout

(f) Supplementary engineering projects

(g) Efficiency

(h) Flexibility of productive capacity

(i) Work schedules

The above problems indicate the complex nature of project installation. Much of the criticism of the public sector in India has been because of the long delays and cost overruns during the construction phase. These have resulted in delayed realization of benefits expected from the projects and poor returns on capital investment.[14]

As against the public sector projects of the engineering nature there may be other projects such as health projects or community development projects. Such projects generally require no construction. The installation stage of such projects would be the making of administrative arrangements to carry out the projects. The existing organizations may be reoriented or strengthened or some new special units may be created for this purpose. The internal technical capability may be utilized or it may be asked for from external sources. Other issues relating to the project installation are the arranging of financial and material resources and fixing up authority responsibility and relationships.

Project Operation

After the installation and/or making the necessary administrative arrangements, comes the stage of actual working of the project. During this stage even greater attention must be paid to planning and control for it is during this stage that the benefits of the earlier investments are reaped.[15] Here the first task of the management team is to develop a detailed plan of organization and administration, including scheduling, budgeting, staffing, continuous evaluation reporting planning for contingencies and the final transition stage. Most of the problems encountered in the operation of a project can be frequently traced back to the shortcomings of these initial plans.[16]

Thus, for effective execution of large and complex projects, it is essential to have a project management team including the consultants who have a clear understanding of the technical requirements as well as necessary management techniques. There should be proper supervision and continuous and constant coordination between all the disciplines involved in the project. Above all it is essential to maintain a high morale and spirit of dedication by all concerned with the projects.[17]

There must be a system of reports and feedback for the successful operation of the project. There must be constant checks against conform plans so as to guide the activities in the intended direction. The plan against which comparison is made is not often an invariant of the activity which once made continues as unchanged for the life of the activity. Therefore if the plan is to change it must be for some reason which generally results from the acquisition of new facts.[18] Similarly, it may be discovered that there are some deficiencies in the equipment which have to be removed or unanticipated developments may necessitate adjustments to the project to optimize its use.

Project Evaluation

Every project is required to be evaluated in terms of its utility—social as well as economic. The results should be examined from the broader views, i.e. in terms of the national objectives enshrined in the development plans. The evaluation is also required in order to utilize the experience for future of contemporary projects of similar nature. It may throw some light on the possible bottlenecks or deficiencies. Since projects are essentially of innovative and experimental nature, the end results are always of vital importance for the ecumenicists and planners. A postmortem of projects may reveal the weaknesses in the original preparation and help to better the future preparations. Thus, there should be systematic evaluation of the projects in a co-ordinated fashion. It should be carried out from all the angle so as to assess the overall successes or failures in regard to the achievement of project objectives his role in the overall national development, i.e. its economic and social advantages or disadvantages, costs involved against the benefits and so on. For effective evaluation, there should be constant monitoring of the project with regular collection of information and processing of information. There also, experts should handle the review task.

The project cycle, from the inception of the project idea to the completion or end of the project, involves a number of complications and problems. Any flaw at any stage may lead to delays or increase in costs. These two problems may be attributed to any or a combination of the following reasons.[19]

(a) Feasibility studies are seldom done in-depth with regard to the assessment of market demand, availability of raw materials of desired specifications suitability of technology and mode of financing.

(b) Detailed time schedule and activity charts are neither prepared in-depth nor monitored properly. This is due to insufficient experience/knowledge in the total comprehension of the programme and application of an appropriate monitoring system.

(c) Cost estimates are made on ad hoc basis without a clear perception of the various items involved and their implications. Only very experienced engineers can visualize and provide for these items in the estimate.

(d) Inadequate estimates naturally call for supplementary fund allocation and result in delay in the execution. Late execution leads to further escalation of costs since inflation is almost an order of the day.

(e) Inexperienced handling to labour problems and spoilage of labour relations may cause serious bottlenecks in construction activities upsetting the project execution schedule.

In a nutshell, the main weaknesses of causing slippage may be the bad definition of a project, poor coordination, lack of competent staff, ad hoc decision making, change in resource availability, changing and conflicting project priorities, no fixed responsibility, bad human relations procedural delays, poor management information system, other organizational deficiencies, unanticipated consequences and so on.

For effective project management, there should be greater emphasis on planning and control training project personnel availability of required materials at the right time and cordial human relations. It is vital for the developing countries that projects are implemented within realistic budgets and time and for this, the authorities must give due importance to the role played by technically competent and cost-conscious planners and project managers.

EXERCISES

1. Discuss in brief different stages of a project.
2. Examine the process of formulation of a project.
3. Write short notes on the following:
   (a) Project installation
   (b) Project operation
   (c) Project evaluation

REFERENCES

[1]   United Nations, *Manual on Economic Development Projects*, New York, 1958, p. 7.

[2]   Goel, S.L., *Modernizing Administrative Management: Management Techniques and Administrative Research.* Arun Publications, Chandigarh, 1981, Vol. II, p. 105.

[3]   *Ibid.*, pp. 105–06.

[4]   *Manual on Economic Development Projects*, *op. cit.*, p. xiii.

[5]   Administration of Development Programmes & Projects, pp. 74–75.

[6]   *Ibid.*, p. 75.

[7] "Programming and Control of Implementation of Industrial Projects in Developing Countries," *United Nations Industrial Development Organization,* Vienna, Industrial Implementation System No.1, New York, 1970, p. 1.

[8] World Health Organization, *Health Project Management Manual* (76550), quoted in Goel, S.L. *Modernizing Administrative Management*, pp. 106–07.

[9] Programming and Control of Implementation of Industrial Projects, *op. cit.*, p. 7.

[10] Sastry, A.S., *Network Techniques in a Public Sector Fertilizer Project*, in Project Management Association, National Symposium on Effectiveness of Project Scheduling and Monitoring, New Delhi, Nov. 14–15, 1980, p. 73.

[11] Programming and Control of Implementation of Industrial Projects, *ibid.*, p. 14.

[12] Administration of Development Programmes and Projects. *op. cit.*, p. 82.

[13] Manual on Economic Development Projects, *op. cit.*, pp. 55–57.

[14] Kitchlu, J.M., "Project Management", in V.A. Pai Panandiker (Ed.), *Development Administration in India*, Macmillan, New Delhi, 1974. p. 85.

[15] *Ibid.*, p. 87.

[16] Administration of Development Programmes & Projects, *op. cit.*, pp. 83–84.

[17] Iyengar, R.K. and Ramamurthy, T.J., Effectiveness of Project Scheduling and Monitoring in *Project Management Association Symposium*, p. 252.

[18] Srivastava, S.S., Garg, R.C. and Prasad, J., "Monitoring and Scheduling of Research and Development Projects" in *Project Management Association*—Symposium, p. 182.

[19] Das, B., Role of Consultants on Planning and Project Management, in *Project Management Association National Symposium*, p. 133.

7

Planning Machinery and Development Planning in India

Planning as an instrument of socio-economic progress has created a new faith in the state. It became popular in the underdeveloped world because of its unique achievements in the field of economic development countries. After the World War II, due to the end of the colonial era and the rapid expansion of scientific and technical knowledge, the underdeveloped and newly emerged countries began a struggle to meet the challenges of development. They adopted a system of economic planning for achieving economic development and social justice.

PLANNING

Planning is a rational process of human behaviour. It means determining what is to be done and how it is to be done. "A plan is a programme of action for achieving define objectives or goals"[1]

Planning is a process of choosing and making things happen that might not otherwise happen. Millett observes, "Planning is the process of deterring the objectives of administrate effort and divining the means calculated to achieve them"[2]. Marshall Dimock defines planning as "the use of rational design as contracted with chance, the reaching of a decision before a line of action is taken instead of improving after the action has started". Simon, Smithsburg and Thompson define it as "the activity that concerns itself with proposals for the future. With the evaluation of alternate proposals and with the methods by which these proposals may be achieved".[3]

A succinct definition of the term has been given by Peter Decker. According to him. "Planning is the continuous process of making present knowledge of their future, organizing systematically the efforts needed to carry out these decisions and measuring the results of these decisions against the expectations through organized systematic feedback".[4]

When planning is taken up for achieving national development tasks, it is termed as development planning. A United Nations publication relates development planning to a teleological-determined manipulation of policy measures and instruments devised so as to stimulate the actors of the socio-economic scene to act in the way most conductive to the achievement of the national socio-economic development objective and goals.[5]

Planning may be of many kinds—economic, social, administrative physical, etc. The nature of planning varies according to its end. When the economic resources of a country are rationally arranged with a pre-determined purpose. It is called economic planning. It involves a careful arrangement throughout, and allocation of economic resources of the country as a whole. It is close to development planning as it always refers to planning by the state rather than any individuals. It is the making of major economic decision—what and how much is to be produced, and to whom it is to be allocated by the conscious decisions of a determinate authority on the basis of a comprehensive survey of the economy as a whole.

Administrative planning, on the other hand, consists of drawing up a programme of operations in advance and the provision of the requisite organizational material and procedure of carrying it out. In the works of Professor White, "Planning as a term used in the context of public administration, is not equivalent to making decisions on basic policy". Planning in the context of administration begins where general policy stops. It is now fully agreed that planning is an administrative process permeating all administrative efforts and is, thus, completely neutral. Administrative planning to improve administrative capability is basic for the success of development plans. The targets and goals of development plans should match the capabilities available in the country.

Need of Planning

The basic reason for adopting planning is to achieve the goals in a desired manner. In particular, it helps to:

(a) offset uncertainty and change

(b) focus attention on objectives

(c) gain economy in operations

(d) achieve efficiency and effectiveness

(e) facilitate control

Planning is of particular importance in developing countries. Where the government nearly always has the responsibility for the accelerated use of the available human and material resources. Long-term programmes based on well-reasoned priorities, are invaluable for such countries as they cannot afford to waste time people or material.[6] These countries face the problems of scarcity of capital. Lack of skilled personnel, lopsided production, backward agricultural system, countrywide poverty with the consequences of a low volume of effective demand and a large labour surplus which have been regarded as the main obstacles for progress and growth in such countries. There is also deficiency of capital, labour and management skills and organization. There is little industrialization, because of lack or daring risk taking temperament and because of shortage of industrial equipment and technical personnel. The objectives of development planning are not the same for all the countries or for a country at all time. What precisely are the objectives placed by the planners before them depends on the stage of economic development, nature of economic development, social, economic and political conditions prevalent at the time and the requirements of a particular situation in a country. The rationale of development planning in developing countries is supported by the following points:

   (a) Economic stability

   (b) Superiority of State's judgment

   (c) Reduction in economic inequalities

   (d) Enhancing national income

   (e) Effective utilization of natural resources

   (f) Capital formation

   (g) Comprehensive development of public and private sectors

   (h) Balanced regional development

   (i) Co-ordination of various development activities

   (j) Socio-economic welfare.

Planning is the basic criterion to carry out development tasks. It is required to promote change, and still is not free from objection. Whereas Lord Keynes, Webbs, Stafford Cripps. A.P. Lerner, Dobb, Barbara Wootton. Lord Beveridege and many more have advocated the case of planned economy. The economists like William Letwin, Van Hayek, Berne, etc. have opposed the idea of planned economy. They put forward the following arguments against planning:

The foremost objection levelled against planning is that it will cause loss of freedom. Planning cannot be successful without strict regulation and control by the State. This will lead to loss of private initiative, loss of consumer sovereignty and even the loss of freedom of occupation. Hayek goes to the extent of calling planning a road to serfdom, leading to a regimented and cruel society.

However, it is not easy to formulate a proper plan. Lack of reliable data and statistics and continuous changes in prices make the task of formulating a plan very difficult. Moreover, in an unplanned economy, every entrepreneur will gain or lose independently, but in a planned economy, a single mistake made by planners will make the entire country surface for it. Furthermore, it is equally difficult to implement a plan properly. Successful implementation requires an alert, efficient and honest administrative structure, which is quite often non-existent in underdeveloped countries.

It is also said that planning will hinder the automatic working of the economy and will make it extremely rigid. This may lead to lack of co-ordination between costs, prices and wages. Moreover, in a market economy a production process ensuring minimum costs or maximum profits is considered to be optimum. In a planned economy, however, this measuring rod is not there. Therefore, it will become difficult to know how efficient our process and technique of production. Some economists also hold that planning will lead to too much standardization and lack of variety. This will rob life of colour and spice.

Finally, it is argued that planning will bring forth the rule of bureaucracy which, in turn, may breed many other socio-economic ills such as red-tapism, corruption, favouritism, etc.

However, if we analyze the whole discussion, we will have to conclude that much of the criticism levelled against planning is uncalled for. It is true that economic planning may involve some political implications and overtones. Yet it is illogical to hold that planning means the end of economic freedom. The experience of France, the USA the UK and other capitalist countries which have adopted planning to some extent shows that planning and democratic way of life can co-exist. Moreover, many other shortcomings of planning can easily be overcome through fareful and sincere efforts.

Pre-requisites of Successful Planning in Developing Countries

Most of the developing countries face similar problems, and thus, require certain essential pre-conditions to make their planning efforts a success. Some of the basic requirements may be discussed under the points as follows:

A sufficiently developed administrative set-up

The development of a country will depend largely on an efficient administrative set-up, planning requires an army of devoted personnel able to maintain a high order of efficiency. Unless there are, at the top of personnel machinery, trustworthy, upright, unselfish men with nationalist outlook planning will invariably fall. For successful and efficient planning, a central planning body is essential which should consist of experts in different lines including experienced administrators. The existence of a strong, competent and incorrupt administrations also need for the proper implementation of the plans.

Sound information system

The availability of adequate, accurate, reliable and up-to-date statistical data pertaining the existing economic situation in the country is an important pre-requisite of successful economic planning. Accurate information about the economic conditions and resources can be collected only if the existing and potential resources are thoroughly surveyed. Without reliable data about the availability of raw-material, capital, human and natural resources including minerals, water power, etc., fixing targets becomes impossible. In the words of Professor Baykov, "Every act of planning, in so far at it is not mere fantastic castle building, pre-suppose as preliminary investigation of existing resources. "Setting up of central statistical organization with a competent staff for collecting statistical data is essential for the formulation of a realistic plan that can be effectively implemented". To quote Professor F. Zweig, "The road to effective planning leads through research and perfect knowledge of factual relationships. Satisfactory statistics, inquiries, reports and cost accountancy, besides good administrative and through-going propaganda, provide for effective planning."

Laying down limited objectives and fixing concrete targets

Too many objectives are not likely to be fulfilled in a planned economy. If planning is to be a success. It should have some basic principle objectives to be achieved within a specified period of time. These objectives should be definite and laid down in an order of priority keeping in view the urgency of the country's economic problems. It is essential that the objectives are not too many in number, and are not like wild dreams of distant ideals, but they should be limited realistic, feasible and within reach. As for instance, the common objective of planning in an underdeveloped economy may be to raise the level of output through industrialization to achieve full employment, to increase national income and per-capita income so as to raise the standard of living of the masses and to bring about a reduction in the inequalities of income and wealth in the society.

For their attainment, objectives are broken down into concrete tangents which are fixed for each industry and for each sector, for agriculture, for transport and communication, for imports and exports and of education and public health. Targets are fixed in terms of the quantity of production such as, so many million tons of steel, fertilizers, kilowatts of power, acres of area to be irrigated, and so on. In a mixed economy, such targets are laid down for the public sector as well as the private sector. Though for the private sector, the targets indicate the job assigned to each sector of the economy. Hence, fixing of targets is essential to achieve the aims or objectives of a development plan.

Socialistic economic organization

If planning is to be successful in an underdeveloped country, it should be preceded by an economic organization that promotes it and does not hinder it. The economic organization must be one that responds to the requirements of planning. Hence, socialist economic organization, in which means of production are socialized, is a basic condition for successful economic planning in a country. The planning experience in some, capitalist countries shows that private enterprise never fervors planning. In the words of Professor Charles Bettelhein, "Effective planning and private enterprise go ill together. For genuine economic planning, socialization of the means of production is needed." He points out how genuine overall economic planning is rendered almost impossible by the existence of a large private sector. First, the existence of a large private sector results in the deficiency and scantiness of statistical information in many fields of basic importance in plan-preparation. Secondly, the private sector makes it difficult, even impossible for the administrative institution to fully mobilize the national resource, and to put them into use to the best advantage of planned economic growth. Thirdly, genuine economic planning requires complete mastery over the prices of main goods as well as over the income. The private sector with its price mechanism may lead to such a re-allocation of national income and of the vestibule resources that the national plan would be defeated. Fourthly, with a private sector much larger than the public sector, it is practically impossible to allocate investments and to select techniques which would be in conformity with the needs of a rapid and planned economic growth. Professor G. Mydal suggests, "The underdeveloped countries, if they are to catch up with the industrially advanced countries of the west, must adopt the Soviet pattern of planning as the fundamental system for their economic development". Professor J.K. Galibraith also state, "In many parts of the world, there is in fact, no real alternative to extensive public enterprise."

Well-formulated and integrated plans

There are different stages of planning, such as drawing up of the plan, its adoption, execution and supervision. Different bodies undertake these functions of planning at different stages. In planning, the principle of separation of functions has to be repeated and maintained, e.g. making of the plan is the task of a body of experts to reach workers of the Planning Commission, the adoption of the plan is the function of the Parliament, the execution of the plan is done by the ministries and the administrative set-up and supervision is again assigned to a special body of experts such as the Plan Evaluation Committee of the Planning Commission. In planning, the administrative principle of separation should not mean lack of co-ordination in the functioning of a plan at different stages. For its ultimate success, a plan must be well-integrated in all respects.

Strong and efficient government

Economic planning pre-supposes the existence of a strong national government with a high degree of honesty and efficiency. If we study the working of planned economy in historical perspective, we shall find that effective planning has seldom taken place in a loose democratic set-up with corrupt and inefficient bureaucratic administrative machinery. Planning has succeeded only in countries where political set-up was authoritarian, and administration— honest, efficient and responsible. According to R.S. Tucker, "Planning as is universally admitted, requires centralized direction equipped to act more promptly and vigorously than parliament or other forms of representative governments have shown themselves able to action the past. "There can be no difference option on the issue that the drawing up of a plan for development must be the function of the central authority or government in consultation and agreement with the state governments the latter are in a better position to chalk out their programmes of development for incorporation in central planning for the country as a whole. But once the plan is drawn up, the Central Government should see to it that there is no slackness to the part of the states in respect of their obligations towards the fulfillment of the objective of the plan.

Mobilization of financial resources

Success of economic planning also depends on proper mobilization of financial resources. In an underdeveloped country, finance is a great snag in planning. Financial resources are usually inadequate and irregular in flow and cannot be effectively developed and mobilized to the required extent. Hence, administrative, fiscal and monetary measures have to be very wisely framed and effectively adopted an order to mobilize resources for the development of backward economies. The principle of profitability has to be retained in the working of public enterprises. They should no longer be run with the traditional no profit or loss motive. Moreover, in democratic countries, loans, government revenue, small savings, etc. are to be mobilized efficiently to finance public sector programmes. Also limited doses of deficit financing and control of inflation and administrative regulations, both direct and indirect, determine the achievements of planning.

Economic controls

Planning and controls have close relationship, and therefore, efficiency and success of economic planning largely depend on the adoption and efficient execution of economic controls, commercial controls as well as physical or quantity controls. Economic controls are particularly essential in mixed economy where both the sectors public and private—pull on scarce resources to meet their requirements of investment. According to J.M. Meade, "Planning is implemented by a series of State controls. Raw materials and capital goods are allocated and licensed to achieve their planned use. Labour is directed to planned employment's and the consumption of products is subjected to rotating and licensing. Full employment is achieved since the plan accounts for all available resources. Equity is assured since by rationing, each citizen is granted a fair share of national product. The social wastes of competition are avoided. "For the success of planning in an underdeveloped country, therefore, a policy of price controls, control of distribution of essential good and scarce raw-materials, import and export controls, exchange controls of capital issues, etc. have to be enforced and implemented effectively. In the absence of economic controls, planning is bound to prove abortive".

Flexibility in planning

A plan should not be rigid. It should be as flexible as possible. All those countries which are planning the development of their economy are in a state of continual change regarding techniques of production, tastes of people and demography, etc. All these changes require new types of skill and tools. A plan, therefore should be dynamic and should adapt itself to continuing changes in the economy. According to Mrs. Barbara Wootton, 'We have to keep in the forefront the fact that every well-conceived plan is going to call for change, even through it must begin from the status quo. Its job is to improve upon what it finds...Every good plan will be different from that which it succeeds, and unless it is drafted to cover only the shortest possible period, it will almost certainly itself need to be revised in the course of execution, so as to meet new circumstances that have arisen between the time of its conception and the date at which it is intended to give place to its successor." Economic planning, to be successful, will have to recognize the need for elasticity and adaptability.

Good international relations

A planned economy should have good relations with other countries of the world. As far as possible, it should not associate itself with any power blocs, and foreign trade relations must be maintained primarily on non-political grounds. Maintaining good relations with the outside world becomes specially important in the context of economic planning in the underdeveloped countries. Success of planning in underdeveloped countries is also conditioned by external factors such as the flow of foreign capital, technical know-how and assistance of numerous types. Hence, a developing country committed to planning must maintain friendly and harmonious relations with other countries of the world.

Public co-operation

Mass co-operation and spirit of sacrifice are also very essential for successful economic planning. An economic revolution or very rapid economic development in a planned economy is possible only by men and women in whom lies the mainspring of progress. People should be roused to the need for an economic effort, and people in power should encourage this urge. When it is not done, planning falls. As Professor W.A. Lewis states, "Popular enthusiasm is both the lubricating oil of planning and the possible."[7] People at all levels, can be made to make sacrifices by foregoing immediate satisfaction of their wants in order to buildup a strong base for their country's economic development provided they are convinced that their sacrifices will bear fruit.

PLANNING MACHINERY IN INDIA

The most important event in the economic history of India since gaining independence from the British in 1947 has been the initiation of the process of planned economic development of the country by the Government of India.[8] In the course of three decades planning and development have become household words in the country today.[9] During these years, India has attempted to bring about rapid economic and social development of the country through a planned effort.

Historical Background

The first effort at introducing social planning in India was made by an individual noted for his pioneering zeal and breadth of vision. Dr. M. Visvesvarayya, in 1934, published a ten-year plan with the objective of doubling the national income.[10] In 1936, he published an essay underlining the desirability and feasibility of planning for industrialization of the country. For the formulation, implementation and administration of the plan, he had suggested the formation of an advisory body of 60 members including political leaders, economists, Businessmen, administrators, etc. and a Planning Commission of 5 to 7 members for day-to-day execution. Though interesting as an intellectual exercise, this could not directly influence any social action, or any government move.[11] Five years later, in 1938 at a conference of the Provincial Ministers of Industries held under the chairmanship of the then congress President, Subhash Chandra Bose, a resolution was passed which stated that industrialization was essential for meeting the problems of poverty, unemployment, national defence and economic regeneration and a comprehensive scheme of national planning had to be formulated as a step towards such industrialization. The Conference also recommended that a commission should be appointed for this purpose, and that it should consist of representatives of the Governments of the Provinces and the princely States in the country, the Federation of Indian Chambers of Commerce and the All India Village Industries Association. The conference also decided to appoint a planning committee with a view to do preliminary work regarding the proportion of a national plan.

Jawaharlal Nehru, the architect of planning India, set up the National Planning Committee towards the end of 1938. The Committee considered all aspects of planning and produced a series of studies on different subjects connected with economic development. The Committee laid down that the State should own or control all key industries and services, mineral resources and railways, waterways, shipping and other public utilities and in fact, all those large-scale industries which were likely to become monopolistic in character. The Committee felt that were likely to become monopolistic in character. The Committee felt that it was not possible to draw up a scheme or national planning without including agriculture. The Committee aimed at doubling the standard of living of the people in 10 years. The Committee appointed 29 sub-committees to study and report on different sectors of the economy and certain special problems relating to national planning. Though the work of the Committee was interrupted by the outbreak of the Second World War, and the arrest and imprisonment of its chairman, a number of sub-committees prepared reports relating to their respective fields. These reports and the work of the Committee generally led to considerable discussion of and interest in the problems of national planning.

Besides this, eight industrialists conceived, "A Plan of Economic Development", which was popularly known as the Bombay plan. There was also a Gandhian plan which was prepared by Shriman Narayan. The world-famous revolutionary, M.N. Roy formulated the People's Plan. These three private development plans were published by the Planning and Development Board which was established by the government in 1944. These plans are of historical importance only, because they were paper plans which were never implemented. Their importance lay in the fact that they indicated the trend of economic thinking on the eve of independence. These pre-independence efforts at planning brought out a certain unity of approach to the problems of national reconstruction as most of the plans included more or less the same objectives to be achieved through similar means.

An interim government, under the leadership of Nehru, was appointed in 1946 as a part of the process of transfer of power from Britain to India. An Advisory Planning Board was appointed by the interim government in October, 1946 with Shri K.C. Neogy as Chairman for reviewing the work that had already been done in the field of planning and to make recommendations for the future machinery for planning. The Board, in its report, submitted in December 1946. Recommended the appointment of a single, compact and authoritative organization for the purpose of planning. The Board also suggested that the proposed Planning Commission should be mainly advisory in character, the final decisions resting with the government. The Commission was to be a non-political body whose members would not fluctuate with changes in political fortunes.[12]

THE PLANNING COMMISSION

The central theme of public policy and philosophy of national planning in India since independence has been the promotion of balanced economic growth, for increasing opportunities for gainful employment; for promoting greater equality in income and wealth and raising living standards and working conditions for the masses.[13] The constitution has declared India to be a welfare state and included the following principles of economic policy:

(a) That the ownership and control of the material resource of the community distributed as best to subserve the common good and

(b) That the operation of the economic system does not result in the concentration of wealth and means of production to the common detriment.[14]

To carry out these principles and to achieve the national developmental goals necessiated the setting up of a planning machinery. On the recommendation of the Advisory Planning Board, the Government of India passed a resolution on 15 March 1950, to establish the Planning Commission.[15] It may be noted here that the Planning Commission was set-up by a movement resolution or statutory instrument which supports its operation even though it has assumed a unique stature and importance in the administrative and government organization of the country.[16]

Functions

The Planning Commission has the responsibility to assess resources, formulate plans, define their stages, appraise progress and make related recommendations on policy and administration. The resolution for creating the Commission referred to the Constitution of India and especially to certain directive principles of State policy, and stated that in view of these and the declared objective of the government to promote and rapid rise in the standard of living of the people a Planning Commission was being set up with the following functions:

(a) To make an assessment of the material, and human resources of the country, including technical personnel, and investigate the possibilities of augmenting such of these resources as are found to be deficient in relation to the nation's requirements

(b) To formulate a plan for the most effective and balanced utilization of the country's resources

(c) On determination of priorities; to define the stage in which the plan should be carried out and propose. The allocation of resources for the due completion of each stage

(d) To indicate the factors which are the hindrance for the economic development, and determine the condition which in view for the successful execution of the plan

(e) To determine the nature of machinery which will be necessary for securing the successful implementation of each stage of the plan in all its aspects.

(f) To appraise from time-to-time the progress achieved in the execution of each stage of the plan, and to recommend the adjustments of policy and measures that such appraisal may show to be necessary

(g) To make such interim or ancillary recommendations as might be appropriate on consideration of the prevailing economic conditions, current policies, measures and development programme, or an examination of such specific problems as maybe referred to it for advice by central or State governments for facilitating the discharge of the duties assigned to it

It should be remembered that the Commission is a staff body responsible for the preparation of national plans for economic development, and is not responsible for the execution of development programmes or plans. The resolution indicated that the Commission would be essentially an advisory body, and would make recommendations to the Cabinet. The resolution stated, the Cabinet, "In framing its recommendations to the Commission will act in close understanding and consolation with the Ministries of the Central Government and the

Governments of the States. The responsibility for taking and implementing decisions will rest with the Central and State Governments."

In more specific terms its functions are:

(a) Assessment of resources

(b) Priorities of allocation of resources

(c) Problems of planning

(d) Formulation of development plans of Central and State Governments

(e) Planning of industrial development

(f) Determination of the nature of the machinery necessary for the implementation of the plan in all its respects

(g) An appraisal from time to time of the progress achieved in the execution of each stage of the plan

(h) Perspective planning

(i) Public cooperation in national development

(j) Publication of the journal *Yojana*[17]

COMPOSITION

The Advisory Planning Board had suggested the setting up of a single and compact organization for the purpose of planning. In its report the Board had suggested the establishment of a small Planning Commission comprising three to five members. In case the membership was to be five, it would consist of:

(a) A person of standing with general experience of public affairs, who would be the chairman.

(b) Two non-officials with knowledge and experience of industry, agriculture or labour.

(c) A government official with knowledge and experience of finance and general administration.

(d) A person eminent in the field of science and technology.

Alternatively, a three-member body would comprise of:

(a) A person of standing with general experience of public affairs, who would be the chairman

(b) A non-official with knowledge and experience of industry

(c) A government official preferably with some experience of finance

Originally, the Planning Commission was set up with Prime Minister Nehru as its Chairman, and five full time members V.T. Krishnamachari, G.L. Mehta, S.K. Patil, G.L. Nanda and C.D. Deshmukh. The composition of the Commission underwent changes from time to time.

The number of full time members has varied between three and seven. The study team of the machinery for planning in its interim report (March 1967) suggested a whole time membership of not more than six to ensure effective teamwork in the Commission. The Administrative Reforms Commission in its interim report of April 1967 however, recommended that the number of whole time members should not exceed seven.

But the government decided to keep the number of full time members including the Deputy Chairman at five. The Planning Commission in 1973 consisted of the Chairman, the Deputy Chairman, the Minister of Finance and four other members—G.S. Pathak, B. Sivarman, B.S. Minhas and S. Chakravarty. The total membership of the Commission as of 1975 was only six having Indira Gandhi as the chairman, P.N. Haksar as the Deputy Chairman, and C. Subramaniam, S. Chakravarty and S. Sivaraman as members. The composition of the Commission again changed in 1977 under the Janata Party government. The membership was as follows

(a) Chairman—the Prime Minister

(b) Deputy Chairman

(c) Part-time Members—(i) Union Home Minister (ii) Union Defence Minister (iii) Union Finance Minister

(d) Full-time Members—three

With the takeover of every new government, a major reshuffle is effected in the Planning Commission. The number of total members (including the Deputy Chairman) is now eight. A major change is that the Planning Minister is not the Deputy Chairman, which has generally been the case. The new composition includes the following categories of members (as per India-2000):

(a) Chairman—Prime Minister

(b) Deputy Chairman (full time)

(c) Four full-time members—Experts

(d) Three part-time members—Ministers

The Secretary belongs to the IAS cadre and the Statically Advisor to the Cabinet is additional *de facto* member of the Commission.

It is observed that ever since the inception of the Planning Commission. Ministers are included as its members. Their inclusion has been objected to by many. The ARO examined the controversy and made the following observations:

"Experience so far gained, however, shows that Ministers, busy as they are with their governmental and parliamentary work, are unable to find time to make a significant contribution to the planning process. Their membership of the Commission has only provided a ground for criticism. If Ministers are member of the Commission, the Commission is likely to be committed to the Minister's stand with regard to executive matters relating to the implementation of the plans. This will affect its capacity to make a critical appraisal and evaluation of the implementation of the plan by the executive. Further, as the Commission has to formulate plans for the whole of the country, the inclusion of some central Ministers as members thereof is likely to expose the Commission to the criticism that the States in which they are interested are placed in a favourable position and that the other States suffer neglection. Such a criticism becomes particularly serIous if the parties in power in some of the States are different from the party in power at the Center." The ARC, therefore, did not favour Ministers the members. On the other hand, the Estimates Committee of the Parliament in its report viewed it desirable that Ministers should continue to be associated with the Commission. It was felt that the idea of the Commission functioning as a completely detached body was not likely to be very useful in practice, and that if the Commission was out of touch with the government for want of close association with the thinking on the broader issues of policy, it may make for ineffectiveness in planning.[18]

It has developed in practice and by convention that the Prime Minister is the Chairman of the Commission. From the very beginning of the Commission, Jawaharlal Nehru was its Chairman. The original resolution about the appointment of the Commission had only mentioned "Shri Jawaharlal Nehru" (not the "Prime Minister") as the Chairman of the Commission. But Lal Bahadur Shastri, who became Prime Minister after the death of Nehru in 1964 assumed change as the Chairman. At present, the Prime Minister is the Chairman of the Commission. However, since the very inception of the Commission, it has become evident that the Prime Minister would not find it possible to discharge his functions the chairman except on a formal sense he could not even attend all the meetings of the Commission. It was also essential for the Prime Minister not to become too closely connected with the Commission so as to be able to take a detached attitude towards its recommendations when they reach the cabinet. It was, therefore, decided to create the office of the Deputy Chairman who would like after the day-to-day functions of the Commission. It was conceived that he would provide the main working link between the Cabinet at the Center, the Chief Ministers of different States and the Planning Commission. He has to led a group of eminent members so as to work as a team. He has the responsibility to ensure some kind of continuity in the overall process of planned development and advising the Prime Minister on the choice of suitable personnel for the membership of the Commission.[19] P.N. Haksar, V.T. Krishnamachari, D.T. Lakdawala and R.D. Gadgil, Dr. Manmohan Singh, Pranab Mukherjee have served as Deputy Chairman of the Commission from time to time.

As regards the full-time member of the Commission, their number varies from time to time. There are generally three to seven full-time members and there may also be some part-time members. The appointment of the members of the Commission is treated as a purely executed decision. The Prime Minister decides, in consolation with the Deputy Chairman, that a particular person is to be appointed as a member and after consulting the person concerned, instructs the Commission to arrange for the assumption of office by the proposed member. Since the beginning, a convention has grown up that the Union Finance Minister should be a member of the Commission. In addition to the Finance Minister, Minister for Planning and some other Union Ministers are needed to be appointed from time to time, as Members of the Commission Ministers are appointed as part-time members. Along the full-time members, persons with experience of administration have always, found a place on the Commission. Apart from this, persons associated with industry, agriculture and commerce have also been included from time to time. No qualifications have been laid down or prescribed for the membership, but the ARC Study Team on the machinery of Planning had suggested certain qualifications and qualities for members to possess. In other words, "The members should be chosen for their expertise, wisdom and knowledge of handling men and affairs. What we need is not narrow specialization, but wide knowledge and experience in major areas of development, such as agriculture and rural economy, industry, commerce, science and technology, economic and other social science, and public administration."[20]

As regards the age of the full-time members, since they are treated as executive appointments equivalent in rank and status to those of Ministers, no minimum or maximum age limits are laid down for them. As far as salary and allowances of the members are concerned, they have the same salary, allowances and other facilities as those of the Union Minister. Members are appointed without any specific period being indicated regarding their tenure. They continue in office as long as they are willing to serve the Commission and their services are considered benefits to the Commission by the Prime Minister. For the members a convention has developed that a Minister, who for any reason ceases to be a Minister, relinquishes charge of his membership of the Commission.

The Commission functions as a collective body. A number of formal and informal meetings are held through which the business of the Commission is transited, the number of meetings varies according to the work that has to be disposed of. The main responsibility for carrying out the work of the Commission devolves in the full-time members and it is they who meet frequently, formally and informally, for disposing of business.[21]

The four full-time members are incharges of each of the following groups:

(a) Industry labour, transport and power group

(b) Agriculture and rural development group

(c) Perspective planning group.

(d) Education, scientific research and social services group.

ORGANIZATION

The administrative organization of the Planning Commission has undergone far reaching changes since its inception in 1950. It was recognized from the beginning that for the kind of work that the Commission had to undertake, its internal organization had to be different from that in normal government ministries or departments. The present organization of the Commission is mainly based on the principles laid down by a group set by it in 1971, as follows:

(a) There should be more coherent grouping of the divisions in the Planning Commission with a clear deliberation of (i) line division dealing with various sectors and their inter-relationship (ii) plan formulation and co-ordination divisions and servicing divisions.

(b) The line divisions need to be strengthened in order that they are fully equipped to undertake (i) long-term sectored planning (ii) participate in the preparation and evaluation of projects and programmes (iii) monitoring of plan performance and (iv) improvements in the information content in their work.

(c) Necessary expertise should be provided in the servicing divisions to provide back-up support for project appraisal, monitoring, evaluation and information.

The Planning Commission has adopted an organization which reflects its expert character. Its internal organization is built around two hierarchies, which may be called the administrative and the technical ones. The administrative hierarchy has the Secretary of the Planning Commission at the top having Joint Secretaries, Deputy Secretaries, Under-Secretaries and other lower staffs under him. These functionaries carry out the normal administrative tasks necessary in an organization. The technical hierarchy, on the other hand, begins with advisers who report directly to their respective members depending on the allocation of work among them. For instance, the Adviser Perspective will be working directly under the member dealing with this subject. The Adviser, who is of the rank of either Additional Secretary or Joint Secretary, is essentially a group co-ordinating functionary, co-ordinating, that is the work relating to the subjects which have been allotted to him. Under him comes the chief whose talk is to undertake a detailed technical examination and analysis of programmes and schemes falling within his sphere of work. The chief is assisted by Directors, Joint Directors and the other staffs. It needs to be pointed out that the organizational structure is characterized by flexibility, and thus, an Adviser may have directly under him a Joint Director, there being no Chief or Director.[22]

The technical hierarchy is manned by experts, such as economists, engineers, statisticians, etc. though some of the Advisers may be drawn from a generalist administrative services like the I.A.S. and so on. The majority of the experts are economists. The Planning Commission is today the single largest employer of the Indian Economic Service. The functionaries on the administrative side are drawn from the A.S.I. and other non-technical central services like the Indian Audit and Accounts Service, Indian Revenue Service, Central Secretariat Service and so on. All taken together, the Planning Commission has a staff about 1150, out of which 450 are officers, others being clerical and lower category staff.[23]

Most of the functions of the Planning Commission are carried out in a number of technical divisions. Presently, there are about 25 such divisions each dealing with an important segment of planning. Various projects and schemes to be incorporated in the plan are scrutinized and analyzed in these divisions. These are generally headed by subject specialists, designated as chiefs or directors. Each division is staffed by both senior and junior research staff.

Descriptions of the technical divisions are as follows:[24]

Agriculture Division

The agriculture division is responsible for agricultural planning, both physical and financial. In particular, it is concerned with subjects such as planning of agricultural production, agricultural marketing, co-operation; and agricultural credit, animal husbandry and dairying; fisheries, forests and soil conservation, rural works, agricultural labour, etc. In addition, special studies on different aspects of agricultural production are initiated from time to time.

Economic, Finance and Resources Division

In regard to the overall aspects of planning, the division examines such issues as are connected with the size of the plan, objectives and priorities and broad economic policy to be pursued for achieving the object of the plan. In regard to resources, the main function of the division is to work out an assessment of financial resources, domestic as well as foreign. The division has also to give an overall evaluation of the progress achieved over a particular period in economic terms. The division has to deal with references received from the central ministries, the State governments and outside bodies and individuals.

Education Division

Problems connected with various types of education, such as general, technical, physical, social, rural, etc. are studied in the education division. In addition, studies on the following subjects are also undertaken in the division:

(a) Scholarships

(b) Library development

(c) School feeding and school health programme

(d) Hindi and regional languages

(e) Cultural activities

(f) National cadet corps

(g) Central assistance to states for education development

Health and Family Welfare Division

Health and family welfare division deals with all aspects of health problems in the country. The following types of studies are initiated in the division to serve as a firm basis for future planning:

(a) Available health facilities

(b) Various diseases prevalent in the country

(c) Vital statistics

(d) Other specific subjects of importance

Industries and Mineral Division

Problems of policy programmes, etc. connected with various industries and minerals including the question of co-ordination with small scale industries, are studied in the industries and minerals division. The subjects dealt with in this division include special studies on various items relating to the development of industries and public enterprises.

Employment and Manpower Division

All aspects of labour and employment problems, including manpower resources and employment are dealt with in the employment and social planning division.

Land Reforms Division

The functions of the land reforms division are as follows:

   (a) To maintain continuous study of problems relating to the ownership, management, cultivation and distribution of land

   (b) To assist the State governments in determining and carrying out programmes of land reforms

   (c) To evaluate and report from time to time on the operation, progress and effects or measures of land reforms

   (d) To recommend such measures and adjustments in land policy as may be with a view to fulfil the directive principles of State policy, prescribed in the Constitution of the country and the programmes and objectives of the plan

   (e) To examine the land reforms proposals of the State governments prior to their introduction in the State legislatures

Perspective Planning Division

It deals with questions of general policy affecting long-term planning and development in the country. It is concerned with problems relating to long range prospects of development of power resources, basic industries, transport services, pattern of agricultural development and employment in relation to increase in productivity.

Programme Administration Division

The programme administration division brings together into common table the public sector plan as a whole, both from the Center and the States. It also prepares and co-ordinates material for periodical reports on the progress of the plan.

Public Co-operation Division

The division deals with the problems relating to the securing of public of co-operation and participation in national development. These problems include widespread understanding of the plan, channeling a voluntary basis the unused time and skill and other spare resources of the people and securing of co-operation through voluntary organizations, universities, professional associations, etc.

Transport Division

Problems relating to planned development in the field of transport, including roads, road transport, railways, ports, etc. are studied in the transport division.

Statistical and Survey Division

The main functions of the statistical and survey division are as follows:

(a) To promote, through various statistics collection agencies in the Union and State Government, the collection, checking and analysis of statistics relating to the plan and the progress of its implementation

(b) To maintain essential statistics needed by the Planning Commission:

(c) To prepare periodical progress reports.

Housing, Urban Development and Water Supply Division

Housing, Urban Development and Water Supply Division deals with policy programmes, etc. relating to various aspects of urban development, housing and construction.

Resources and Scientific Research Division

The resources and scientific research division is responsible for dealing with problems relating to planned development of scientific research in the country. The division also collects necessary information regarding various natural resources including land, forest and mineral resources which is vital to plan formulation.

The other general divisions are plan co-ordination division power and energy division monitoring and information division, irrigation and command area development division, social welfare division, socio-economic research unit, international economic unit project appraisal division, communication, information and broadcasting division backward classes division, and rural development and co-operation division.

Apart from the general and technical division, a number of working groups are appointed. These groups comprised ten to fifteen members including administrators, economists and technicians from various central ministries and divisions of the Planning Commission as a means of co-ordinating the work of the ministries with its own in formulating plans for different sectors of the economy. The number of working groups varies from time to time. For instance, at one time, the number was 44. These groups make through investigation into the problems assigned to them relating to different aspects of the economy, and prepare reports suggesting measures to tackle the given problems and policies and programmes needed for achieving the targets.

Links of the Planning Commission with the Parliament

The Planning Commission has important links with the Parliament through the Prime Minister (who is the Chairman of the Commission) and also through the Minister of Planning. In the beginning, the Prime Ministers was the only spokesman of the Commission in the Parliament. In 1953, it was decided to appoint the Minister of Planning to act as the spokesman of the Commission in the Parliament, and G.L. Nanda who was already the Deputy Chairman of the Commission, was given this portfolio. The Minister is sometimes assisted by one or two Deputy Ministers. In addition to the normal accountability of the Commission to the Parliament which is ultimately reflected in the Parliament having the right to vote, the demands for meeting the expenditure on the Commission, the Parliament is consulted in various ways on the policies and programmes that are formulated by the Commission. The practice has been that both the Houses of the Parliament hold discussions on the draft outlines of the Five Year Plans and later, on the final reports on the Five Year Plans. Sometimes, more elaborate procedures are also followed. For example, at the time of formulating the Third Five Year Plan in 1960. Five Committees of the draft plan. The subjects allotted to these Committees were:

       Committee A – Policy, resources and allocation
       Committee B – Industry, power and transport
       Committee C – Agriculture and rural economy
       Committee D – Social services
       Committee E – Technical, manpower and scientific research

Each Committee has to consist of such members of the Parliament as wished to participate in the discussion of the subjects allotted to that Committee. The membership of the Committees varied from 158 in the case of Committee C to 34 in the case of Committee E.[25] Apart from this, some informal Committees may also be constituted comprising members of the Parliament belonging to different political parties for the purpose of discussing with them and keeping them in touch with the thinking about Five Year Plans. In addition to these discussions of the Five Year Plans when they are formulated, the Parliament also holds discussions on regular basis for reviewing the progress of the Plans.

An Informal Consultative Committee of the Parliament also serves as an important link between the Parliament and the Planning Commission. This was established in 1954 with members from both houses, at budget sessions and twice in the monsoon and winter sessions. But in actual practice, the Consultative Committee relating to the Planning Commission usually meets once in a session.

Links of the Planning Commission with the Union and State Governments

The subject of Planning is included in the concurrent list of the Constitution which means both the Union and the State governments can legislate on it. This is a clear recognition of the fact that planning is and can only be a national subject which is of interest to both the governments. If the Planning Commission is to formulate its plans and implement them successfully and effectively. It must secure active co-operation, close collaboration and much goodwill of the Union and State governments. This necessitates close organizational links between the Planning Commission, on the one hand, and the Union and State governments on the other hand.[26] At the same time, it is purely an advisory body and can only make recommendations to the Union and State governments. However, as the position that the plans have come to occupy in the economic and administrative life of the country, the Union Ministers and State governments are also depending on the Commission for support and advice. Because of the importance that has come to be attached to the advice of the Commission in matters relating to the economic field, important matters should be referred to the Commission for advice.

At the highest level, the link between the Union cabinet and the Planning Commission is provided by the Prime Minister, the real chief executive who is also the Chairman of the Commission. This link with the cabinet is further strengthened by the inclusion of some Union Ministers in the Planning Commission. Though the Prime Minister does not attend all its meetings and is not associated with its day-to-day business yet his being the Chairman adds to the prestige and influence of the Commission. However, he attends the meetings dealing with the problems of over policy while the task of looking after the day-to-day business has been left to the Deputy Chairman of the Commission. The Finance Minister usually attends meetings that are concerned with the key problems of economic and financial policy, but it is understood on both sides that his membership of the Commission and his participation in its deliberations does not commit the Ministry of Finance to the proposals put forward by the Commission. The advantage claimed from these arrangements is therefore, not that the Commission's views are automatically accepted by the Cabinet but that there is a possibilities of co-ordinate thinking at various stages so that there is not much room left for controversies and difficulties that may delay plan formulation and implementation.

Another important link between the Union Government and the Commission is the Cabinet Secretary. He is expected to provide the principal formal link. From the very beginning, the Cabinet Secretary had been the ex-officio Secretary to the Commission. But this arrangement was criticized by the Estimates Committee,[27] and in 1964, the Government put an end to this position and appointed a full-time Secretary to the Commission. However, the practice of the Cabinet Secretary as the Principal Secretary of the Commission was reviewed in 1973. The main advantages claimed from this arrangement are that the Secretary of the Commission being also the Cabinet Secretary is able to get the views of the ministries, and in his dual capacity, can do things by way of discussion on difficult questions at the official level at the meetings of Secretaries, etc.

Similarly, there are other officers performing dual functions. The Chief of the Labour and Employment Division in the Commission is also working as Labour Adviser in the Ministry of Labour and the Joint Secretary in charge of the land reforms division in the Commission is also Joint Secretary in the department of agriculture. Another important link between the Union government and the Commission used to be that the Chief Economic adviser of the Ministry of Finance was also the Economic Adviser of the Commission. But these practices are not being followed now. Similar links are, however maintained by a number of officers of the Commission through their membership on various Committees of the government through their membership on various Committees of the government and vice-versa. Moreover, some of the key officers of the Commission, especially those at senior levels, are drawn from the services of the Government of India and the State governments, and they are expected to help in establishing mutual understanding between the officers of the Commission and those in the Central and State governments.

An important requirement of effective planning is the availability of statistical data. The Central Statistical Organization of the Government of India, which was organized at the same time as the setting up of the Commission, works in close relationship with it.

NATIONAL DEVELOPMENT COUNCIL

As India is having a federal constitution, therefore it is very important that there should be close co-operation between the Planning Commission and the state. There should be a forum where the Central and State leaders may meet and discuss their common problems. Before independence, the Advisory Planning Board under the Chairmanship of K.C. Neogi had recommended to set up a consultative body representing the provinces, the princely states and some other interests to advise the Planning Commission. Later on, the formation of such a body was recommended in the First Five Year Plan (draft outline); which observed "In a country of the size of India, where the States have under the Constitution, full autonomy within their own sphere of duties, it is necessary to have a forum such as a National Development Council at which from time to time, the Prime Minister of India and the Chief Minister of the State can review the working of the Plan and of its various aspets."[28] The National Development Council came into existence in August 1952 as a result of the resolution issued from the Cabinet Secretariat.[29] The main functions of the NDC, as set out in the resolution are:

(a) To review the working of the National Plan from time to time

(b) To consider important questions of social and economic policy affecting national development.

(c) To recommend measures for the achievement of the aims and target setout in the National Plan including measures to secure the active participation and co-operation of the people, improve the efficiency of the administrative services, ensure the fullest development of the less advanced regions and sections of the community and through sacrifice, borne equal and build up resources for national development.[31]

The National Development Council has been evolved as an administrative agency to achieve the fullest co-operation and co-ordination in planning between the Central Government and State government and to bring about uniformity of approach and unanimity in the working of the National Plans.[31]

Composition

The National Development Council comprises the Prime Minister of India the Chief Minister of all the States and the members of the Planning Commission. The Prime Minister who is the Chairman of the Planning Commission acts as the Secretary of the Council. The Union

Ministers and State Ministers in-charge of the related subjects are also invited to participate in its deliberations. Some concerned officers and outside experts may also be invited. The NDC meetings are held at least twice a year: meetings are frequent when the Five Year Plans are being formulated. The Council is always kept informed about the progress of the plans. The size of the NDC is quite big which reduces the utility of this body as a forum for effective discussion. As a result, in 1954, the Council set up a smaller standing committee. The Committee meets in between the meetings of the NDC to review the policies underlying the plan and its progress. Apart from this, the NDC often seeks the assistance of some adhoc Committees, to which it entrusts the investigation of certain specific problems.

In 1993, there were six Committees of the NDC set up to go into some of the critical areas of development

(a) Committee on austerity

(b) Committee on population

(c) Committee on employment

(d) Committee on micro-level planning

(e) Committee on literacy

(f) Committee on medical education

Such committees place their reports before the NDC for final decision and recommendation.

The agenda of a particular meeting of the NDC consists of

(a) Items suggested by the Planning Commission itself

(b) Items suggested by the Central Ministers

(c) Items suggested by the State Governments

The meetings of the NDC start with an address from the Prime Minister. The Secretary of the council prepares a memorandum on each item of the agenda which is circulated among the members in advance.

Evaluation

The National Development Council gives its advice at various stages of the formulation of a plan, and it is only after its approval has been obtained that a plan is presented to the Parliament for consideration. The council has been largely responsible for giving Indian plans a truly national character. Its functioning, since its inception, reveals that there is hardly any matter of importance which it is not competent to discuss. Its pre-occupations are many and varied, and a perusal of its original terms of reference fails to provide a total picture of its actual functioning.[32] It has been quite successful in bringing and linking the Union Government, the Planning Commission and the various State governments. It has served a good forum for discussions and free exchange of ideas, and has created a sense of high responsibility on the part of the State Governments for making the plans a success. It has developed a very earthy convention of not putting its resolutions to vote and taking decisions almost unanimously. In addition, it concerns itself with important questions of social and economic policy affecting national development

It has laid stress on balanced development in different parts of the country and to this end, it has favoured decentralized industrial production, setting up of suitable indicators of general development as well as a continuous study of the problem of diminishing regional disparities. It has also favoured the introduction of Panchayati Raj system. In the words of the former Vice-Chairman. V.T. Krishnamachari, "It provides a forum which the Union Ministers and Chief Ministers of States discuss the plans at important stages in their formulation. Plans are also approved at its meetings after completion and before they are presented to the parliament and the State legislatures. In this way, the national character of the plans is emphasized. The Council also considers social and economic policies affecting the country from a national point of view so that where necessary, uniformity may be secured. In this way, it gives a lead to the country on broad issues of policy and promotes collective thinking and joint action on matters of national importance."

On the other hand, divergent views have also been recorded which have made it doubtful whether the NDC has fulfilled the desired purpose. Many have described it as a super cabinet comprised of policy makers in power. It includes the heads of governments of different States and Union Territories and most of the Council has at times been described as a mere rubber stamp on decisions already taken by the Center. The fact that most of the State governments, during the last 35 years, belonged to the same party as ruled at the Center was mainly responsible for this phenomenon.[33] Moreover, there is the all-powerful headship of the Prime Minister to browbeat the voice of any dissident Chief Minister. We may recall an incident of the post-1967 period when the Marxist Home Minister of West Bengal (Jyothi Basu) tried to move this body in a direction desired by the non-Congress Chief Ministers but was detested by the Congress Prime Minister. With the return of the single dominant party system, again under the towering leadership of late Mrs. Indira Gandhi, the NDC was treated as hardly anything else than a bigger platform where the State Chief Ministers assembled to put their formal seal of approval on the lines laid down by their Prime Minister.

It can be said that the real effectiveness of the NDC is not very easy to assess, as matters connected with it are all State secrets and not publicly known. At least, it is true that the NDC is not purely an advisory body. At matters stand, the Council is actively and extensively associated with policy making. The Council occupies an obviously outstanding position in the Indian federation. Its advice naturally receives the highest consideration by both the Center and the States which otherwise lack any legal sanction.[34]

Comparing the NDC with the Planning Commission, it has been pointed by some that the NDC is superior to the Planning Commission in view of the fact that, while the latter is just a policy-making body, the former is the decision-making authority. Brecher writes in the biography of Pt. Nehru, "The NDC was established as a supreme administrative and advisory body on planning.... It lays down policy directives invariably approved by the Cabinet. Since the inception, the NDC and its standing committees have virtually relegated the Planning Commission to the status of a research arm.[35]

The Administrative Reforms Commission suggested to make the NDC a supreme political body which gives broad guidance in the often with regular sub-committees and should both just rubber-stamp the plan formulation.[36] The ARC also recommended reconstitution of the NDC and redefinition of its function. The NDC should consist of the Prime Minister, the Deputy Prime Minister (if any), the Central Ministers of finance, food and agriculture, industrial development and company affairs, commerce, railways, transport and shipping, education, labour, employment and rehabilitation, home affairs and irrigation and power, the Chief Minister of States and the members of the Planning Commission. The functions should be as follows:

(a) To prescribe guidelines for the formation of the national plan

(b) To consider the national plan as formulated by the Planning Commission

(c) To assess the resources required for implementing the plan and to suggest ways and means for raising them

(d) To consider important questions of social and economic policy affecting development

(e) To review the working of the plan from time to time and to recommend such measures as are necessary for achieving the aims and targets articulated in the national plan.[37]

Programme Advisers

Another link between the Planning Commission and the States is maintained through the Programme Adviser. Just after the commencement of the Planning Commission and the Five Year Plans. It was realized that no machinery was available in the Commission for making an assessment of the implementation of development plans in the States. It was essential to develop an agency in the Commission which would be sufficiently knowledgeable about the problems, prospects and actual developments in various States to be able to advise the Commission and the Union Ministers on the proposals forwarded by the State. Government for the annual as well as Five Year Plans. It was therefore, decided in 1952 to appoint three senior officers as advisers on programme administration. The approach was that the advisers would be primarily touring officers and would try to study at first hand the working of development schemes included in the Five Year Plan, giving necessarily greater attention to the more important projects in which the Union Government gave specific financial or other assistance. In the course of their work, they would give special attention to the problems of administration, finance and public co-operation in implementing the plan. They were expected to keep the Planning Commission as well as the Central Ministries fully posted with the progress of the centrally-aided and centrally-sponsored schemes. The original idea was that for purposes of the advisers should function as the co-ordinating officers for purposes of the formulation of the Five Year and Annual Plans of States. Advisers are ordinarily expected to spend about 15 days in a month on tour in the areas allocated to them. In the course of these tours, they hold discussions at the State headquarters with the development. Planning and Finance departments of the States, reviewing the progress of the Plan in different sectors and particularly of those projects which are assisted by loans and grants from the Union Ministries. The discussions at the headquarters are expected to be supplemented by field inspection of projects.

For small periods, the number of the posts of Programme Advisers was raised to four. It was proposed that the persons to be selected for this post should be of considerable seniority and selected with special care. Most of the persons appointed to these positions have been quite senior. However, the institution of Programme Advisers has not worked in the manner originally expected. In the first plan, there has been a high turnover of persons occupying this post. Between 1952 and 1968, as many as 18 persons had worked as Programme Advisers, and many of them, hardly for 2 years. Secondly, a few officers have linked to work in this capacity in preference to positions of the ministries. They have tended to use this position as a stop-gap arrangement to reach a higher position in the Secretariat or elsewhere. Thirdly, not many of these officers have had close contacts with the Planning Commission or with the planning process before appointment. Fourthly, the members of the Commission have shown a tendency to deal directly with the State governments without necessarily keeping the Programme Advisers in the picture. Fifthly, the State governments have not found these Advisers to be a very effective channel of communication between themselves and the Commission. Lastly, the original intention that the Advisers would to tour the States under their charge for about fifteen days in a month has not been borne out in practice. A suggestion was, therefore, put before the Reforms Commission that the institution of programme Advisers be scrapped and their work entrusted to the members of the Planning Commission. The Administrative Reforms Commission turned down this suggestion and made the following recommendations:

(a) The institution of the Programme Advisers should continue

(b) Their tenure should be fixed for at least five years

(c) The Advisers should be persons with wide knowledge and experience and should possess the qualities of a mediator and a negotiator. Their selection should not be the officers of any particular cadre.

(d) The Programme Advisers should supervise evaluation work in addition to their other duties.

The Government of India has accepted the above recommendations with some modifications. Thus, the tenure is to vary between three to five years. Secondly, the government has not accepted that the Programme Advisers would be available for such association with evaluation work as may be considered necessary.

Advisory Bodies

Apart from the technical work in connection with planning there is need especially in an economy of the size and complexity of India, to consult on general policy from time to time, other knowledgeable people, especially non-official experts, at various stages of formulation as well as implementation of the plans. An attempt is made to have such consolations through a number of standing bodies variously known as Council Panels, Advisory Committees and Consultative Committees. Some of these bodies are discussed as follows:

Programme Evaluation Organization (PEO)

There are no attached or subordinate offices under the Planning Commission. There is however, an organization known as the Programme Evaluation Organization which functions as an independent unit of the Commission. It was originally established in October 1952 for making a systematic and periodic assessment of the methods and results of the Community Development Programmes and national extension movements under an agreement between the Government of India and the Ford Foundation. Since he termination of the grant from the Ford Foundation in 1956, the entire cost of the organization has been met by the Union Government. The functions of the organization were later extended to cover a number of other important programmes, especially in the field of rural development. The independent wing of the Commission, the PEO, works under its general guidance and direction. It is headed by a Director who is assisted by two Deputy Directors, a number of research officers another stall. It also has an elaborate field staff, which act as the eyes and ears of the Planning Commission.[38] There are five regional evaluation offices and 39 field units known as project evaluation offices under the administrative control of the organization. The main functions of the Programme Evaluation Organization are:

(a) To study the progress of a programme and to measure its impact on the socio-economic life of the rural people

(b) Pointing out those extension methods which are proving effective and which are not and to ascertain the reasons for success or failure in respect of different items of the programme

(c) To indicate the direction in which improvements may be sought, undertake normal checking and inspection work which is part of the day-to-day administration. It prepares its evaluation report on the basis of the data supplied by the Project Executive Officers. Block Development Officers or District Officers, etc. However, it undertakes studies with a view to provide an independent and detached assessment of a programme by a body not concerned with its implementation. The results of these studies are presented in reports which are considered by the Planning Commission and the concerned ministries for follow up action. The evaluation reports are of two types:

(i) Survey reports, which are purely study reports based on the facts collected by field officers.

(ii) Main evaluation reports, making a general review of the programme and giving a detailed description of its work in certain specified evaluation centuries. At present, there are about 40 evaluation units in different parts of the country which are devoting themselves to studies and investigations bearing on specific problems.

Committee on Plan Projects (CPP)

The Taxation Enquiry Commission emphasised in 1953–54 the need for a thorough and careful enquiry into the whole question of public expenditure and recommended that such inquiries should be undertaken and entrusted to sufficiently high-powered bodies.[39] The proposal was discussed at a meeting of the National Development Council in May, 1956. The Council approved the proposal and subsequently a Committee on Plan Projects was established with the Union Home Minister as its Chairman. The Union Minister of Planning and Finance and the Deputy Chairman of the Planning Commission are its members. In addition, the Prime Minister as the Chairman of the National Development Council nominates two Chief Ministers of States as members of the Committee for each class of projects. The Union Minister concerned with a project or a class of projects under investigation is also a member of the Committee.

The Committee on plan projects has undertaken studies of various specific problems through specially appointed teams with a view to evolving methods and techniques of raising levels of efficiency and achieving economies particularly in construction costs.

In particular, the Committee has the following functions to perform:

(a) To organize investigations including inspections, in the field of important projects, both at the Center and in the States, through specially selected teams

(b) To initiate studies with the object of evolving suitable forms of organization, methods, standards and techniques for achieving economy, avoiding waste and ensuring efficient execution of projects

(c) To promote the development of suitable machinery for continuous efficiency audit in individual projects and in agencies responsible for their execution

(d) To secure the implementation of the suggestions made in reports submitted to the Committee on Plan Projects and to make the results of studies and investigations generally available

(e) To undertake such other tasks as the National Development Council may propose for the promotion of economy and efficiency in the execution of the plans

The Committee now devotes its main attention to studies relating to management and administration and to economics in construction costs. It works through several teams and groups, which are composed of technical personnel and eminent public men with experience of the subjects detailed for study.

Planning Formulation

As mentioned earlier, the Planning Commission has the responsibility to prepare the plans under the guidance of the National Development Council. Also engaged in the exercise are the working groups and advisory panels of the Planning Commission, the Reserve Bank and other bodies, the ministries of the Central Government, the State Governments, and above all, the Parliament. The process of plan formulation may be divided into the stages as follows:

(a) In the light of broad social economic and political objectives of the government the Planning Commission lays down tentative goals to be achieved over a long period, say of 15 or 20 years. Such a perspective plan takes into account, not only the economic trends of the past, but also the innovations and changes taking place in the field of science, technology and organization. Surveys and futuristic studies provide the basis for the preparation of the perspective plans.[40] Perspective planning is the responsibility of the perspective planning division. After the approval of these long-term goals by the government, the Planning Commission formulates certain tentative goals or targets to be achieved during the five years plans.

(b) The process of formulating a particular plan starts above three years before the commencement of the plan. Initially, for deciding the broad objectives and the strategy to be formulated for working these out, the commission holds frequent discussions with the Central and State Ministries, the Reserve Bank of India, the panel of economists and other advisory bodies including the consultative committees of the Parliament, questions connected with resources for the plan, current revenues public loans, small savings, etc. and the limits of deficit financing are examined with the Finance Ministers of the Union and the States and the Reserve Bank of India.[41]

(c) Simultaneously, studies are undertaken to examine the state of the economy and to identify the social, economic and institutional shortcomings. All these are given for detailed discussions to various working groups one each for the important sectors like agriculture industry, health, education, transport and communication, etc. These groups consist of economics, technicians, high level administrators and representatives of ministries. In the state subjects, working groups are set up in each state to work in close contact with the concerned central groups. These working groups indicate the targets of production which can be achieved with the technical and other resources available irrespective of financial limitations—with specific projects, costs, etc. For instance, in the field of community development, it may be explained how schemes for rural development and welfare are built up from the village upwards, for being incorporated in the state working groups proposals. Similarly, the programmes for industries in the public sector are initiated by the respective wings under the ministries concerned. Those for the private sector are prepared by organized bodies representing individual industries. The Planning Commission considers these proposals in consultation with the development councils for the industries for which these exist. These councils consist of representatives of the employees, labour and consumers. Plans for industries in the public and private sectors are carefully co-ordinated.[42]

(d) On the basis of the reports of the working groups, the Planning Commission formulates the general approach to the next Five Year Plan. The financial and physical targets are brought together and a plan, embodying priorities is, prepared. For this, there are frequent discussions with the ministries and with the Federation of Industries and other representative organizations. The plan, as settled, is placed in the form of a short memorandum before the Cabinet and the National Development Council (NDC) which indicates the rate of growth and the broad priorities to be assumed for the purpose of further work for the preparation of the plan. The ARC in its final report has suggested that the Planning Commission, when seeking guidelines from the NDC for the formulation of the national plan, should give a tentative framework of the plan considered feasible by it and also indicate other alternative approaches calling for different degrees of effort. The basic factors involved such as the rate of growth, the resources required and the sacrifices involved, should clearly be brought out. Detailed work for the formulation of the plan should proceed in the light of the guidelines given by the NDC. The formulation of the Fifth Plan has followed the procedure recommended by the ARC.[43]

(e) After the approval of the Cabinet and the NDC, an attempt is made to work out the general dimensions of the plan in the light of the tentative rate of growth indicated by the NDC. This stage ends with the preparation of a draft outline which indicates the main features of the plan under formulation. The draft is published for public criticism. It is discussed in the press, universities and other interested political and economic circles.

(f) In a democratic country, every action of the executive has to be approved by the legislature. Therefore, the draft reaches the parliament where it is considered by the committees and by the parliament as a whole. The number of committees varies from plan to plan. The observations made by the members are explained carefully.

(g) In a democratic country, every action of the executive has to be approved by the legislature. Therefore, the draft reaches the parliament where it is considered by the committees and by the parliament as a whole. The number of committees varies from plan to plan. The observations made by the members are explained carefully.

(h) Further approval of the plan is interlinked with the approval of the budget. While the Planning Commission makes only demands and allocates revenues, the Finance Minister has to perform the thankless task of raising money for the demands thus made. Budgets are annual, but the plan projects are long drawn out commitments whose requirements and results cannot be properly estimated in a short period of one year. Sometimes, a plan means more or less a budget, but in the developing countries like India, it is more than a budget.[44]

(i) In the next stage, the Planning Commission arranges detailed discussions with the Union Ministries and States on the plans prepared by them. These plans show the expenditure on schemes and projects to be carried over from the previous plan and new ones. The financial resources to be provided by the states themselves and the quantum of central assistance are also discussed. These discussions last several months. Discussions are also held with representatives of major organized industries in the private sector through various Development Councils as well as the Chamber of Commerce and Industry. In the light of the points thrown up during all these discussions, the Planning Commission revises the draft outline, bringing together the principle features of the plan, the policy directives and the issues which may require further consideration before the plan is finally drawn up. It is again placed before the National Development Council for approval.

(j) In the concluding stage of plan formulation, a detailed report is prepared and every chapter in the draft is edited and is sent to the ministries. When completed, the report is placed before the Cabinet and the NDC. The report is then submitted to the parliament for final approval. Resolutions are moved in both the houses by the Prime Minister. Discussions are held in both the houses for several days and many members take part in them. Similarly, the plans for the States are discussed in the local legislatures. The plans become effective after they are approved in the Parliament and the State Legislatures.[45] The approved plans go to all the concerned authorities and organizations for implementation.

Plan Implementation

Proper implementation of the plan is a very significant part of the total planning process. A very well-formulated plan is not of a much use if it is not matched by equally good implementation. Most of the plans are not totally successful due to weak implementation. In India, plans are implemented on annual basis. This is done because Five Year Plan cannot be implemented as a whole and for effective implementation, it is supplemented by an exercise in annual planning provides for flexibility in the implementation of the plan programmes in accordance with the development of the economic situation from time to time.[46] It sets out the programme of development to be implemented every year with sufficient details.

The plans are implemented by the administrative ministries of the Central Government and of the State Governments. The governments should work out in full detail the administrative and operational implications of each programme and ensure its proper phasing. For a development plan and for the programmes and projects comprising it, time phasing is very important which in turn the heavily depends upon the economy's administrative and organizational capacities. But the implementation of plans has mostly been poor in India and the main reasons responsible for this are—administrative inefficiency, defective and complicated procedures and weak co-ordination at different levels of administration. The implementation of plans has also suffered a good deal for want of attention to their detailed phasing and planning. Apart from this, other defects in plan implementation are pointed out as slow pace execution, absence of trained personnel with the requisite caliber and experience, increase in cost and non-adherence to time schedules, lack of co-ordination in the related sectors of the economy, and failure to secure widespread support and co-operation from the people.

To overcome the weaknesses of plan implementation, a number of measures are suggested. During the initial stages of planning in India, the first Five Year Plan stated that the essential conditions for successful planning should be:

(a) A large measure of agreement of the community as to the ends of policy

(b) Effective power, based on the active co-operation of the citizens, capacity and quality.[47]

(c) An efficient administrative set-up with personnel requisite capacity and quality

It has been prescribed in all the plan documents to make large scale improvements in the organization set-up and management procedures in administration to remove the basic drawbacks in the plan implementation. In the words of the second plan document. "If the administration machinery, both at the Centre and in the States does its work with efficiency, integrity and with a sense of urgency and concern for the community, the success of the plan would be assured."[48] For the proper implementation of the plans, there should be effective co-ordination among various ministries at the Centre and between the Centre and State

Governments. In the words of the Third Five Year Plan document. "The plan has to be implemented at many levels—national, state, district, block and village. In each of them in relation to tasks assigned, there has to be a co-operation between different agencies and an understanding of the purposes of the plan and the means through which they are secured. In a vast and varied structure organized on effectively between different levels, and at the same level between different agencies.[49]

Implementation, being mainly and administrative exercise, the following administrative improvements have been suggested to meet the challenge of development planning:

- Simplification of the procedure of work
- Avoidance of delay
- Proper fixation of individual responsibility
- Reduction of costs
- Proper emphasis on administrative research and evaluation
- Radical changes in the procedure of work of the Ministry of Finance
- More delegation of financial powers to the spending ministries
- Emphasis on pre-budget scrutiny
- Reorganization of ministries
- Better co-ordination among the ministries/departments of the Government of India
- Development of methods of cutting red-tapism[50]

It can be said that planning cannot succeed unless planners consider it an integral part of task to establish the kind of administrative system which can formulate and carry out development plans realistically. But this is rendered with difficulty by the persistent gap between the kind of administrative reform which is needed and which is possible. Basic to the proper implementation of the plan programme is the pre-investment planning. Another task of importance is the need for efficiency and economy in project construction followed by requisite efficiency in their administration so that it is possible to get increased output from investment in the programmes. The need of reorganize planning and administrative procedures to achieve respective action and initiative at each point in implementation cannot be over-emphasized. Further, the existing system on reporting and progress and shortcomings in implementation takes cognizance of the dynamic character of the plans and programmes, and unless these are managed according to the twin principle efficiency and justice, there is planning machinery and development planning in India.

Every likelihood of a gap arising between the plans and their implementation. The need of the day is to eliminate this gap.[51]

Plan Evaluation

The formulation, implementation and evaluation of plans go side by side. A regular evaluation helps to improve the future plans and programmes. Evaluation covers the survey of the progress of the schemes with a view to ensure their fulfillment in due time and assessing the extent of success or failure, measuring the real impact of programmes. For this purpose, two important organizations are attached with the Planning Committee on plan projects. The help of leading universities and other research bodies is also secured to undertake evaluation studies. As a result of such studies certain problems have been identified and further studies are also taken up with a view to remove the shortcomings and to make the programmes more effective.

Regarding the progress in the implementation and working of important projects, discussions take place in the Parliament and the State Assemblies in practically all the session. During the budget session, the Parliament and the State Assemblies, the working of the plan in the Union and the State is systematically reviewed as the annual plans from part of the budgets in the Union and the States. The reports of the Estimates Committees and Pubic Accounts Committees the Parliament and the State legislatures devote much attention to the working of the plans in individual sectors of the economy and these are discussed at a considerable length. In these and other ways, interest in the plans is always maintained at a high level. The Planning Commission publishes periodical progress reports on the working of the plans, which are invariably discussed.

The Administrative Reforms Commission has recommended that there should be a careful review of the progress of the developmental programmes under execution and also a reasonably accurate appreciation of the private economic acidity.[52] putting further emphasis on the proper evaluation of plans and programmes. The Commission observed.

This has been a tendency to assess the performance of a project more in terms of progress of expenditure than in terms of physical achievements. This is bound to give a misleading picture. Further, the time lag between the completion of the field work and finalization of the evaluation report is too long and this vitiates the usefulness of the findings. There is no systematic follow-up and check of how far these reports are being made use by different agencies. It is necessary to strengthen the existing evaluation machinery to remove these defects. The Planning Commission should have an evaluation wing which should include the present personnel of the Programme Evaluation Organization as well as the staff in the Committee on plan projects engaged in evaluation work.

Regarding the State programmes, the evaluation should be entrusted to the State Planning Boards. However, even in respect of such programmes, the Commission could undertake a few studies on a sample basis."[53]

STATE LEVEL PLANNING

The subject of economic and social planning is included in the concurrent list of the Indian Constitution which means that both the Center and States can make plans in their own spheres. As there is a plan for the country as a whole, similarly there are separate plans for each constituent unit. There are certain special characteristics of State Planning which make it different from Central Planning.[54]

The differences are given as follows:

(a) State Planning is the grass root planning. The planner's task is not merely to formulate schemes, but to motivate the people to implement these schemes. Detailed knowledge of local conditions, needs and aspirations of the people is necessary.

(b) The State being close to the beneficiaries, a sizeable part of the State resources is spent on projects which have psychological impact than economic benefit.

(c) Each State has its own problems and its own stage of development. No plan can be applied to whole of India on a uniform basis as there is a wide disparity between States in both social and economic matters.

(d) States are also dependent on the Center for financing their plans and this heavy reliance makes them readily comply with the directions of the Planning Commission and the Central ministries.

(e) States do not have any elaborate machinery for planning. States generally submit a list of their wants to the Planning Commission, and leave it to the latter to sort them out and relate them to pattern of priorities.

(f) The scope of the State plans is limited to the additional development outlay of the State sector only and covers fewer areas of economic and social activity.

(g) As we move below the national, formulating and implementation come closer.

(h) The nature of the national plan is comparatively less promotional and more of capital investment, but the State plans are oriented towards increasing agricultural production, building up of the infrastructure, and are directed towards enhancing production in the diffused sectors of the economy.

The main institution responsible for the preparation of State plan is the State Planning department which works directly under the Chief Minister of the State. The department is responsible of liaison between the Planning Commission and various departments of the State government, co-cordination of their programmes for development and formulation of the development plan for the State as a whole.[55] On the other hand, it is age of the major tasks of the Commission to ensure that all these plans are mutually consistent, compatible with the projected total investment and in conformity with centrally established priorities. The State planning units, therefore, are essentially subordinate as they formulate the plans in the light of the main guidelines received from Planning Commission and the general directives of the Council of Ministers of the State. The planning department consults sister departments as well such advisory bodies may be set up for the different sectors and the development and planning bodies set up in the districts. To start with, some States established whole planning came up and to assist it, most of the States established development Boards of planning advisory boards.

Planning Boards

In March 1962, the Planning Commission suggested to the State Governments to set up a State Planning Board in each State, which should be on the lines of the Planning Commission. The Board should assist the State Government in the formulation of the main policies and solution of the basic problems of implementation. The Planning Commission also advised that each board could have the Chief Minister of its State as its Chairman and State Minister of Finance as a member. Apart from this it could have two or three full-time members who possess special experience, knowledge of planning and economic problems. The Planning Commission viewed that the boards would be able to carry out the task of planning in more comprehensive manner than the individual departments which are mainly concerned with the implementation of specific projects or the boards would also facilitate improvement in the quality of planning by bringing about closer collaboration between the Planning Commission and the States in drawing up the plans for long-term development.

In 1966, the Administrative Reforms Commission (ARC) also recommended the constitution such boards to formulate the Five Year Plans and to evaluate plan performance. It recommended that the boards should have their own Secretariats to help them in the adequate discharge of these functions. The Commission said "In our view, the basic reason for the absence of temporal, spatial and intersectional phasing of state plans is the absence of temporal, adequate planning machinery at the state and lower levels. In absence of such a planning agency, the work of project and programme planning could not be taken up in a scientific manner and on a continuous and systematic basis, and planning has to be largely confined to financial planning with very little attention paid to the actual results of plan investment.[56]

The Administrative Reforms Commission's investigation revealed that about eight states, viz., Bihar, Gujarat, J&K, Kerala, Odissa, Punjab, Rajasthan and West Bengal had organized State Planning Boards and Councils. On an examination of the functioning of these agencies, the ARC observed "They have best served as Public Relations Committees," The appointment of the Boards or other similar bodies has thus not helped in the past to strengthen either the planning machinery or the process of planning in the states."[57] The study team of the ARC recommended a three-tier planning machinery—a state agency, sectoral (departmental) planning agencies and regional and district planning agencies. Accepting the recommendations of set up planning boards and strengthen the planning machinery in general.[58]

A number of states consequently undertook measures to set up or to strengthen their Planning Boards of similar bodies. However, Odissa and Gujarat appeared to be pioneers in establishing state planning agencies. Having done this as early as 1962. Most of the other states established planning agencies in the late sixties or early seventies.

Composition

The State Planning Board are composed of a Chairman, a Vice Chairman and some members, like the Prime Minister at the Center, the Chief Minister generally serves as the Chairman of the State Planning Board. In the event of President's Rule in a state, the Governor serves as the Chairman. The Vice/Deputy Chairman is generally occupied by the Finance Minister of the state concerned. It is only in a few states that this post is sometimes filled by a non-official expert.

The number of members of the planning boards varies from state to state. It ranges from 1 to 40. In 1984, the number of Board members in different states was as follows[59]: Nagaland–1, Assam–3. Bihar and Kerala–4 each, Tamil Nadu–6, Haryana–8, Rajasthan–11,

West Bengal–13, Punjab–19, and Maharashtra–36. These members include ex-officio, non-official and part-time members. Most of the States include experts in the boards. The ex-officio members are generally Chief Secretaries to the Government, Planning Secretaries, Finance Secretaries, Development Commissioners and so no. Among the non-officials, expert are usually economists, scientists, educationists and other professional. There is no uniformity in the proportion of ex-officio and non-official or expert members in different states. In a number of states, 50 per cent of the total members are experts while in some states, there is an overdose of economists.

Planning Machinery and Development Planning in India

In a number of states, there is a post of Member Secretary which is generally filled by the Secretary of planning development. The tenure of the members in most States is unspecified. The State governments generally appoint the members (by invitation) on the basis of their eminence in public life and their academic background.[60]

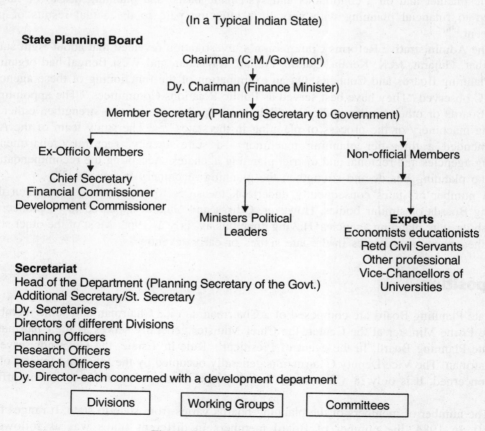

Figure 7.1   State planning machinery

Functions of the planning boards

The basic functions of the planning boards at the state level are more or less in line with those of the Planning Commission. These functions, which were also recommended by the ARC, are as follows:

(a) To make an assessment of the State resources and formulate plans for the most effective and balanced utilization of those resources

(b) To determine plan priorities of the State within the framework of the priorities of the national plan

(c) To assist the district authorities in formulating their development plans within the spheres in which such planning is considered to be useful and feasible and co-ordinate these with the state plan

(d) To identify factors which tend to retard the economic and social development of the State, and to determine the set of conditions for the successful execution of the plans

(e) To review the progress of the implementation to the plan programmes and recommend such adjustments in policies and measures as the review may indicate

Secretariat

In a number of states, planning boards do not have any independent secretariat at their disposal. Instead, in these states, the planning department or the planning wing in the secretariat of the State Government provides the necessary assistance. Some of the states having a fullfledged secretariat for planning are—Assam, Bihar, Kerala, Punjab, Tamil Nadu, etc.[61] The secretariat in these states is divided into nine divisions. In Punjab (1984), the three divisions were:

(a) Perspective planning division

(b) Plan monitoring and information division

(c) Man power planning division

While the perspective planning division was headed by a Director, the other two divisions were headed by a Deputy Director and a Senior Research Officer. A novel feature found in Punjab is that eight working groups and five committees are constituted in the planning board, each with a term of 2 years. The working groups are concerned with the following

(a) Financial resources

(b) Agriculture, minor irrigation and soil conservation

(c) Power and rural electrification

(d) Industries

(e) Employment and manpower planning

(f) Area planning and development of backward areas

(g) Irrigation and flood control

(h) Science and technology

Committees Responsible for Development Planning in India

The five Committees are responsible for economic co-ordination, perspective planning, plan review and evaluation, monitoring, and building construction.

Each Committee and working group has a Chairman (who is often a part-time member of the board), several members and convener. The members of the planning boards are also members of the Committees and working groups. The other (expert) members are drawn from the fields of economics, industry and education. The Planning Secretary is the convener of all the working groups and committees. The present strength of Planning Board Secretariat stands over 100 in Punjab. As compared with this, the figure for UP stand over 350, for Tamil Nadu it is 85, for Bihar it is 40, for MP it is 16 and for Gujarat it is 4. In Punjab, about 2 per cent of the personnel constitute academic and directing staff; 45 per cent research and administrative staff; and the rest supporting staff.[62]

In a number of states, including Punjab, it is the planning department which is responsible for annual and Five Year Plan formulation, review of economy, responsible for the day-to-day affairs relating to planning guidance of the technical departments in plan formulation, holding discussions, and so on. Presently, it is only in a few states that there exists a separate secretariat for the Planning Board and the planning department. In Punjab, presently, there is a common secretariat. Besides, the Board and Department, the planning organization consists of planning cells as well, which are located in the major development departments.

In most of the States, the State planning boards are advisory bodies. Whereas, the planning departments are executive departments in charge of actual plan formulation. Implementation monitoring, evaluation and appraisal. The link between the two is provided by the head of the department who is also a member of Board and by the common secretariat.

Working

The overall working of the planning machinery of the state level is not satisfactory. Despite the Planning Commission's frequent recommendations for developing an effective state planning organization by establishing board more or less on the pattern of the Planning Commission and the ARC's recommendations to this effect. A number of states have not set up planning board as recommended. The States are apparently not convinced of the necessity of having any elaborate planning set-up.[63] Most of the states which have set-up planning machinery have not provided sufficient organizational support to it. They have either insufficient or untrained staff. The personnel working in the state planning set-up lack training in planning techniques. Besides, there is an overdose of administrators in these bodies and the number or professionals are either very little or they do not have much say in the working. The criteria for resources for different programmes is virtually based on political and ulterior considerations rather than on the needs, desires and expectations of the beneficiaries. It has rightly been pointed out that in most states, the planning boards, like several autonomous corporations, have been made sanctuaries for disgruntle, defeated or troublesome politicians who tend to treat plan funds as discretionary grants inevitably, such political accommodation has led to minimum involvement of economic experts who alone should comprise State Planning Boards.

Planning Process at the State Level

Every State plan is the outcome of a compromise between the State and the Center, worked out through discussions with, the National Development Council, deciding on the scope, objectives and priorities of the forthcoming plan. The Planning Commission, after working out the details for both the Central sector and the State sector, communicates them to the respective States Governments. At the State level, each department prepares a tentative plan on the basis of proposals from the districts. These are discussed by the Secretaries and Ministers. After discussion, the plan is presented to the Cabinet sub-committee and is subsequently discussed by the state planning board. After its approval, the plan becomes a draft plan, and its copies are sent to the Planning Commission and the Central Ministries. There, the State representatives, (normally, the Chief Minister) the Planning and Finance Ministers are invited by the Planning Commission to discuss the draft plan which means a lot of bargaining[64]. The plans become binding only after acceptance by the State cabinets and approval by the State legislatures. The implementation of the plans is the responsibility of the state.

In the overall process of the formulation of a five-year plan, the role played by the state planning board is quite important. It reviews the economy of the state, assessing its resources, constituting working groups and guiding and participating in their deliberations. The planning department, on the other hand, scrutinises and finalizes the proposals. The work done by the technical department, matters because, the outlines provided by them in shape of their proposals basically remain (more or less) the same till the finalization of the plan.

District planning

Indian has a rich experience of local approach to socio-economic development ever since the Community Development Programme was launched in 1952. For the proper planning at the local level, the Planning Commission issued guidelines to the States in 1954 in regard to the preparation of plans concerning agricultural production, industries and co-operation. During the period of the Second Five Year Plan (1950–61) an effort was made not only to decentralize the administration at the district and block levels but also to promote the establishment of a three-tier system of the village, block and district panchayats. In 1969, the Planning Commission issued another set of guidelines for the formation of district plans. The planning at the district level is useful because of the following reasons:

(a) Grass-root planning is more effective for the best use of land and manpower

(b) A district or a block is a compact area in which conditions are likely to be homogenous

(c) People's participation is possible

(d) It may help to strengthen democratic values

A former Deputy Chairman of the Planning Commission, Professor D.T. Lakdawala is of view that local planning has the great advantage of compelling the planners to look more closely and concretely at the problems at local levels, and to devise measures for the optimum utilization of natural and manpower resources to suit local potentials, needs and problems.[65]

At the local level, planning may be undertaken at the district and block levels. This is done jointly by the officers of the various departments and the members of district councils or block councils and may be with the help of non-official representatives. The district officers are responsible for necessary co-ordination at the district and block levels, respectively. Those district and block planning authorities who are given a tough idea of the assistance that is likely to be available from outside make an assessment of their own resources and needs to formulate the programme for the development of their respective areas.[66]

Thus, the idea of decentralized district level planning has for a long time been regarded as an idealistic approach to planning in India. By the fifth Five-Year Plan, most of the states began to achieve this ideal. Maharashtra emerged as the pioneer of district planning in India. Only a few states like UP, Kerala, Haryana, Punjab and J&K paid routine attention to district level planning.[67] In most of the states, district planning is unit within the framework of state planning. District outlays are allocated from the divisible outlays provided for the State plan. In Maharashtra, district planning is quite advanced and has a very elaborate machinery, the apex organization being the district planning and development council, In Haryana, Gujarat and Nagaland, there are district planning boards in UP, Tamil Nadu, District Planning Cells, in Rajasthan District Planning Committees, and so no. These are generally headed by the District Collector of the Minister from the District, In Maharashtra, Rajasthan, UP, Tamil Nadu and West Bengal, these organizations are empowered to formulate district plans white in a number of other states, are only advisory in nature.[68]

The District Planning Advisory Boards: These are in charge of advising district authorities on the priorities to be adopted and the programmes to be taken up for a systematic socio-economic development of the district and of paying due attention to the backward pockets and potential area of the district.

The District Planning Committees: These have more specific functions to perform, namely to assist in the formulation of long-term district programmes/schemes and ensuing smooth implementation.

The District Executive Councils: They are chiefly concerned with the formulation of district perspective plan.[69]

However, it has been observed that the working of the above set up is more on paper than in reality. The system of district planning is yet to gain ground, It requires more innovation, experimentation, training, commitment and willingness of political and administrative leadership.

In 1977, a high level committee was appointed to inquire into the working of the Panchayati Raj institutions and to suggest measures to strengthen them so as to enable an effective decentralized system of planning and development. The Committee, headed by Ashoka Mehta, a former Deputy Chairman was of the Planning Commission, concluded that there was considerable scope for decision-making at the district level. The Committee was of the view that the district level was broad enough to consider policy options and was immediately below the State—a strategy level for economic planning. According to the Committee, the structure of the Panchayati Raj institutions provided suitable machinery for the effective functioning of multi-level planning. Progress had already been achieved in institutionalizing and standardizing the technique and procedure for district planning. When the district was made the key unit of decentralization, the task became easy.

The Planning Commission also appointed a working group under the chairmanship of Professor M.D. Dantwala, an eminent economist, to prepare guidelines for block level planning in the country. The working group made it very clear from the beginning that district block/level planning could be visualized only as a part of the same exercise. The remoteness of the planning agencies from the area of implementation and the vastness of geographical coverage had been hampering the matching of sectoral financial allocations with location specific as well as potential needs and standing in the way of proper distribution of the gains of developments. The remoteness of the planning agencies from the area of implementation and the vastness of geographical coverage had been hampering the matching of sectoral financial allocations with location-specific as well as potential needs and standing in the way of proper distribution of the gains of development. The purpose of block-level planning was to accelerate the process of decentralization in the hope that a more systematic planning effort with a smaller coverage would not only help to speed up the development process but also improve it qualitatively, by making it more responsive to the need of the community. In the opinion of the working group, block-level planning was not to be viewed as an isolated exercise but as a link in a hierarchy of levels from a cluster of villages below the block level to the district, regional and state level. The group recognized the block as a unit of planning. The block was sufficiently small in terms of area and population to enable intimate contact and understanding between the planners, those responsible for the implementation of the plan and the people. It could also provide an observation platform in close proximity of the beneficiary group and help to understand more clearly the needs of the people and the factors inhibiting the socio-economic growth. According to the working group, the plan for the block had to be related, on the one hand to the plans the district and the state levels, and on the other, to the plans for the sub-units consisting of clusters of villages within the block.[70]

Earlier, the study team of the Administrative Reforms Commission had suggested an elaborate arrangement for planning at the district level and even suggested the creation of a special machinery for regular consultation between the planning agencies in the districts and the State Planning Boards. But in its final report, the Commission did not consider that any elaborate machinery for planning in the district was necessary. "At the operational level, planning cannot be divorced from implementation. A District plan would necessarily have to be in the nature of identifying the local resources and meet the local needs. The best arrangement, therefore, would be that same set of persons who are responsible for implementation are also made responsible for planning. We would, therefore, like the work relating to planning at the district level to be handled by the developmental set-up in the district."[71]

Some features of plan formulation or the planning system in India have emerged over the years. These are as follows:

(a) Planning in India is highly centralized, and this centralism acquires an arresting nature when considered in the background of the federal system of government under the Constitution. The centralist thrust has received powerful impetus from historical and environmental factors, such as the hang-over of the unitary arrangements of governance till the enforcement of the present Constitution, single party dominance, centralization of financial resource, etc. Once a tradition of centralist planning was built up, it began to feed upon itself with the passage of time.[72]

(b) The second feature of planning is its bureaucratic nature. This characteristic is an implicit in preceding one, but has become a prominent feature. The planning process does not seek to involve citizen participation in any organised way. When slackness in execution is noticed, the remedy is discovered in still greater bureaucratization.[73]

(c) Another feature of Indian planning is that while at the aggregative level, concepts of national planning tend to be sophisticated and advanced and economic models of perspective planning and material balances are prepared. Planning at the ground levels is extremely weak in the absence of techno-economically sound projects. The technique of project-planning is not yet adequately appreciated by the development administrators at the district level. The district planning as practiced in an Indian district is thus primarily a process of data collection at the lower levels in which implications of such data for various programmes are worked out (informational decentralization). The final decision-making power is not delegated to the lower levels. It is liable to be generalized, because we place this outcome, inter alia, on the model prescribed by the planning itself.[74]

(d) There is a sort of absence of regional planning in the Indian planning mechanism. Planning in India has been sectoral rather than spatial. As a result, regional or area-planning in the scientific sense of the term has never been introduced in the country so far. The plans at the state, district, block or village levels are no more than break-up or sectoral programmes or, more accurately, schemes of departments.[75]

(e) The planning procedures are also highly sophisticated. The process of plan formulation is enormously complex and plan implementation leaves the equally vital task of evaluation unmentioned for which the commission has the assistance of two specialized agencies—the programme evaluation organization and the committee on plan projects. Although the machinery available is adequate yet it has not been used with vigour and understanding.[76]

(f) Planning of plan implementation is not undertaken at any level particularly at the national level. The concern of the planners regarding implementation mechanism, if any, is more of a postscript or a tailpiece than a product of interacted thinking. Plans have failed because of defective and half-hearted implementation efforts. Planning cannot succeed unless the planners consider it an integral part of their task to establish some kind of administrative system which can formulate and carry out development plans realistically. Unless the implementation takes cognizance of the dynamic character of the plans and programmes and unless they are managed according to the twin principal of efficacy and justice, there is every likelihood of a gap arising between the plans and their implementation. The need of the day is to eliminate this gap.[77]

STRATEGY OF DEVELOPMENT IN INDIAN PLANNING

The political independence of the country in 1947 was accompanied by the partition which broke up the Union into two complementary economies of India and Pakistan. Creating severe problems relating to the sources of raw material, and upsetting the structure of production, consumption and trade in the country. All these factors led to economic chaos superimposed on the fundamental problem of the poverty of the masses. The problem of transforming such an underdeveloped country into a self-generating economy required the adoption of a meaningful strategy of economic development. Under the circumstances, given the adherence to democracy expressed in the Constitution of India. The Government of India realized the need for conscious and deliberate efforts to break the vicious circle of poverty by planning for the economic development of the country. The Planning Commission was set up and made responsible for drawing up Five Year Plans aimed at attaining self-sustaining economic growth within a few decades.

Since the commencement of planning, Five Year Plans have been a major instrument of public policy in India. Even during the period 1966–69, when there was no approved Five Year Plan, an earlier draft plan served as guide for annual plans. The objectives of planning and its social premises were derived from Directive Principles of State Policy set up in the Constitution in 1950. Each plan has served at the same time as an appraisal of the past, and as a guide map for action in the future and also a means for reformulation and strengthening of basic national policies in the light of experience and evaluation.[78]

The First Five Year Plan covered the period 1951–1956 (April 1951 to March 1956). The First Plan, was no plan but was a collection of a few projects which were already in operation or were about to be taken in hand. There was no strategy of developments as such. Though the development of agriculture and transportation and communications was given a higher priority. It was only with the Second Five Year Plan that there was a clear enunciation of the strategy of development of Indian planners. Professor Mahalanobis, who was the real architect of Second Plan, was responsible for introducing a clear-cut strategy for development based on the Russian experience. This strategy emphasized investment in heavy industries to achieve rapid industrialization, which in turn, was a basic condition for rapid economic development. For Jawaharlal Nehru, 'the development of heavy industry was synonymous with industrialization. The purpose of this investment strategy was so achieve self-sustained growth by diverting an increased proportion of investment into the establishment of machine-building industries.[79]

The main aims of the plan were:

(i) an increase of 25 per cent in the national income; (ii) rapid industrialization with particular emphasis on the development of basic and heavy industries; (iii) large expansion of employment opportunities; and (vi) reduction of inequalities in income and wealth and a more even distribution of economic power.

The Third Five Year Plan (1961–62 to 1965–66) aimed at securing a marked advance towards self-sustaining growth. Its immediate objectives were to secure an increase in the national income by over 5 per cent per annum and at the same time ensure pattern of investment which could sustain this rate of growth during subsequent plan periods; achieve self-sufficiency in food grains and increase agricultural production to meet the requirements of industry and export; expand basic industries like steel, chemical, fuel and power and to establish machine-building capacity, so that the requirements of further industrialization could be met within a period of ten years or so mainly form the country's own resources; utilize fully the main-power resources of the county and ensure a sustained expansion in employment opportunities; and establish progressively greater equality of opportunity and bring about reduction in disparities of income and wealth and a more even distribution of economic power. The working of the Second Plan had shown that the rate of growth of agricultural production was the main limiting factor in Indian economic development, and thus, the experience of the first two plans suggested that agricultural be assigned a top priority. Consequently, the Third Plan emphasised that agricultural production should be expanded as far as possible and rural economy be diversified, so as to reduce the pressure of population on agriculture.

After plan holiday due to the situation created by the Indo-Pakistan conflict, two successive years of severe drought, devaluation of the currency, general rise in prices and erosion of resources available for plan progress, the country resumed formalized national economic planning with the formulation of the Fourth Year Plan covering the period 1969–74. The Fourth Plan set before itself two principal objectives viz. growth with stability and progressive achievement of self-reliance. It aimed at raising the standard of living of the people through programmes which at the same time were designed to promote equality and social justice. The plan laid particular emphasis on improving the condition of the less privileged and weaker sections of the society especially through the provision of employment and education. Efforts were also directed toward reduction of concentration and a wider diffusion of wealth, income and economic power.[80]

The Fifth Five Year Plan was formulated at a time when the economy was facing severe inflationary pressures. The major objectives of the Plan were to achieve self-reliance and to adopt measures for raising the consumption standards of the people living below the poverty line. The plan also gave high priority to bringing inflation under control and to achieve stability in the economic situation.[81] The Sixth Plan (1978–83) formulated by Janata Party Government did not intend to follow the GNP approach to development, but sought to reconcile the objectives of higher production with those of greater employment so that millions of people living below the poverty line might benefit therefrom. The Sixth Plan, therefore, redefined the following principal objectives of planning to be achieved within a period of ten years:

(a) the removal of unemployment and significant under-employment;

(b) An appreciable rise in the standard of living of the poorest section of the population;

(c) Provision of some basic need of the people in those income groups by the State, i.e. elementary education, healthcare, rural roads, rural housing for the landless.

The Congress (I) Government led by Mrs. Indira Gandhi which came to power in January 1980, decided to terminate the Sixth Plan formulated under the patronage of the Janata Party

Government. It declared that a new plan for 1980–85 would be formulated and with this end in view, the Planning Commission was reconstituted. Several eminent economists like Professor K.N. Raj, Professor Raj Krishna, etc. suggested that there was no need to reformulate the Sixth Plan, as the new plan could not be different from the one that has been framed, unless there are to be major changes in development policy. The choice before the country was very limited and no time should be wasted in preparing a fresh plan[82]. But the Government was determined to present a new plan. The new Sixth Plan mainly aimed at the following:

(a) A significant step in the rate of growth of the economy, the promotion of efficiency in the use of resources and for the achievement of economic and technological self-reliance

(b) A progressive reduction in the incidence of poverty and unemployment

(c) A speedy development of indigenous sources of energy, with emphasis on conservation and efficiency in the use of energy

(d) A progressive reduction in inequalities—social, economic and regional in the face of development

(e) Promoting the active involvement of all sections of the people in the process of development through appropriate education, communication and institutional strategies

A careful comparison of the two documents, the original Sixth Plan (1978–83) reveals that there is similarity in their approach, since the options open to planners were rather few. Professor Raj Krishna, former member of the Planning Commission, has been arguing that over the years, a large degree of consensus has been achieved in our objectives planning and the direction in which the economy should move. Consequently, for the planners in the Yojana Bhavan, whosoever, they may be, the degree of between is limited. This explains why one can discern a close similarity between the two drafts of the Sixth Plan—one prepared by the Janata Party Government and the other by the Congress (I) Government.

The most outstanding feature of the planned Indian economy is the total absence of policy frame. It would not be unfair to say that Indian planners are deliberately avoiding the construction of such frame and that from plan to plan, there is definite regression in this respect. The results that in the aggregate, the economy operates as almost a laissez fair economy.[83] However, the successes have been the field of public investment in irrigation, power, transport, etc. and in basic industries and to some extent in the extension the diversification of educational and health services. These required no policy support and depended on the availability of resources and the appropriate administrative and technical skills. Therefore, even though planning might have been defective and costs high in particular cases, substantial progress has been in the creation of a diversified industrial complement in the private sector. A field of partial success has been that of agricultural production. The overall increase in production over the years has been substantial and in some crops highly significant. However, the attempt to guide the direction of production has proved in fructuous and the failure has been large in the crucial area of increased production of food grains.[84] Considering another view point, the planning process has been able to create a social and economic infrastructure, provide an industrial base by fostering the development of heavy and basic industries and give employment to every able-bodied to reduction in the concentration of income and wealth.

According to the Sixth Plan, the benefits form the economic infrastructure have accrued largely to relatively affluent segments of population. Our pattern of investment, particularly in the provision of social infrastructure, been biased in favour of urban areas. Many segments of population, like the scheduled castes and tribes have not shared fully the benefits of growth. The plan further mentions "We must face the fact that the most important objectives of planning have not been achieved, the most cherished goals seem to be almost as distant today as they were when we set out on the road to planned development. These aims are implicit in all our plans more explicit in the formulation of our development strategy—are universally accepted by the Indian people. They are the achievement of full employment, the eradication of poverty, and the creation of more equal society."[85] The Seventh Plan (1985–90) has also emphasised these aims. The Eighth Plan was launched amidst economic reforms and changed political scenario (1990–95) and revised for 1992–97. The Ninth Plan (1997–2002) launched in the 50th year of India's independence is based on a careful stock taking to provide appropriate direction and balance for the socio-economic development of the country.[86] The Tenth Plan (2002–07) commenced with the objectives which had greater participation of the NDC in their formulation. Some of the highly important steps were during the plan which undoubtedly points out a change in the planning policy mindset of the economy. Eleventh Plan (2007–12) emphasized the idea of inclusive growth.

Planning has been subjected to a number of criticisms right since its inception in the country. With the passage of time, not only the number of criticism increased, but more importantly, the shortcoming of planning were pointed out. Although after considerable delay, but the Government took note of the shortcomings besides taking some major steps. The criticisms stand even today, but with one difference that the Government is not only conscious of them but also trying to do away with them.

In a democratic political system, almost every issue of socio-political importance is influenced by politics. It is more the case of less matured democracies. The some stands true for the process of planning in our country. Greater politicization of the planning process culminated in such a design that at times economic planning served the opposite purpose! For example, we know that planning is a tool for promoting regionally balanced growth but in India in the process of serving vested political interests of the Centre, it resulted into promoting an imbalanced growth.

By early 2000, we saw greater political maturity emerging in the Indian political system, and the Centre come ahead to forget politics in the name of the economic development. Real economy can never be devoid of real politics, neither it is desirable in a democracy, but political economy should be able to promote the right cause in a constructive way and not the other way round.

Thus, we see that the Governments in the recent years have tried to address the major criticisms of planning in India. More such constructive steps with better results are expected in future. More aware informed citizens will lead to better planning in future, there should not be any doubt about in it.

EXERCISES

1. Examine the need of planning in India.
2. Discuss in brief pre-requisites of successful planning in developing countries.
3. Evaluate the role of planning commission in India.
4. Write shorts notes on the following:
   (a) National Development Council
   (b) State Level Planning
   (c) District Planning

REFERENCES

[1] United Nations, Development Administration, Current Approaches and Trends in Public Administration for National Development, New York, 1975, p. 63.

[2] Millet, J.D., *Management in Public Service*, McGraw Hill, New York, 1954, p. 55.

[3] Simon, H.A., Smithburg, D.W. and Thompson, V.A., *Public Administration*, Alfred Knopf, New York, 1967.

[4] Drucker, Peter F., "Long Range Planning Challenge to Management Science, April 1959, p. 233.

[5] United Nations, Proceeding of Interregional Seminar on Organization and Administration of Development Planning Agencies, 1974, Vol. I, p. 113.

[6] Jain, R.B., *Contemporary Issues in Indian Administration*, Vishal Publication, Delhi, 1976, p. 23.

[7] Lewis, W. Arthur, *Development Planning: The Essentials of Economic Policy*, George Allen, London, 1966, p. 23.

[8] Wadhava, Charan D. (Ed.), "Introduction", Some Problems of India's Economic Policy, Tata McGraw-Hill, New Delhi 1977, p. 3.

[9] Adiseshias, Malcolm S., "Planning and Development," in Sudesh Kumar Sharma (Ed.), *Dynamics of Development Concept*, Vol. II, 1978, p. 279.

[10] Visveswaraya, M., *Planned Economy for India*, Bangalore Press, Bangalore, 1934.

[11] Jain, R.B., *Contemporary Issues in Indian Administration*, Vishal Publication, Delhi, 1976, pp. 246–47.

[12] Report of the Advisory Planning Board Delhi, 1947, p. 24.

[13] Jain, R.B., *Contemporary Issues in Indian Administration,* Vishal Publication, Delhi, 1976, pp. 246–47.

[14] *The Constitution of India*, Part II, Art. 35 (b. c).

[15] Government of India, Cabinet Secretariat, Resolution No. 1 P. (c)/ 50.

[16] Avasthi, A., *Central Administration*, Tata McGraw Hill, New Delhi, 1980, p. 193.

[17] Lok Sabha Secretariat, Subjects for which Ministries and Departments Of Government of India are Responsible, New Delhi, May 1966, p. 179, quoted in Maheshwari, S.R., *Indian Administration*, Orient Longman, New Delhi, 1968, p. 96.

[18] Estimates Committee, Twenty First Report (1957–58) and Twenty Fifth Report (1962–63).

[19] Interim Report of the Study Team on The Machinery for Planning, March 1967, pp. 29–30.

[20] *Ibid.*, p. 27.

[21] Paranjape, H.K., *The Planning Commission—A Descriptive Account*, Indian Institute of Public Administration, 1964, p. 24.

[22] Maheshwari, S.R., *Indian Administration*, Orient Longman, New Delhi, 1968, p. 86.

[23] Panadiker, Pai (Ed.), *Development Administration in India,* Macmillon, New Delhi, 1974, p. 7.

[24] Indian Institute of Public Administration, *The Organization of Government of India*, Somaiya Publications, New Delhi, 1971, pp, 451-55.

[25] Paranjape, H.K., *The Planning Commission—A Descriptive Account,* Indian Institute of Public Administration, *1964,* pp. 56–57.

[26] Avasthi, A., *op. cit.,* p. 201.

[27] Estimates Committee, Twenty First Report and Twenty Fifth Report.

[28] Planning Commission, First Five Year Plan: A Draft Outline, Government of India, New Delhi, 1975, p. 253.

[29] Cabinet Secretariat, Resolution No. 62/C.F./50. New Delhi, 6th August, 1952.

[30] *Ibid.,* p. 67.

[31] Sen, S.R., "Planning Machinery in India", *Indian Journal of Public Administration*, Vol. VII, No. 3, July–September, 1961, p. 233.

[32] Maheshwari, S.R., *Indian Administration*, Orient Longman, New Delhi, 1968, p. 113.

[33] Avasthi, A., *Central Administration*, Tata McGraw-Hill, New Delhi, 1980, p. 204.

[34] Maheshwari, S.R., *Indian Administration*, Orient Longman, New Delhi, 1968, p. 115.

[35] Brecher, M. Nehru, *A Political Biography*, London, Oxford University Press, 1959, p. 521.

[36] Sharma, S.K., *Dynamics of Development,* Delhi Concept, 1980, p. 69.

[37] Maheshwari, S.R., *The Administrative Reforms Commission*, Lakshmi Narain Agarwal, Agra, 1972, pp. 96–97.

[38] Sen, S.R., "Formulation of the National Plan—the Basic Process and the Machinery" in Panandiker, V.A. Pai, *Development Administration in India,* The Macmillan, New Delhi, 1974, p. 65.

[39] Report of the Taxation Enquiry Committee, 1953–54, New Delhi, 1954, Vol. 5, p. 34.

[40] Dubhashi, P.R., "The Process of Planning", in *Yojana,* Vol. 28. No. 23, Dec. 16–31, 1984, p. 30.

[41] Krishnamachari, V.T., "Planning for Economic Development" *Gazetteer of India,* Vol. III, Economic Structure and Activities, Ministry of Education and Social Welfare, Publication Division, New Delhi, 1975, p. 16.

[42] *Ibid.,* p. 17.

[43] Jain, R.B., "Planning in the Third World," *Indian Journal of Public Administration,* Spl. Number of Planning Systems, Vol. XXX, No. 3,

[44] Sharma, S.K., *Dynamics of Development, op. cit.,* p. 45.

[45] Krishnamachari, V.T., *op. cit.,* pp. 19–18.

[46] Maheshwari, S.R., *The Administrative Reforms Commission,* Laxmi Narain Aggarwal, Agra, 1972, p. 21.

[47] Planning Commission, First Five Year Plan, Draft Outline, 1951.

[48] Planning Commission, Second Five Year Plan, Government of India, New Delhi, 1956.

[49] Planning Commission, Third Five Year Plan, Government of India, New Delhi, 1961.

[50] Bhambri, C.P., *Public Administration in India,* Vikas Publishing, New Delhi, 1973, p. 94.

[51] Agarwal, P.P., "Some Aspects of Plan Implantation", *Indian Journal of Public Administration,* Vol, 19, New Delhi, January–March 1973.

[52] Administrative Reforms Commission, p. 21.

[53] *Ibid.,* p. 41

[54] Sharma, S.K., *op. cit.,* pp. 70–71.

[55] Sen, S.R., "Formulation of National Plan....." *op. cit.,* p. 66.

[56] The Administrative Reforms Commission, *op. cit.,* p. 92.

[57] *Ibid.,* p. 54

[58] Somasekhara, N., *State Planning in India,* Himalaya Publishing, Bombay, 1984, p. 158.

[59] *Ibid.,* p. 161.

[60] *Ibid.,* pp. 163–64.

[61] *Ibid.,* p. 165.

[62] *Ibid.,* pp. 166–69.

[63] Indian Institute of Public Administration, Report of Workshop on Planning at the State Level, New Delhi, 19–21 May, 1968, quoted in Jain, R.B., pp. 256–57.

[64] Sharma, S.K., *op. cit.,* p. 71.

[65] Lakdawala, D.T., Inaugural Address. Seminar on Block Level Planning and Full Employment, New Delhi, 17–18, August 1977.

[66] Sen, S.R., "Formulation of the National Plan," *op. cit.,* pp. 66–67.

[67] Somasekhara, *State Planning in India,* Himalaya Publishing, Bombay, 1984, pp. 104–105.

[68] *Ibid.,* pp. 205–207.

[69] *Ibid.,* p. 151.

[70] Planning Commission Report of the Working Group on Block Level Planning, New Delhi, 1978.

[71] Administrative Reforms Commission in Maheswari, *op, cit.,* p. 100.

[72] Maheswari, Shriram "Administering the Planning System," *Indian Journal of Public Administration,* Vol. XXX. No. 3. July–September 1984, pp. 6.3–6.4.

[73] *Ibid.,* p. 604.

[74] Jain, R.B., "Planning in the Third World", *op, cit.,* p. 557.

[75] *Ibid.,* p. 556.

[76] *Ibid.,* p. 565.

[77] Agarwal, P.P., "Some Aspects of Plan Implementation", *Indian Journal of Public Administration,* Vol. XIX, No. I, January–March 1973, pp. 16–25.

[78] Tarlok Singh, "Development Planning in South Asia," *Indian Journal of Public Administration,* Vol. XXX, No. 3, July–September, 1984,

[79] Datt, Ruddar and Sundharam, K.P.M., *Indian Economy,* S. Chand and Co., New Delhi, 1982, pp. 121–22.

[80] Research and Reference Division, India-1980, Publication Division. Ministry of Information and Broadcasting, Government of India, 1980, p. 202.

[81] *Ibid.,* p. 166.

[82] Datt, Ruddar and Sundharam, K.P.M., *Indian Economy, op. cit.,* p. 225.

[83] Gadgil, D.R., "Planning Without a Police Frame", *Economic and Political Weekly,* Bombay, Vol. II, Nos. 3, 4 & 5 (Annual Number, Feb, 1967) pp. 253–64.

[84] *Ibid.,* p. 181.

[85] Planning Commission, Draft Sixth Five Year Plan (1978–83), New Delhi, p. 2.

[86] India-2000-A Reference Annual, Publication Division, GOI, New Delhi, 200, p. 374.

Chapter

8

Administration of Social Welfare

As discussed in the preceding chapters development has been defined by experts as a phenomenon of change and growth. The change has to be socio-cultural while the growth can be measured in terms of per capita income, GDP and GNP. The government can initiate and monitor this change leading to growth or the vice versa. Once the infrastructure becomes conducive to the elimination of poverty and illiteracy, the welfare measures can be launched for the weak and the deprived and also for the welfare of the people in the main stream. The Constitution tries to identify these weaker sections or deprived people as members of Scheduled Castes and Scheduled Tribes. The later developments have added members of the OBC (other backward classes) minority communities and handicapped individuals. According to Kaka Kalelkar Report, women as a class are backward in India and all sorts of welfare programmes for these deprived or underprivileged groups constitute the core of welfare administration. Thus, broadly speaking, development administration and welfare administration are intimately interlinked, but they cannot be called synonymous.

We define a welfare state as one which is wedded to the principle of promoting the general happiness and welfare of the people. In a restricted sense, it means, "a community where state power is deliberately used to modify the normal play of economic forces so as to obtain a more equal distribution of income for every citizen. A basic minimum, irrespective of the market value of his work and property." In this sense, a welfare state regards itself as an agency of social service than as an instrument of power. To some, the concept of a welfare state was an economic proposition, to others, it was an institutional arrangement for the solution of the problem of poverty, Professor Marshall interpreted it as a compromise between individualism and collectivism. The former confers on the individual an absolute right to receive welfare, the latter imposes a duty on the state to promote and safeguard the whole community, which may transcend the aggression of individual claims.[1]

If it means anything at all to an average man, it may be said to mean at least the following: A civil community in which the instrumentalities and the authority of government are employed to establish, maintain and the guarantee to its citizens certain specific conditions of physical and sociological protection. Beneficial services and institutionalized opportunities that are considered to be essential to the general public welfare of the State and to the corresponding personal well-being of each on several count as follows:

(a) They emphasize its over aspect of security and ignore the vital principle liberty on which it founded

(b) They view the welfare state out of the historical context in which it developed

(c) They ignore the empirical thrust of the concept and tend to see it as a vindication of one ideology or another

(d) They tend to universalize the concept[2]

The basic philosophy of the Welfare State rests upon several important and rational assumptions. Some of which are clearly in harmony with democratic ideologies. The concept is deliberately advocated as an extension of democratic values within the functional structure of the state. A Welfare State is expected to perform miracles of security and liberty, liberalism and conservatism, and individualism and equalitarianism. It is supposed to guarantee freedom from personal obligation and at the same time to provide for certainty of social compulsion. And it is expected that the government will have sufficient authority and enough mechanism to perform these miracles without making the citizens too much aware of its pressures or its costs and without reducing his freedom or ignoring the uniqueness as it is a system wherein the government agrees to underwrite certain levels of employment, income, education, medical aid, social security and housing for all its citizens. In general, the Welfare State may have the following elements.

(a) An extensive and all-embracing scheme of social security against the normal risks and hazards of life (social insurance, assistance, etc.)

(b) The provision of many free services by State, (education, medical aid, etc.)

(c) The maintenance of full employment regardless of cost

(d) A considerable degree of equality of incomes founded upon redistributive taxation, minimum-wage legislation, etc.

(e) The public ownership of many utilities and leading industries

(f) Improvement in the quality of life rather than alleviation of sufferings, distress and want as a new trend in a Welfare State

Socialism as a Welfare Ideal

The capitalist economy, by its very nature, is not in a position to bring about the desired pattern of income distribution. Such an economy is based on class antagonisms and private vested interests. The optimum pattern of distribution can be realized only in a socialist economy because of the social ownership of the means of production. Private property, which is the root cause of all inequalities, is happily abolished under socialism. The existence of a steeply progressive system of taxation coupled with a well-conceived social security system helps to bring about an egalitarian income distribution in a socialist economy. The capitalist economy, on the contrary, not only fails to bring about optimum distribution but also to realize even optimum production. A socialist economy, on the other hand, secures not only optimum distribution, but also optimum production. A socialist economy is a planned economy and as such, it secures a balanced, co-ordinate and optimum development of a country's resources for raising the living standards of the masses. However, a rising standard of life or material welfare, as it is sometimes called, is of course not an end in itself. Essentially, it is means to a better intellectual and cultural life. The task before an underdeveloped country is not merely to get better results within the existing framework of economic and social institutions, but to mould and refashion these so that they contribute effectively to the realization of wider and deeper social values.[3]

Advantages and disadvantages

Advocates of the welfare state thinks that it minimizes, sufferings, encourages creative initiative, provides security against poverty, illness, unemployment, and socio-economic injustice, and establishes the ties of love among the members of a community.

The critics, on the other hand, feel that it inhibits the growth of human personality, curbs incentive, self-reliance, self-respect, individual freedom and so on. At the same time, it is a costly affair putting a heavy burden and strain on governmental machinery.

Socialistic Pattern Society in India

When India attained independence, she inherited a war ravaged and backward economy. Millions of people were up-rooted due to the partition of the country. In 1951, hardly 16.7 per cent of the people were literate and only 42.6 per cent of the children were enrolled at the secondary level. Girls' education was in a poor state. In 1950–51 only 5.38 million girls were enrolled at the primary level, 0.53 million at the middle level and 0.17 million at secondary level. Unemployment, underemployment, malnutrition, disease and poverty affected a very large part of the population. Medical facilities were at their lowest ebb. One doctor was available for every 6,445 people. The total number of hospital beds available was 1,13,000 or 31 beds per one hundred thousand people. There were only 9,608 hospitals and dispensaries in the country.

After the attainment of independence, the process of economic development and social justice ushered by planned development through the national plans and the spread of egalitarian ideas have brought in welcome changes in the lives of millions of people. The federal political structure, the body of civil and criminal law, a well-knit administrative system, a developing economy and secular approach to public life now provide substance and reality to India's nationhood. The democratic structure of the country based on adult franchise has been followed since independence both at the Centre and in the States. A system of democratic decentralization, establishing Panchayati Raj institutions from the village to the district level has been adopted to institutions the process of participation by the people in the national progress. For the legal accomplishment of these tasks, appropriate provisions were made in the Constitution framed in 1950. The Preamble to the Constriction states:

"We, the people of India, having resolved to constitute India into a Sovereign, Socialist, Secular, Democratic, Republic and to secure to all citizens: Justice-social, economic and political; Equality of status and of opportunity and to promote among them all fraternity assuring the dignity of the individual and the unit and integrity of the Nation ... ."

The idea of a Welfare State is more fully defined in Article 41 of the Constitution which runs as follows: "The State shall, within the limits of its economic capacity and development, make effective provision for securing the right to work, to education, and public assistance in the case of unemployment, old age, sickness disablement and other cases of undeserved want,"

A little further, Article 46 lays down that "the State shall promote with special care, educational and economic interests of the weaker sections of the people and shall protect them from social injustice and all forms of exploitation."

The Directive Principles of State Policy (Article 37 to 51) are a clear cut evidence of a welfare state par excellence. Though these are not directly enforceable by court yet the principles therein laid down are nevertheless fundamental in law-making and governance of the country.

The provision in the Constitution relevant to social welfare are:

(a) Provisions Relating to General Social Welfare

    1. Fundamental Rights
       (i)   Equality before law
       (ii) Abolition of unsociability
       (iii) Prohibition of traffic in human beings and forced labour.

    2. Directive Principles of State Policy
       (i)   State to secure social order for the promotion of welfare of the people
       (ii) Promotion of educational and economic interests of the interests of the Scheduled Castes, Scheduled Tribes and other weaker sections
       (iii) Duty of the State to raise the level of nutrition and the standard of living and to improve public health

(b) Provisions Relating to Children

    1. Prohibition of discrimination on grounds of religion, race, caste, sex or place of birth
    2. Prohibition of employment of children in factories, etc.
    3. The State shall so direct its policy that (i) the health and strength of workers, men and women and the tender age of the children are not abused to enter avocations unsuited to their age or strength, (ii) childhood and youth are protected against exploitation and against moral and material abandonment
    4. Provision for free and compulsory education for children
    5. Duty of the State to raise the level of nutrition and the standard of living and to improve public health

(c) Provisions Relating to Women

    1. (i) Prohibition of discrimination on grounds of religion, race, caste, sex or place of birth
       (ii Equality of opportunity in matters relating to public employment
       (iii) Prohibition of traffic in human beings and forced labour

2. (i) Men and women equally have the right to an adequate means of livelihood
   (ii) Equal pay for equal work for both men and women
   (iii) Health and strength of workers, men and women and the tender age of children are not abused and citizens are not forced by economic necessity to enter avocation unsuited to their age or strength
   (iv) Childhood and youth are protected against exploitation and against moral and material abandonment

3. Provision for just and humane conditions of work and maternity relief.

(d) Provisions Relating to Social Defence

(e) Provisions Relating to the Disabled

1. Right to work, to education and to public assistance in certain cases.

(f) Provisions Relating to Prohibition
The State shall endeavour to bring about prohibition of consumption, except for medical purposes, of intoxicating drinks and of drugs, which are injurious to health.

(g) Provisions Relating to the Aged
The State shall, within the limits of its economic capacity and development, make effective provisions for securing the right to work, to education and to public assistance in case of unemployment, old age, sickness and disablement and in other cases of underserved want.

(h) Provisions Relating to Distribution of Legislative Powers on matters regarding Social Welfare

Items have been listed under three lists—the Union List, the State List and the Concurrent List.

These values or objectives of socialism in Indian have been summed up in the phrase socialist pattern of society.

The socialist pattern of society is not to be regarded as some fixed or rigid pattern. It is not rooted in any doctrine or dogma. Each country has to develop according to its own genius and traditions. Economic and social policy has to be shaped from time-to-time in the light of historical circumstances. It is neither necessary nor desirable that the economy should become a monolithic type of organization offering little play for experimentation either as to forms or as to modes of functioning. Nor should expansion of the public sector mean centralization of decision-making and of exercise of authority. In fact, the aim should be to secure an appropriate devolution of function and to ensure to public enterprises is a field in which considerable experimentation will be necessary, and this holds, in fact, for the entire socialist pattern. What is important is a clear sense of direction, a consistent regard for certain basic values and a readiness to adapt institutions and organizations and their rules of conduct in the light of experience.

The accent of the socialist pattern is on the attainment of positive goals; the raising of living standards, the enlargement of opportunities for all, the promotion of enterprise among the disadvantaged classes and the creation of a sense of partnership among all sections of the community. These positive goals provide the criteria for basic decision. The Directive Principles of State Policy in the Constitution had indicated the approach in broad terms; the socialist pattern of society is a more concretized expression for this approach. Economic policy and institutional changes have to be planned in a manner that would secure economic advance along democratic and egalitarian lines. Democracy, it has been said, is a way of life rather than a particular set of institutional arrangements. The same could well be said of the socialist pattern.

Within this broader approach, the Second Five Year has been formulated with reference to the following principal objectives:

(a) A sizeable increase in national income so to raise the level of living in the country

(b) Rapid industrialization with particular emphasis on the development of basic and heavy industries

(c) A large expansion of employment opportunities

(d) Reduction of inequalities in income and wealth and more even distribution of economic power

These objectives are interrelated. A significant increase in national income and a marked improvement in living standard cannot be secured without a substantial increase in production and investment. To this end the building up of economic and social overheads, exploration and development of minerals and the promotion of basic industries like steel, machine, building, coal, and heavy chemicals are vital. For securing and advance simultaneously in all these directions, the available manpower and natural resources have to be used to the best advantage. In a country, in which there is relative abundance of manpower. expansion of employment opportunities becomes an important objective in itself. Further, the process and social inequalities and should be achieved through democratic means and processes. Economic objectives cannot be divorced from social objectives and means and objectives go together. It is only in the context of plan which satisfies the legitimate urges of the people that a democratic society can put forward its best effort.

The excessive emphasis on any one of objectives may damage the economy and delay the realization of the very objective which is being stressed. Low or static standards of living, underemployment and unemployment, and to a certain extent even the gap between the average incomes and the highest incomes are all manifestations of the basic underdevelopment which characterizes an economy depending mainly on agriculture, Rapid industrialization and diversification of the economy are thus the core of development.

Investment in basic industries creates demand for consumer goods, but it does not enlarge the supply of consumer goods in the short run; nor does it directly absorb any large quantities of labour. A balanced pattern of industrialization. Therefore, requires a well-organized effort to utilize labour for increasing the supplies of much needed consumer goods in a manner which economizes the use of capital. A society in which labour is plentiful in relation to capital has to develop the art and technique of using labour-intensive modes of production effectively, and to much social advantage, in diverse fields. Indeed, in the context of prevailing unemployment, the absorption of labour becomes an important objective in itself.

Economic development has in the past often been associated with growing inequalities of income and wealth. The gains of development accrues in the early stages to a small class of businessmen and manufactures, whereas the immediate impact of the application of new techniques in agriculture and in traditional industry has often meant growing unemployment or underemployment among large numbers of people. In course of time, this trend gets corrected partly through the development of countervailing power of trade unions and partly through state action undertake in response to the growth of democratic ideas. The problem before underdeveloped countries embarking upon development at this late stage is to so plan the alignment of productive resources and of class relationships as to combine development with reduction in economic and social inequality; the process and pattern of development has, in essence, to be socialized. There are existing inequalities of income and wealth which need to be corrected and care has to be taken to secure that development does not create further inequalities and widen the exiting disparities. The process of reducing inequalities is two-fold. It must raise incomes at the lowest levels and it must simultaneously reduce income at the top. The former is, basically, the more important aspect, but early and purposeful action in regard to the second aspect is also called for. Development along these lines has not so far been attempted on any signification scale under democratic conditions. There are not historical parallels or plans of action which could be regarded as providing an answer to this special problem, and these problems will have to be faced pragmatically. It will call forth a great deal of flexibility and experimentation in the matter of techniques.

Social Welfare Services

The term social welfare services has been used to refer to these and other special services when they are established for the benefit of individuals or groups who by reason of physical, mental or social handicaps are not able to derive benefit from the existing services in the community and fail to make their own contribution to the life of the community. These services seek to help the handicapped individuals of groups to develop their own capacities for utilizing existing services and also for making their contribution to society in the same way as other members of the community do.

Some of the major services are discussed as follows:

Welfare of children

The national policy for children adopted by the government in August, 1947 describes the country as a supremely important asset. It enjoins on the state the responsibility for their nurture and solicitude. There is a National Children's Board to provide a focus and a forum to ensure continuous planning review and co-ordination of all the essential services for the children. Similar boards have been constituted in almost all the states. A number of schemes and programmes have been introduced by the government for the welfare of children. Which include: Integrated child development services, services for children in need of care and protection, crèches for working and ailing mother's children, nutrition programmes, national awards in the field of children's welfare, national children's fund, UNICEFS programmes, etc.

Welfare of the physically handicapped

Initially, there were no special services for the people who suffered from physical disability. If they happened to be poor and destitute, besides being handicapped, they were taken care of in the homes of the destitute. Now there are various programmes for about 16.15 million[5] disabled people in the country. These programmers are related to early detection and treatment, education, training and rehabilitation of disabled persons namely, the blind, the deaf, the orthopaedically handicapped, the mentally retarded and leprosy cured persons.

Welfare of women

In 1971, GOI appointed the National Committee on the status of Women, and submitted its report in 1974. The National Plan of Action for Women introduced in 1976 provides guidelines in formulating policies and programmes for the welfare and development of women in the country. To keep a watch on the implementation of policies and programmes for women. A national committee, a steering committee and an inter-departmental co-ordination committee were set up. The major schemes for women welfare include hostels for working women, functional literacy for adult women, training courses for rehabilitation of women, vocational training programmes, etc.

Social Defence Services

Problems of social disorganization emerging in the wake of industrialization and urbanization are manifest in the form of juvenile delinquency, drug addiction, alcoholism, crime of various types, immoral traffic in women, etc. In order to control these problems, a number of programmes of social defense have been launched. These include: Delinquency control (under the Children Act. 1960), prison welfare schemes, suppression of immoral traffic, beggary prevention, prohibition and drug abuse, etc. The National Institute of Social Defence functions as the central advisory body in this regard.

Welfare of SCs/STs and backward classes

According to the 1991 census, about 24.56 per cent of the country's population comprised of scheduled castes and scheduled tribes. In addition, some state governments have also specified other categories of people as the' other backward classes and denote flied nomadic and semi-nomadic communities. The Constitution has prescribed certain protective measures and safeguards for these classes and a number of programmes and schemes were introduced under the various Five Year Plans.[6]

Welfare of minorities

The Constitution of India protects the interests of minorities and recognizes their rights to conserve their languages, scripts or culture and establish and administer educational institutions of their choice. The Government has notified five communities namely, Muslims, Sikhs, Christians, Buddhists and Zoroastrians as minorities at the national level. As per census of 2001, the minority groups constitute nearly 18 per cent of the total population of the country.

1. *National Commission for Minorities:* A Minorities Commission was set up in January 1978, which reviews the implementation of policies of the Union and the State Governments towards minorities and submits annual reports to the Government. The National Commission for Minorities Act, 1992 was passed by the Parliament. Under this Act, the National Commission for Minorities was constituted on 16 May 1993 with statutory status replacing the erstwhile Commission. The Commission has a Chairperson, a Vice-Chairperson and five members to be nominated by the Central Government. The National Commission has been reconstituted with effect from 21 January 2000.

2. *Commissioner for Linguistic Minorities:* The Commissioner for Linguistic Minorities appointed under Article 350-B of the Constitution investigates all matters relating to the safeguards provided for linguistic minorities. He looks into representations and complaints received, from various associations and individuals belonging to linguistic minorities. The Commissioner has his headquarters at Allahabad, with regional offices at Kolkata, Belgaum and Chennai. So far 35 reports have been laid before the Parliament. The Programme for Welfare of Minorities has the objective of securing life and property of minorities and for providing special consideration for minorities in public employment and ensuring non-discrimination in development programmes and grant of financial benefits. The programme is being implemented by the State Governments and Union Territories and the concerned Central Ministries/Departments.

3. *National Minorities Development and Finance Corporation:* A National Minorities Development and Finance Corporation has been set up by the Government of India with a share capital of ₹ 500 crore to provide economic and developmental activities for the benefit of backward sections among the minorities, preference being given to occupational groups and women among minorities. The Government of India have raised the level of its contribution from ₹ 125 crore to ₹ 300 crore subject to pro-rata contribution from the State Governments/ UT Administrations towards the share capital of the Corporation. During 1999–2000, the Corporation disbursed ₹ 60.78 crore as loan covering 22,510 beneficiaries. The cumulative assistance provided by the Corporation since 1994–95 amounts to ₹ 224.34 crore for 66,891 beneficiaries.

Besides these, there are also a number of programmes and services started by the Government for the welfare of the aged, the girl child, the urban and rural poor and for other disadvantaged or weaker section of society.

EXERCISES

1. Discuss in brief meaning and nature of administration of social welfare.
2. Examine social welfare services.
3. Write short notes on the following:
   (a) Welfare of children
   (b) Welfare of physically handicapped
   (c) Welfare of women
   (d) Welfare of SCs/STs and backward classes

REFERENCES

[1]   Marshall, T.H., *"Sociology on the Cross Roads"*, 1963, p. 246 quoted in Robson, William A. *Welfare State and Welfare Society*, George Allen and Unwin London, 1976, p. 12.

[2]   Shankhdher, M.M., *The Concept of Welfare State*, Deep and Deep, New Delhi, 1995, p. 255.

[3]   Seth, M.L., *Principles of Economics*, Lakshmi Narain Agarwal, Agra, 1981, p. 793.

[4]   Mainly based upon Government Reports and Documents, India–84, Gazetteer of India, Five Year Plans, etc.

[5]   *India 2000*, Publication Division, GOI, New Delhi, p. 269.

[6]   Details of the constitutional provisions, other schemes, legislation and administration.

International Aid and Technical Assistance Programmes

A pledge is contained in Article 55 of the U.N. Charter to "promote higher standards of living, full employment and conditions of economic and social progress and development." Accordingly, the United Nations has supported the development efforts of less developed countries. Four successive Development Decades have been proclaimed since the beginning of 1960. During the 1960s, both the General Assembly and the Economic and Social council increasingly stressed the need for a unified approach to economic and social planning to promote balanced and sound development. In 1974, the General Assembly in its special session gave a call for the New International Economic order. In the late 1980s and early 1990s, the emphasis shifted to more market-oriented approaches to economic and social development, without ignoring the important role of the state in improving the human conditions.

The United Nations and various organizations related to it are making global effort for socio-economic development of the developing countries through programmes ranging from technical cooperation, and comprehensive development planning to special projects in individual field such as trade, industry and agriculture. Increasing priority has been given in assisting the developing countries in programmes dealing with social implications such as human resource development, eradication of poverty, population activities, drug abuse control, crime prevention and advancement of women.

Several programmes have been launched by the United Nations for technical cooperation for development. The most significant of these programmes is the United Nations Development Programme (UNDP). According to a UN publication, it is the world's largest, multilateral source of grant funding for development cooperation. It was created in 1965, and by 1991 its funds totalling about 1.5 billion US dollars came from voluntary contributions of Member-States and affiliated agencies of the UNO. Forty-eight nations Governing Council composed of the developed and developing countries approves major programmes and policy decisions. UNDP has its offices in 115 developing countries, including one in New Delhi, it works with 152 government to promote higher standard of living, faster and equitable economic growth, and environmentally sound development. UNDP also works extensively with non-governmental organizations (NGOs). During 1995, it provided financial and technical support for over 6,000 projects to train human resources and transfer technology.

Some other programmes started by the United Nations include development of science and technology, utilisation of natural resources and generation of energy, protection of environment, human settlements, tackling of world food problems and comprehensive healthcare programmes.

In addition to the efforts made for development of poorer nations, the United Nations has been engaging itself, through numerous agencies called the inter-governmental agencies related to United Nations in the task of social and economic cooperation. Article 55(b) provides for UN commitment to seek, solutions of international economic, social, health and related problems; and international cultural and educational cooperation... "The co-ordination of the work of a large number of inter-governmental agencies is done by one of the principle organs viz. the Economic and Social council. Seventeen of these agencies are designated as the specialized agencies. These include: International Labour Organization, Food and Agriculture Organization, the World Health Organization, the United Nations Educational, Scientific and Cultural Organization, the World Bank, the IMF, and the United Nations Industrial Development Organization. The specialized agencies report annually to the ECOSOC. Besides, the International Atomic Energy (IAEA), created in 1957, reports annually to the General Assembly, and if necessary to the Security Council and the ECOSOC. The General Agreement on Tariffs and Trade (GATT) was, and the World Trade Organization (WTO) is multilateral agreement which lays down rules of international trade.

THE UN AGENCIES

The UN agencies have such commendable work in the area of social and economic cooperation that the primary task, of the UN, of maintenance of international peace and security appears to have taken secondary place, particularly after the end of the Cold War. It is impossible to examine in detail the role and performance of all the agencies in this small section. However, a brief reference is unavoidable in fact necessary to the contribution of some of them.

ILO

The International Labour Organization (ILO) is the oldest of agencies, and it seeks to promote social justice for working people all over the world. Through its programme of technical cooperation, the ILO experts assist member-countries in such field as vocational training, management techniques, manpower planning, employment policies, social security cooperatives and small-scale handicraft agencies.

FAO

The aims of Food and Agriculture Organization (FAO) are to raise level of nutrition and standards of living, and to improve the production, processing, marketing and distribution of all food and agricultural products. FAO is the lead agency for rural development, and works for freedom from hunger. The primary task of the UNESCO is to contribute to peace and security in the world by promoting collaboration among nations through education, science, culture and communication. Its activities include advancement of basic education for all. Its cultural activities are concentrated mainly on safeguarding cultural heritage, promoting the cultural dimension of development and preservation of cultural identities and promotion of books and reading material.

WHO

The World Health Organization has been working for attainment by all people of the highest possible level of health, in cooperation with the children's fund (UNICEF) it has been trying to eradicate certain diseases that are often fatal for children. For example, it has fully succeeded in eradication of small-pox, and serious efforts are bring made to make the world free of polio and contain and (if possible) eradicate malaria. The WHO offers help in fighting the epidemics whenever they occur.

IMF

The International Monetary Fund (IMF) came up in 1944 whose Articles came into force on the 27th of December 1945 with the main functions as exchange rate regulation, purchasing short-term foreign currency liabilities of the member nations from around the world, allotting special drawing rights (SDRs) to the member nations and the most important one as the bailor to the member economies in the situation of the BoP crisis.

The main functions[1] of the IMF are as given:

(a) To facilitate international monetary cooperation;

(b) To promote exchange rate stability and orderly exchange arrangements;

(c) To assist in the establishment of a multilateral system of payments and the elimination of foreign exchange restrictions; and

(d) To assist member countries by temporarily providing financial resources of correct maladjustment in their balance of payments (BoPs).

Every member nation has two seats in the IMF, one of the Governor and the other of the Alternate Governor. The Union Finance Minister is the ex-officio Governor of India in the IMF and the RBI Governor is the Alternate Governor.

The total SDR quota of IMF is SDR 212 billion with India having an SDR of 4.1582 billion (1.961 per cent share) including its constituency countries viz. Bhutan, Bangladesh and Srilanka[2].

India's relative position based on the SDR quota is 13th, however, based on voting share India together with its constituencies is ranked 21st. The 12th round of the SDR quota review in 2003 by the IMF left India's share unchanged.

The SDR 4.1582 billion quota of India in IMF comprises three segments—

(a) A rupee securities of SDR 3.46635 billion

(b) A cash holding of SDR 203 million and

(c) A credit trenches position (in foreign currency) of SDR 488.88 million.

The SDR position of member countries keeps changing on account of the sovereign short-term instruments purchased by the IMF from the member nations around the world—reimbursed by the concerned member nations. This function of the IMF makes it behave like a central bank for its member countries on foreign lands.

The financial resources of IMF consists primarily of the subscription (quotas) of its 184-member countries. Quotas are determined by a formula based on the relative economic size of the members. IMF has the authority to create and allocate to its members international financial reserves in the form of SDRs.

The main financial role of the IMF is to provide temporary credits (3 to 10 years) to members experiencing BoP crisis. In return, members borrowing from IMF agree to undertake policy reforms[3] to correct the problems that underlie the BoP difficulties. The amounts that IMF members may borrow are limited in proportion to their quotas.

After India signed the Extended Fund Facility (EFF) with IMF in 1981–82, it has borrowed many times from it to mitigate its BoP crisis, last being in 1991.

IMF publishes the *World Economic* outlook twice a year, as well as the annual International *Capital Markers*.

WORLD BANK

The World Bank (WB) Group today consists of five closely associated institutions propitiating the role of development in the member nations in different areas. A brief account is as follows[4]:

IBRD

The International Bank for Reconstruction and Development is the oldest of the World Bank institutions which started functioning (1945) in the area of reconstruction of the war-ravaged (World War-II) countries, and later for the development of the middle-income and creditworthy poorer economies of the world. Human development was the main focus of the developmental lending with a very low interest rate (1.55 per cent per annum)—the areas of focus being agriculture, irrigation, urban development, healthcare, family welfare, dairy development, etc. It commenced lending for India in 1949.

IDA

The International Development Agency (IDA) which is also known as the soft window of the WB was set up in 1960 with the basic aim of developing infrastructure support among the member nations, long-term lending for the development of economic services. Its loans, known as credits are extended mainly to economics with less than $895 per capita income. The credits are for a period of 35–40 years, interest-free, except for a small charge to cover administrative costs. Repayment begins after a 10-year grace period. There was no human angle to its lending. But now there remain no hard and fast differences between the purposes for the IBRD and IDA lending.

Every year developing nations make enough diplomatic attempts to carve out maximum loan disbursal for themselves. India had been the biggest beneficiary of the IDA support. The total support (IBRD + IDA) for India had been $65.8 billion till date[5].

IFC

The International Finance Corporation (IFC) was set up in 1956 which is also known as the private arm of the WB. It lends money to the private sector companies of its member nations. The interest rate charged is commercial, but comparatively low. There are many attractive features of IFC's lending. It finances and provides advice for private public ventures and projects in partnership with private investors and, through its advisory work, helps governments of the member nations to create conditions that stimulate the flow of both domestic and foreign private savings and investment.

It focuses on promoting economic development by encouraging the growth of productive enterprises and efficient capital markets in its member countries. It participates in an investment only when it can make a special contribution that compliments the role of market investors (as a Foreign Financial Investor, i.e. FFI). It also plays a catalytic role, stimulating and mobilizing private investment in the developing world by demonstrating that investments there too can be profitable.

We have seen a great upsurge in the IFC investments in India which has undoubtedly strengthened the foreign investors confidence in the Indian economy.

MIGA

The Multilateral Investment Guarantee Agency (MIGA), set up in 1988 encourages foreign investment in development economies by offering insurance (guarantees) to foreign private investors against loss caused by non-commercial (i.e. political) risks, such as currency transfer, expropriation, and war and civil disturbance. It also provides technical assistance to help countries disseminate information on investment opportunities.

ICSID

The International Centre for Settlement of Investment Disputes (ICSID), set up in 1966 is an investment dispute settlement body whose decisions are binding on the parties. It was established under the 1966 convention on the settlement of Investment Disputes between States and National of Other States. Though recourse to the centre is voluntary, but once the parties have agreed to arbitration, they cannot withdraw their consent unilaterally. It settles the investment disputes arising between the investing foreign companies and the host countries where the investments have been done.

India is not member (that is why the Enron issue was out of its preview). It is believed that being signatory to it encourages the foreign investment flows into an economy but risks independent sovereign decisions, too.

ASIAN DEVELOPMENT BANK

The Asian Development Bank (ADB), with an international partnership of 63-member countries, was established in 1966 and has headquarters at Manila, the Philippines. India is a founder member of ADB. The bank is engaged in promoting economic and social progress of its developing member countries in the Asia-Pacific region. Its principal functions are as follows:

(a) To make loans and equity investments for the economic and social advancement of its developing member countries

(b) To provide technical assistance for the preparation and execution of development projects and programmes and advisory services

(c) To respond to the requests for assistance in co-ordinating development policies and plans in developing member countries and

(d) To respond to the requests for assistance and co-ordinating development policies and plans of developing member countries

India's subscription to the bank's capital stock as on 31 December 2004 is 6.424 per cent of all the member countries.[6]

India started borrowing from ADB's Ordinary Capital Resources (OCR) in 1986. The bank's lending has been mainly in the energy, transport and communications, finance, industry and social infrastructure sectors.

India has contributed US $2.91 million in convertible currency (upto the end of 2004) to the Technical Assistance Special Fund (TASF) of the ADB.[7]

The bank has extended technical assistance to India in addition to loans from its OCR window. The technical assistance provided include support for institutional strengthening, effective project implementation and policy reforms as well as for project preparation.

India holds the position of Executive Director on the Board of Directors of the Bank— its Constituency comprises India, Bangladesh, Bhutan, Lao PDR and Tajikistan. The Finance Minister is India's Governor on the Board of Governors of Asian Development Bank of Secretary (EA) is the Alternate Governor.

WORLD TRADE ORGANIZATION (WTO)

The World Trade Organization (WTO) came into being as a result of the evolution of the multilateral trading system starting with the establishment of the General Agreement on Tariffs and Trade (GATT) in 1947. The protracted Uruguay Round negotiations spanning the period 1986–1994, which resulted in the establishment of the WTO, substantially extended the reach of multilateral rules and disciplines related to trade in goods, and introduced multilateral rules applicable to trade in agriculture (Agreement on Agriculture), trade in services (General Agreement on Trade in Services GATS) as well as Trade Related Intellectual Property Rights (TRIPS). A separate understanding on WTO dispute settlement mechanism (DSU) and trade policy review mechanism (TPRM) was also agreed upon.

WTO and INDIA

India is a founder member of both GATT and WTO. The WTO provides a rule based, transparent and predictable multilateral trading system. The WTO rules envisage non-discrimination in the form of National Treatment and Most Favoured Nation (MFN) treatment to India's exports in the markets of other WTO members. National treatment ensures that India's products once imported into the territory of other WTO members would not be discriminated vis-à-vis the domestic products in those countries. MFN treatment principle ensures that members do not discriminate among various WTO members. If a member country believes that the dues benefits are not accruing to it because of trade measures by another WTO member, which are violative of WTO rules and disciplines, it may file a dispute under the Dispute Settlement Mechanism (DSM) of the WTO. There are also contingency provisions built into WTO rules, enabling member countries to take care of exigencies like balance of payment problems and situations like a surge in imports. In case of unfair trade practices causing injury to the domestic producers, there are provisions to impose anti-dumping or countervailing duties as provided for in the anti-dumping agreement and the subsidies and countervailing measures agreement.

WTO Membership

Presently, WTO has 149 members. This includes China and Nepal whose accession was approved by the WTO ministerial conferences held on Doha and Cancun in November 2001 and September 2003, respectively. Saudi Arabia became the 149th member of the WTO at the Hong Kong Ministerial Conference in December 2005. The Kingdom of Tonga, whose accession was approved by the WTO Ministerial Conference held in December 2005, is yet to complete its domestic ratification before it becomes a WTO Member. There are presently around 30 countries in the process of accession to the WTO.

WTO Ministerial Conferences

The highest decision-making body of the WTO is the Ministerial Conference, which has to meet at least once every two years. It brings together all members of the WTO, all of which are countries or separate customs territories. The Ministerial Conference can take decisions on all matters under any of the multilateral trade agreements. Since the coming into being of the WTO in January 1995, six Ministerial Conferences have been held, namely Singapore (9–13

December 1996); Geneva (18–20 May 1998); Seattle (30 November–3 December 1999); Doha (9–14 November 2001); Cancun (10–14 September 2003); and Hong Kong, China (13–18 December 2005). US, Japan and Korea continue to oppose this. They feel that the fact-based debate on the subject should continue.

On the issue of GI-extension, India proposed higher GI Protection on all products other than wines and spirits. This protection should be given at the same level as it is available to wines and spirits under the present TRIPS Agreement. A result on this issue has implications for a large number of farmers and artisans; a higher protection will fetch better market realization for these people and would give them better market access. This will increase their welfare—an issue important for the present development round. It may also be mentioned that while we have an interest in the GI-extension issue, given that a large proportion of GIs in our country are either agricultural items or handcrafts items, we certainly do not want that the obligation of setting up a multilateral GI register should result in an increase in the financial burden or should result in any obligation, which proves to be onerous to handle.

Trade and Environment

The Doha Ministerial Declaration had provided a negotiating mandate on certain issues of trade and environment. On the issue of a relationship between existing WTO rules and specific trade obligations set out in MEAs [para 31(i)], India believes that trade and environment should be mutually supportive of the objective of achieving sustainable development. India is one of the proponents of the Multilateral Environment Agreements (MEAs), and is a party to all the major MEAs. The discussions so far in the Committee on Trade and Environment (CTE) have been on submitting national experiences, so as to come up with a bottoms-up approach on the subject. Though a number of countries have given their experiences, but no actual conflict has come to notice so far between the existing WTO rules and specific trade obligations set out in MEAs.

On Para 31(iii) regarding reduction or, as appropriate, elimination of tariff and non-tariff barriers to environmental goods and services, India has proposed the adoption of an environmental project approach. This approach achieves clearly identified environmental benefits, and eliminates, or at least reduces, dual or multiple uses. It brings in synergy between environmental goods and services. This approach clearly addresses the Doha mandate of Para 31(iii). Developed countries, on the other hand, have advocated the adoption of a list approach for seeking tariff reduction on environmental goods. The list approach seeks to apply a sectoral approach to the NAMA negotiations—an objective which goes against the gain of development. Besides, it does not ensure the flow of environmental benefits, which is central to the mandate. Also it focuses only on goods, and does not address the issues of environmental services. Further, most of the goods in the list have been found to have dual or multiple uses. The Hong Kong Ministerial Conference Declaration reaffirmed the mandate of Para 31 of the Doha Declaration, and instructed the member countries to complete the work expeditiously to fulfill the mandate. India feels that it needs to address these issues carefully and develop a mechanism so that the mandate is fulfilled in the best possible manner.

Trade Facilitation

Trade facilitation is the only subject from the bundle of four Singapore Issues on which negotiation had started pursuant to the WTO's July Framework Agreement of 2004. [The modalities for negotiations are set out in Annexure D of the July Framework Agreement.] India's participation in the negotiations has been positive and constructive. India has also placed emphasis on compliance issues through an effective cooperation mechanism between customs administrations. India has made a joint proposal with the US to have a multilateral mechanism for information exchange. Negotiations are also looking at the aspect of technical and financial assistance for capacity building in developing countries. The Hong Kong Ministerial Declaration on Trade Facilitation is a good basis for further negotiations on this subject. A large number of measures have been submitted so far as negotiating proposals in the Negotiating Group on Trade Facilitation (NGTF).

Dispute Settlement Understanding (DSU) Review

The Doha Ministerial Conference mandated negotiations on Dispute Settlement Understanding (DSU) aimed at clarifying and improving disciplines under the DUS. These negotiations are outside the single undertaking. The DSU negotiations reached a certain textual basis in May 2003 but there was no consensus on that text. Subsequently, negotiations have been continuing without, however, reaching any convergence. In the Hong Kong Ministerial Declaration, Ministers have instructed for rapid conclusion of these negotiations.

Regional Trading Arrangement (RTAs)

The negotiations aimed at clarifying and improving disciplines and procedures under the existing WTO provisions applying to Regional Trading Arrangements are under way in the Negotiating Group on Rules. An agreement was reached by Members within the Negotiating Group on Rules on improving the transparency process of RTAs. The decision, however, needs to be approved by the Trade Negotiation Committee/General Council.

India's Stand on WTO

India attachés utmost importance to a rule-based multilateral trading system. India will continue to protect and pursue its national interests in these negotiations and work together with other WTO Members, towards securing a fair and equitable outcome of these negotiations and also ensuring that the development dimension is fully preserved in the final outcome as mandated at Doha and reiterated in the July Framework Decision of August 1, 2004 and the Hong Kong Ministerial Declaration. Many of the elements and principles agreed so far are concrete expressions to deliver on the development promises of the Doha Round, including the elimination of the structural flaws in agricultural trade. The outcome of the negotiations should not undermine the ability of developing countries, like India, to safeguard the livelihood and food security of their poor farmers or to develop their industries and services sectors.

India has fully cooperated with the United Nation's System in its multifarious activities. India's concern for peace has been reflected in her repeated calls for disarmament and complete and comprehensive war on all nuclear testing. It is ironical that, on account of their discriminatory nature, India has not found it possible to sign either the Non-Proliferation Treaty (NTP) or agree to the CTBT. In view of threat to its security, India was forced to conduct five nuclear tests in May 1998, acquiring capability to make nuclear weapons. In the area of development India is one of the main contributors to the UNDP. The central funding agency of the United Nation Systems. There are in all 18 agencies that have their country offices in India. They have been cooperating with India and working together as a family at the country level in areas of common human development concern so as to be able to build capacity and add tangible value to national initiatives. India's commitment to the United Nations System can still be best summed up in the words of Jawaharlal Nehru spoken decades ago. He had said, "We have always been a staunch supporter of the UN. As a member of that august body. India has taken its full measure of responsibility in all aspects of United Nations activities. The United Nation is the one hope of the world for bringing peace and freedom to humanity".

EXERCISES

1. Discuss the significance of International AID.
2. Critically examine the role of International Monetary Fund and World Bank.
3. Write short notes on the following:
   (a) Asian Development Bank (ADB)
   (b) World Trade Organization and India

REFERENCES

[1]   *Basic Facts About the United Nations,* UN, New York, 2000, p. 55 and p. 137.

[2]   *India 2007,* Publication Division, Government of India, New Delhi.

[3]   Such facility from it is available once the member country has signed the agreement with the IMF called as the Extended Fund Facility (EFF). Popularly, this is known as the "Conditionalities of the IMF" under which India started its Economic Reform Programme in 1991–92 once it borrowed from the IMF in the wake of the BoP crisis of 1990–91.

[4]   Based on *Basic Facts About the United Nations, op. cit.,* pp. 52–55 & *India 2004, 2005, 2006, 2007 and 2008,* Publication Division GOI, N. Delhi.

[5]   *India 2008,* Publication Division, Government of India, New Delhi.

[6]   *Ibid.*

[7]   *Ibid.*

Chapter

10

Bureaucracy and Development Administration

Most developing countries are engaged in bringing about rapid socio-economic development. The effort is to modernize the societies by introducing changes in almost all the sectors including social overheads, infrastructural facilities and productive enterprises like industry and agriculture. Social services such as health, education and water supply, infrastructure like roads and communication facilities, electricity and market centres, and productive activities in industry, agriculture, animal husbandry and forestry are being developed within definite planning frameworks. Development goals are being set and programmes and projects formulated and implemented to achieve the goals within a specific time-horizon. There is universal concern in the developing countries to improve the standard of living of large masses of people who have so far been denied even the basic requirements of decent living. It is this concern for rapid socio-economic development that sets the background for any discussion on the relationship between bureaucracy and development administration.

Development, in this context, is an exceedingly complex enterprise involving correct diagnosis of problems, setting right priorities, planning action programmes, mobilizing adequate resources, creating new organizations and improving the capacity of existing ones and implementing programmes and projects within a definite time frame. The complex of activities connected with the development enterprise is essentially a governmental responsibility. Private sector may be induced to fall in line with general public policy, but the brunt of development work would naturally devolve on the public sector. Hence, a high degree of public administrative competence is of paramount importance in pushing through speedy development measures. As an indispensable aid to nation-building, the role of public administration is now universally acknowledged, and this is reflected in the emergence of a sort of new administrative science in recent times called development administration.

ROLE OF BUREAUCRACY

Although the vital role of the public sector in bringing about rapid socio-economic changes is generally acknowledged, there are many misgivings about the role of the bureaucracy in development administration. Bureaucracy has often been characterized as a soulless, inflexible machine which seems to be unsuited to the dynamic needs of social transformation. It is commonly associated with red tape, rigidity and never-ending rules and regulations. Historically, it has been observed that bureaucracy antedates development administration and does not fit in with the requirements of modernization. Conservation rather than change is the essence of bureaucracy. Culturally also, as the critics have maintained, the bureaucratic form of organization does not suit the needs of the traditional societies that are currently going through a process of change. Bureaucracy has also been criticized as urban-oriented and elitist in nature and unrelated to the needs of rural areas where most of the people of the developing countries live. Above all, development has been looked at as essentially a matter of shrewd political management of a society. Bureaucracy, in this context, has often been considered a threat to political leadership and an undesirable monopolizer of power. It has even been suggested that development calls for a degree of debureaucratization and steady institutionalization of popular participation in the management of development.

Clarification of Concepts

A discussion on the role of bureaucracy in development administration must first clarify the two concepts: bureaucracy and development administration. Relationship between the two can be better comprehended after the concepts have been properly understood.

Bureaucracy is essentially a normative model which emphasizes the structure of the organization. The concept of bureaucracy was fully developed by the German philosopher, Max Weber, in the early part of this century. In Weberian analysis, bureaucracy refers to the sociological concept of rationalization of collective activities. it describes a form or design of organization which assures predictability of the behaviour of employees. According to Weber, bureaucracy is superior to any other form in decision precision, stability, discipline and reliability. It makes possible a high degree of calculability of results for the heads of the organization and for those acting in relation to it. So bureaucracy compares to other organizations as does the machine with non-mechanical mode of production. Certain design strategies are built in the bureaucratic form of organization as follows:

(a) All tasks necessary for the accomplishment of goals are divided into highly specialized jobs. Thus, division of labour and specialization are ensured in the organization.

(b) Each task is performed according to a consistent system of abstract rules, ensuring uniformity and co-ordination of different tasks.

(c) Each member in the organization is accountable to a superior for his and his subordinates' actions. The principle of hierarchy is thus emphasized.

(d) Each official conducts the business of his office in an impersonal formalistic manner.

(e) Employment is based on technical qualifications and is protected against arbitrary dismissal. Promotions are based on seniority and achievement.

To the extent that these characteristics are highly articulated in an organization, that organization approaches the ideal type of bureaucracy. From Weberian formulation, one can deduce a set of structural properties and another set of behavioural characteristics. Structurally, a bureaucratic form of organization exhibits the following characteristics:

1. *Division of labour:* The total task of the organization is broken down into a number of specialized functions.

2. *Hierarchy:* As a structural principle hierarchy manifests itself in a number of levels of differentially graded authority. It creates a system of superior-subordinate relationship under which supervision of the lower offices is done by the higher ones.

3. *System of rules:* The rights and duties of the employees and the modes of doing work are governed by clearly laid down rules.

4. *Rule specificity:* Every role in the organization is clearly earmarked with specific job descriptions. Organizational expectations are reflected in job specificity.

The set of behavioural characteristics can be described as follows:

1. *Rationality:* Bureaucracy represents a rational form of organization. Hence by definition, it leaves no room of irrationality. Decisions are taken on strict evidence. Alternatives are considered objectively to choose a decision path.

2. *Impersonality:* A bureaucracy form of organization does not entertain irrational sentiments. Official business is conducted without regard for persons. It is a machine-like construct, and as such it is characterized by high degree of impersonality.

3. *Rule-orientation:* Depersonalization of the organization is achieved through formulation of rules and procedures which lay down the way of doing work. The employees are to strictly follow the rules in the discharge of their duties.

4. *Neutrality:* As a corollary of impersonality, this characteristic implies biaslessness. Bureaucracy as an instrument serves any kind of political regime without being aligned to it. It has commitment to work only and to no other value.

DEVELOPMENT ADMINISTRATION

The other concept of development administration is of a recent origin due mainly to the work of a group of American experts on comparative administration. Edward Weidner, one of the pioneers in this area, defined development administration as "an action-oriented; goal-oriented administrative system". As already mentioned, planned change to bring about rapid socio-economic transformation has become a kind of administrative ideology in the developing nations. The crux of development administration is societal change.

As Fred Riggs has characterized it, development administration refers both to administrative problems, and governmental reform. The problems relate to governmental tasks connected with agricultural, industrial, educational and medical progress. "Reforms of governmental organizations and bureaucratic procedures have necessarily to go with the administrative processes connected with problem solving."

The characteristics of development administration can be identified as follows:

Change orientation

The distinctive mark of development administration is its central concern with secio-economic change. This special orientation distinguishes development administration from regulatory or general administration which is basically concerned with maintenance of the status quo.

Result orientation

Since changes have to be brought about rapidly and within a definte time horizon, development administration has to be result oriented. Its performance is overtly related to productivity in terms of increase in per capita income, provision of health and welfare facilities, etc.

Commitment

Commitment to change and concern for timebound programmes constitute the organization role expectations in development administration. Administrators are expected to be involved and emotionally attached to jobs they are called upon to perform.

Client orientation

Development administration is overtly client-oriented. It has to be positively oriented towards satisfying the needs of specific target groups. So their satisfaction is an important criterion for evaluating performance. The people in development administration are not the passive beneficiaries. They are looked at as active participants in the public programmes. This close nexus between public and administration is an essential attribute of development administration.

Temporal dimension

Development Administration attaches special importance to time. Since socio-economic changes have to be brought about as quickly as possible, the timeliness of all activities assumes considerable significance.

EVALUATION OF BUREAUCRACY

The characteristics of a bureaucratic form of organization can be reiterated as existence of rules, division of work, hierarchical arrangement of offices, selection of technically-trained officials, separation of ownership from management, adherence of rights to offices and not to incumbents and meticulous recording administrative acts in writing.

The bureaucratic from of organization has been quite useful at a certain point of time in history. It could establish standards of integrity and professional competence. It helped weeding out of corruption and nepotism. It provided much desired stability. In a slowly changing pre-industrial society, bureaucracy was therefore, a useful organizational model.

Its capacity for adaptation to change is, however, rather low. In the developing countries where speedy change is needed to bring about socio-economic transformation, bureaucracy is a misfit. As Trist comments, "The nineteenth century cannot be repeated in developing countries in the last third of the twentieth. A fallacy is to suppose—that large-scale organizations in these countries must, initially at least, be regimentally constructed in the bureaucratic mode that is beginning to decline in the advanced countries. Evidence is mounting that the pre-industrial traditions of many developing countries enable transbureaurcratic styles to be learnt more quickly than in some advanced countries where a great deal of unlearning must first take place". Some of the criticisms levelled against bureaucracy point out its weaknesses as an organizational form. Its role in development administration has been questioned in this connection. The Weberian model, according to the critics, is subject to the dysfunctional consequences of failing to take into account the individual or behavioural aspects of the people who work within the organization system. It has been observed that the organizational design at best can function in a stable environmental situation. In an unstable environment, as in the course of management of development, the structure will be unsuitable to meet the demands of the situation.

Some thinkers like Robert K. Merton, Alvin Gouldner, Robert V. Prethus, Warren Bennis have questioned the role of bureaucracy in the developmental administration. Warren Bennis goes to the extent of saying that bureaucracy is likely to go out of use in the wake of new social system. Mohit Bhattacharya states, "The Weberian model, according to the critics, is subject to dysfunctional consequences of failings to take into account the individual or behavioural aspects of the people who work within the organizational system. It has been observed that the organizational design at best can function in a stable environmental situation. In an unstable environment, as in the course of management of development the structure will be unsuitable to meet the demands of the situation."[1]

It may be pointed out that in many developing countries, the economic and political situations are unstable. Joseph La Palombara writes, "The time is evidently past when public officials are expected to sit on the developmental sidelines, limiting their roles to fixing of general rules and to providing certain basic services and incentives for those private entrepreneurs who are the major players in the complicated and exciting game of fashioning profound changes in economic and social system.... The bureaucracies except for minor and other changes, have confined their roles to the fixing up of legal framework. They have remained more or less bound by hierarchy, functioning in accordance with predetermined laws, rules and procedures." Dwivedi and Jain wrote, "Most studies of public administration in developing countries have stressed the viewpoint that the band of officials who have been brought up and trained in the colonial administrative culture, wedded to Weberian characteristics of hierarchy, status and rigidity in the adherence of rules and concerned mainly with the enforcement of law and order and collection of revenues, were quite unfit to perform the duties expected in the changed situation of an administration geared to the task of development."[2]

The conclusions of Burns and Stalker in course of their study of a group of manufacturing concerns in Scotland and England are significant in this context. They identified two distinct systems of management: The Mechanistic and the Organic. The mechanistic system of management closely resembles the Weberian model with its accent on division of tasks, hierarchy, role-specificity and vertical communication. It was considered suitable for stable conditions. By contrast, the organic system of management fits in well with unstable environmental conditions. To quote Burns and Stalker, "Organic systems are adapted to unstable conditions, when problems and requirements for action arise which cannot be broken down and distributed among specialist roles within a clearly defined hierarchy. Individuals have to perform their special tasks in the light of their knowledge of the tasks of the firm as a whole. Jobs lose much of their formal definition in terms of methods, duties, and powers, which have to be redefined continually by interaction with others participating in a task. Interaction runs laterally as much as vertically. Communication between people of different ranks tends to resemble lateral consultation rather than vertical command".

The critics point out that the structure, as envisaged in the Weberian formulation, might suit the routine and repetitive tasks. The organizational design will produce dysfunctional consequences in terms of human behaviour, if jobs are devoid of innovation and creativity.

Robert K. Merton, the eminent social scientist, was the first to point out that although close control by the rule favours reliability and predictability of behaviour, at the same time it accounts for lack of flexibility, reliability and predictability of behaviour, and their tendency to turn means into ends. The instrumental and formalistic aspects of the bureaucratic job become more important than the substantive ones (e.g., good service to the people), and the effectiveness of the whole system suffers accordingly. Excessive formalism will be counter productive specially in rural development where the clients are mostly illiterate and are not conversant with government rules and regulations. Another writer, Selznick, converses the central dilemma in bureaucracy as arising out of the need for delegation of power to organizational sub-systems. The increasing complexity of organizational tasks makes decentralization and delegation of responsibility to the intermediaries inevitable. But such a measure brings forth the organizational paradox of goal displacement, the bifurcation of interest between the central system and its decentralized sub-units.

In his classical study, Alvin Gouldner advances the thesis that bureaucratic techniques produce their own reactions. Gouldner found that the organizational rules tended to define the minimum levels of acceptable behaviour. As managers become aware of their subordinates' behaviour, they respond by issuing additional rules and procedures. This leads to tension between the managers and subordinate and, in the process, displacement of organizational goals.

There have been other writers on bureaucracy (for instance presents), who are of the view that the Weberian model is a product of alien culture not quite suitable for transplantation in the developing societies. Presthus in his study of the Turkish coal mines observed that in some of the traditional societies there are highly bureaucratized government organizations, but their behavioural consequences and manifest goals are mainly a function of the particular social context in which the bureaucratic apparatus exists. A study of the state level administration in India also revealed clear linkage between administrative culture and social environment. The administrators admired inter-personal behaviour, morality and honesty more than qualification, competence or intelligence. Observers of bureaucracy in developing countries have noticed behavioural aberration reflecting societal culture of the countries studied. It has been pointed out that where the need to fulfil development programmes was most urgent, much of the bureaucratic pursuit was directed towards activities other than achievement of goals. Where management of change is the basic purpose, a new-look development bureaucracy has been suggested in replacement of the Weberian model.

At the extreme end are social scientists like Warren Bennis, who predict that bureaucracy is likely to go out of use in the wake of new social systems. According to Bennis, the forecast is based on the evolutionary principle that every age develops an organizational form appropriate to its genius. The vacuum created by the eclipse of bureaucracy, according to him, will be filled up by temporary work-systems which will be more adaptive to rapid social changes.

The concept of bureaucracy of the Weberian variety has been criticized as being the product of a specific historical, social and political milieu. To overcome this limitation, Fred Riggs introduced his ecological model of public administration. Public administration, according to Riggs, is subject to many influences from the social environment. These influences in a traditional society (agrarian) to a modern one (industrial) can be analyzed from various sectors of society, such as social structure, economy, culture and ideology, the communication network and the political system. Riggs formulated his own model of public administration which he termed sala administration embedded in the prismatic society—a society which is neither traditional nor modern. In the sala model, unofficial influences play important role in recruitment, interest articulation and decision-making. There is no agreement about norms and values; what prevails is polynormativity and normlessness. The bureaucratic behaviour is traditional behind the façade of western institutions.

In the Indian context, the role of bureaucracy in development administration has come in for searching inquiry. Very often, the bureaucracy has been equated with law and order and regulatory administration and its suitability for development situation has been questioned. Bureaucracy has been looked at as having the hang-over of the colonial era. It has been generally criticized as authoritarian in outlook and power monopolizer.

Another line of criticism based the arguments on the elite-background of the members of the bureaucracy. Coming from a narrow social base, they are unable to appreciate the problems of development and are tuned to the administrative requirements of rural development.

The bureaucracy has also been criticized for not demonstrating enough commitment to development needs and programmes. Where development calls for full-throated support, bureaucracy has generally taken shelter under conservative neutrality.

At the other end, bureaucracy has been found both efficient and effective in crisis management. In times of drought and flood, the performance of bureaucracy has generally been satisfactory both in terms of results and people-orientation. The politician and the bureaucrat have worked together in crisis situations to provide relief to the people. Hence, any general indictment of bureaucracy as something dysfunctional for development administration will go against available evidence.

A recent study by Pai Panadiker and Kshirsagar brings out some interesting findings about the relationships between bureaucracy and development administration. The study suggests propositions like the following:

(a) Bureaucracies involved in the developmental tasks at the field level, such as in agriculture necessitating mass participation and with more educated personnel, tend to be structurally less rigid and behaviourally more flexible than headquarter bureaucracies (secretariat-based).

(b) Bureaucracies essentially in a regulatory and other non-developmental agencies will tend to be structurally more rigid and behaviourally less flexible.

The importance of the study lies in pointing out that what we need is not only a generalized bureaucratic model but also a range of sub-models in which the various characteristics of bureaucracy play varying roles.

From the point of view of development administration, the study seems to suggest that there is no basic conflict between bureaucratic structure and development scale. But it did find a sharply negative relationship between bureaucratic behaviour and developmental scale. The study concludes in an optimistic note that: "a more carefully and deliberately adapted bureaucracy would possibly be more flexible and capable of being positive towards the developmental requirements".

CHANGING ROLE

Development administration, as pointed out earlier, is essentially change-oriented. It has, therefore, to be flexible and adaptable to meet quickly changing circumstances. In unstructured situations, decision-making has to be much more situational, innovative and creative. Development situations, it has been suggested, require risk taking and achievement orientation. Organizational rules and procedures should not, therefore, be allowed to get precedence over target achievement instead of magnifying the systematic characteristics of bureaucracy, a view point has been advanced that the development job should be looked at more as a function of individual administrative behaviour and style of operation. Status which is at the core of bureaucratic hierarchy needs to be replaced by service-motivation in development administration. The criticisms against bureaucracy, as mentioned before, reveal some of its structural weaknesses as well as the behavioural consequences that flow from the structure. In any large-scale administrative arrangement, bureaucracy cannot be thrown overboard. Its dysfunctional ties need to be identified and corrected. The changing role of bureaucracy in development administration is characterized in such phrases as development bureaucracy, and non-Weberian model of bureaucracy.

Development administration calls for both qualitative and quantitative changes in bureaucratic policies, programmes, procedures and methods of work, organizational structures and staffing patterns, number and quality of development personnel of different types and patterns of relations with clients of administration.

To fit bureaucracy into developmental tasks, changes are needed both on structural and behavioural fronts. Structurally, de-emphasis of hierarchy has been suggested to get rid of the conventional organizational pyramid which leads to centralization and creates tension and interpersonal conflicts.

As a corollary, there is a need to redesign organizations to enable collegiate decision-making and promote collaborative problem-solving.

Most of the development activities take place at the field level away from the capital city or headquarters administration. Decentralization of authority is therefore necessary to enable the field units to take decisions on the spot, as far as possible, without waiting indefinitely for central clearance. Decentralized decision-making is facilitated by creating separate, fairly autonomous units of administration at the field level.

Communication or flow of information is the life blood of an organization. In pushing through measures for socio-economic development, the organization has to have free flow of messages and information unhindered by the status—levels within it. Speedy and effective decision-making needs the support of reliable information through free flow of communication.

If the personnel structure of bureaucracy is essentially status-based, it is likely to be an impediment to development tasks. Structured class distinctions with accompanying disparities in the conditions of service adversely affect the morale and motivation of the personnel. Merit has to be accepted as the basic criterion of work evaluation and accessibility to higher positions in the organization should be on this consideration. A development bureaucracy is not an insular inward-oriented organization that does not take care of the people and the political leadership. Development has to depend a lot on political management, as the impulse for change comes more often from the political leadership. To accept the supremacy of the politician and to work alongside him as a co-partner in development enterprise are the in-built requirements of development administration.

Last but not the least, bureaucracy has to work very closely with the people under a general rubric of service ethic. Popular participation in development has to be looked at as a resource and the bureaucracy has to elicit popular support for the developmental tasks. The traditional concept of people as passive beneficiaries has thus to be replaced by the newer concept of people as active participants.

Corresponding behavioural changes are needed to make the bureaucracy change-oriented, result-oriented and people-oriented. In fact, it is in this context that raining of civil servants has assumed much significance in most developing countries. To the extent, popular participation in administration will become a reality, this is bound to bring in a good deal of pressure on the bureaucracy to change.

EXERCISES

1. Assess the developmental role of bureaucracy.

2. Examine changing role of bureaucracy in administration.

3. Write short notes on the following:
   (a) Bureaucracy and political development
   (b) Bureaucracy and policy making

REFERENCES

[1]   Bhattacharya Mohit, *Bureaucracy and Development Administration,* Uppal Publishing House, New Delhi, 1979, p. 13.

[2]   Dwivedi, O.P. and Jain, R.B., *Indian Administrative State*, Gitanjali Publishing House, New Delhi, 1985, p. 8.

Chapter
11
Educational Administration

Whenever education is considered from the point of view of development, its purpose must be to rationalize or modernize attitudes as well as to impart knowledge and skills. These challenges far greater in the underdeveloped countries where attitudes and institutions that hinder development have become so firmly rooted. Hence, the educational policy in these countries must have the central purpose of directing and apportioning educational efforts so as to give maximum impetus to national development.[1]

Like the enjoyment of health, access to education has acquired recognition as a human right. Article 29 of the Universal Declaration of Human Rights is very explicitly on this score:

"Everyone has right to education, education shall be free, at least in the elementary and fundamental stages". UNESCO's Constitution stresses the need to raise the level of education and strive to achieve the ideal of educational opportunity without regard to race or sex or any distinction, economic or social.[2]

The expenditure on education shows some special characteristics:

(a) Owing to the long gestation period, the benefits from the investment in education do not occur immediately

(b) A decision once implemented in this field cannot be reversed without grave loss

(c) The burden of the education falls more on the recurrent expenditure which constitutes a severe budgetary strain

(d) Unlike the more directly productive fields the objective of educational policy cannot be precisely defined

(e) A wrong investment in material capital can be scrapped when it proves too expensive to salvage, but wrong pieces of human capital cannot be scrapped

They tend to be self-perpetuating and might even disrupt social infrastructure. The growing problem of unemployment of educated persons due to the production of too much of wrong type of human capital is an instance of this danger.[3]

EDUCATION IN INDIA

In India, the high value attached to education through the whole span of life and deep respect for learning were firmly enshrined in her traditional culture. The Brahmanic, Buddhistic, and Islamic systems of education had much in common: learning was based upon religious texts and the authority of tradition was over-ridding. These traditional systems were mainly designed to transmit culture from one generation to another and to preserve the hierarchical character of society. They did however, emphasize the value of education for enrichment of personality and the quality of life, especially for the upper classes, and maintained an established order of institutions and beliefs in the society.

During the British rule, the system of education remained basically as an alien system of imparting literacy to a few and useful knowledge to the elite in a foreign larguage for creating a class of people who could be relied upon to maintain and strengthen the might of the British Raj in India. This system suffered from many defects, which paralyzed the originality of thinking and the urge to creativity among the Indians. It made a sharp break with the past and remained for more than a century a foreign implantation without any relationship with the roots of the Indian Culture and the traditional values of the people. The colonial system was alien in concept, limited in scope and rigid in character.

Though with the passage of time, some concessions were made in favour of the native learning and spread of literacy, the contents proved worse and gave rise to divisions and inequalities in the society. It was the nationalist movement of the late nineteenth century, which generated strong criticism of the colonial system. Both the national leaders and the educationists condemned this system. There emerged several constructive solutions and experiments, which made some original contribution to educational thoughts and practice. However, their influence was limited and the colonial system dominated the scene until the advent of independence.

At the time of independence, there was mass illiteracy in India, mainly in the rural areas. The problem was not only to spread literacy or expand education, but something more, i.e. to improve the socio-economic conditions of the masses and find new skills for higher output, in order to use education as an engine of economic progress.

The Constitution of India contained important provisions concerning education and defined the divisions of responsibility between the union government at the Centre and the states. The Constitution makes education a state subject according to entry 11 to list II of state functions. The jurisdiction of the state for education is limited only by the provisions of entries of 63, 64, 65 and 66 of List I and entry 25 of List III. These entries read as follows:

List I—Union Functions

Entry 63. The institutions known at the commencement of this Constitution as the Banaras Hindu University, the Aligarh Muslim University and the Delhi University and any other institution declared by Parliament to be institutions of national importance.

Entry 64. Institutions for scientific or technical education financed by the Government of India wholly or in part and declared by Parliament to be institutions of national importance.

Entry 65. Union agencies and institutions for

    (a) Professional or vocational or technical training, including the training of police officers; or

    (b) The promotion of special studies or research; or

    (c) Scientific or technical assistance in the investigation or detection of crime.

Entry 66. Co-ordination and determination of standards in institutions for higher education or research and scientific and technical institutions.

List III—Concurrent Functions

Entry 25. Vocational and technical training of labour

Apart from these main provisions of the Constitution defining the direct responsibility of the union government in the field of education there are several provisions bearing on education. Article 45 of the Constitution, which is also a directive principle of State policy, provides that "the State shall endeavour to provide, within a period of ten years from the commencement of the Constitution for free and compulsory education for all children until they complete the age of 14 years." Various provisions for safeguarding the educational and cultural interests of the minorities notably Articles 28, 29, 30, 337, 350 A and 350 B have a bearing on education. The provision of safeguards for the advancements of the weaker sections of the community like the scheduled castes and scheduled tribes is reflected in Articles 15, 17, 29, 46, 338, 339 and 340. Article 46, which is a Directive Principle of State Policy, provides that "the States shall promote with special care the educational and economic interests of the weaker sections of the people and in particular of the Scheduled Castes and the Scheduled Tribes and shall protect them from social injustice and all forms of exploitation". Several other provisions have an indirect bearing on the development of the education, e.g. Articles 14, 15, 16 and 24. Provisions concerning the official language of the Union notably Articles 343 and 351 place additional responsibilities on the union government. Article 351 provides that "it shall be the duty of the union to promote the spread of Hindi language, to develop it so that it may serve as a medium of expression of all the elements of the composite culture of India and to secure its enrichment by assimilating, without interfering with its genius the form, style and expression used in Hindi and other languages of India".

During the post-independence period, both the union government and the state authorities were continuously involved in the search for a modern system of education responding to the needs of the times. The quest was pursued by a process of consensus expressing itself through national commissions conferences, committees councils and all India institutions. Thus was evolved a national pattern of education which surveyed the national scene, examined special problems of national importance and character, formulated measures and recommendations for action and appraised and evaluated progress from time to time. Commencing with the various committees before independence which led to the formulation of a post-war educational development plan embodied in the Sargent Report the different stages of education were reviewed. Notable among these were the University Educational Commission (1948–49) under the chairmanship of Sarvapalli Radha Krishnan the Committee on Elementary Education

(1950–52) the Secondary Education Commission (1952–53) the Rural Higher Education Committee (1954–55) the Committee on three-year Degree Course (1956–58) the Assessment Committee on Basic Education and the National Committee on Women's Education (1958–59). The process of transforming the national system of education (1958–59). The process of transforming the national system of education culminated in the work of the Indian Education Commission, which was appointed in 1964 and reported to the government in 1966. The findings and recommendations of these committees were carefully considered by the union and the state governments and were the subject of thorough discussions by India bodies such as the Central Advisory Board of Education the All India Council of Secondary Education, the All India Council of Elementary Education and the University Grants Commission. The results of these deliberations were reflected in varying measures in all educational developments since independence.

Shortfalls

Making a review of the progress the Sixth Plan stated that despite a network of educational institutions with over 3 million teachers and a high annual budget, it has not been possible so far for the education system to achieve the goal of universal education of all children upto the age of 14 years as enshrined in the Directive Principles of the Constitution. The total enrolment in elementary education has increased. Nevertheless for every three children enrolled in primary and middle schools, one eligible child is left behind. Over 80 per cent of the children not enrolled so far are confined to a dozen States who have not been in a position to allocate the necessary economic resources to achieve the goal of universalization according to the present system of elementary education.

About 38 per cent of the SC children and 56 per cent of the ST children are yet to receive elementary education. As revealed by the fourth educational survey, the non-availability of schools is not a major constraint in this regard, but socio-economic compulsions in families particularly in the rural areas and among the weaker sections not too-relevant nature of curricular programmes and lack of essential facilities in schools seem to be some of the more important factors contributing to the slow progress. Even the existing facilities for elementary education are not optimally utilized. Over aged and under aged children account for around 20 per cent of enrolment. Nearly, 64 per cent of the children who are enrolled in Class I drop out by the time they complete Class V. This represents economic loss in resource utilization educational inefficiency and low productivity not to mention the long-term social loss to the individual child and the family on account of the incomplete development of the farmer's educational career.[4]

(a) Significant improvements have taken place in the enrolment of girls and SCs/STs.

(b) Significant improvements have taken place in the area of higher education.

(c) A number of programmes have been started including steps to check drop outs.

(d) The 83rd Constitutional Amendment Bill has been introduced in the Rajyasabha to make the right to education a Fundamental Right and a fundamental duty.

Table 11.1 Achievement in the Field of Education

Items	1950–51	1996–97
Literacy rate	16.6	56 (Estimated)
Enrolment in Primary Education (6–11 yrs) lakhs	192	1104
Middle Level (11–14 yrs)	31	411
Rural Population Provided with Elementary Edu.	—	94%
Number of Primary Schools (Lakhs)	2.23	7.75
Number of Teachers (Lakhs)	6.24	29.86
Expenditure on Education (Percentage of GDP)	0.7	3.8

(e) The Ninth Plan central outlay for education is ₹ 20,381.64 crore, which is higher than the Eighth Plan outlay of ₹ 7,443 crore by 2–7 times.

In the areas of secondary and higher education facilities have been expanded during the last three decades. Nonetheless the reforms for qualitative improvement and system reorganization as envisaged in the National Policy on Education (1968) are yet to be completed effectively. This is particularly so for the integration of the practical aspect in the educational programmes and for the planned growth of the programmes directed towards gainful employment to be implemented in close cooperation with all the developmental agencies inter-sectional linkages are yet to be brought about and co-ordination established between work places, schools and development activities for fostering appropriate manpower development programmes.[5]

This has resulted, among other things, in an undesirable growth of facilities for general higher education, specially at the undergraduate stage in arts, commerce and humanities and in the consequent increase in the incidence of unemployment among the educated.[6]

The Seventh Five Year Plan

Although the Indian education scene since independence has been characterized by massive quantitative expansion at all levels, but it is still to undertake the kind of transformation envisaged in the national policy (1968). It is faced with a staggering backlog, the level of illiteracy is as high as 63 per cent vocationalization of secondary education has yet to make headway there is very significant pressure on the higher educational system and a decline in the standards of quality. There is an urgent need for a new design for education.[7]

Despite a number of high-sounding reforms and 50 years of planned efforts the bitter reality is not hidden from us. We can't close our eyes and ears to the state of affairs existing in our educational institutions and the day-to-day vehement criticism levelled against our system of education. The educated unemployment in the youth, growing indiscipline among the students, negative attitude among the teachers, indifference among the parents and lack of faith in education among the people in general are some of the problems vexing the heads of the intellectuals in the country. We may talk of our achievements in terms of the expansion of education, but we have missed excellence in it and hence, all this hue and cry, chaos and confusion and ultimately no peace and happiness in life.[8]

NEW EDUCATION POLICY

Because of the increasing problems as discussed above and the failure of the earlier national education policy the government decided in January 1985 to chalk out a new education policy in order to help the country both scientifically and economically to enter the 21st century. Towards this effect a document "Challenge of Education A Policy Perspective" was placed before the Parliament in August 1985 which was to provoke a discussion on certain issues relevant to the formulation of a new education policy. The document has been honest in confessing that the objectives of the 1968 policy have remained unachieved. It has frankly and openly criticized the policies which were followed the decisions which were deliberately avoided. It has also pointed out how the education budget used to be inadequate. It has not hesitated to criticize the miserable condition of elementary education in the country unsatisfactory female education and the 77 per cent school drop outs. The existing system of examination which makes a mockery of examinations has not been spared. That too has been criticized.[9]

A large number of suggestions from organizations and individuals were received in the Ministry in response to be made by the Prime Minister relating to the formulation of a new education policy. In pursuance of the recommendations of the Conference of State. Education Ministers, National Groups of Ministers of Education on:

(a) Manpower projections and vocationalization

(b) Financial resources

(c) Examination reforms were constituted under the Chairmanship of the Union Minister for Human Resource Development to examine in depth the various issues relating to the formulation of the new education policy and evolve strategies for its implementation.[10]

The National Policy of Education (1986) was followed by the Programmer of Action (POA) 1986 and a revised National Policy in 1992 and POA (1992).

The main contents and the thrust of the new education policy have been given below as follows: [11]

"Education has continued to evolve, diversity and extend its reach and coverage since the dawn of human history. Every country develops its system of education to express and promote its unique socio-cultural identity and also to meet the challenges of the times. There are moments in history when a new direction has to be given to an age-old process. That moment is today".

"The country has reached a stage in its economic and technical development when a major effort must be made to derive maximum benefit from the assets already created and to ensure that fruits of change reach all sections. Education is the highway to that goal."

"India's social and political life is passing through a phase which poses the danger of erosion to long accepted values. The goals of secularism socialism and democracy and professional ethics are coming under increasing strain."

"Life in the coming decades is likely to bring new tensions together with unprecedented opportunities. To enable the people to benefit in the new environment will require new designs of human resource development. The coming generations should have the ability to internalize new ideas constantly and creatively. They have to be imbued with a strong commitment to human values and to social justice. All this implies better education. Besides, a variety of new challenges and social needs make it imperative for the Government to formulate and implement a new education policy for the country. Nothing short of this will meet the situation".

NATIONAL SYSTEM OF EDUCATION

It implies that upto the given level all students irrespective of caste, creed, location or sex, have access to education of a comparable quality. To achieve this, the Government will initiate appropriately founded programmes. Effective measures will be taken in the direction of the common school system recommended in the 1968 policy. Minimum levels of learning will be laid down for each stage of education. Steps will also be taken to foster among students an understanding of the diverse cultural and social systems of people living in different parts of the country.

Education for Equality

The new policy will lay special emphasis on the removal of disparities and to equalize educational opportunities by attending to the specific needs of those who have been denied equality so far. Special provisions have been made for the education of the SCs/STs the handicapped, the minorities, etc.

Adult education

A vast programme of adult and continuing education will be implemented through various ways and channels including the following.

    (a) Establishment of centres in the rural areas for continuing education.

    (b) Worker's education through the employers trade unions and concerned agencies of the government

    (c) Post-secondary education institutions

    (d) Use of radio, TV and Films

    (e) Creation of learner's groups and organizations

    (f) Programmes of distance learning

(g) Organizing assistance in self-learning

(h) Organizing need and interest based vocational training programmes.

The National Policy on Children specially emphasizes investment in the development of the young children, particularly children from the sections of the population in which the first generation learners predominate.

Non-formal Education

A large and systematic programme of non-formal education will be launched for school drop outs for children from habitations without schools, and for working children and girls who cannot attend schools the whole day.

Elementary, secondary and higher education and vocationalization

All these areas are to be revitalized and implemented properly. Higher education provides people with an opportunity to reflect on the critical social, economic, cultural, moral and spiritual issues facing humanity. It contributes to national development through the dissemination of specialized knowledge and skills. It is therefore, a crucial factor for survival. Being at the apex of educational pyramid it has also a key role in producing teachers for this educational system.

Delinking Degress from Jobs

A beginning will be made by delinking degrees from jobs in selected areas. The proposal cannot be applied to occupation specific courses like engineering, medicine, law, teaching, etc.

Technical and Management Education

Although the two streams of technical and management education are functioning separately, it is essential to look at them together, in view of their close relationship and complementary concerns. The reorganization of technical and management education should take into account the anticipated scenario by the turn of the century, with specific reference to the likely changes in the economy, social environment production and management processes the rapid expansion of knowledge and the great advances in science and technology.

Reorienting the Concept and Process of Education

This includes stress on the maintenance of culture and art, value education, development of languages, availability of low-priced quality books, use of media and educational technology, mathematics teaching, science education, sports and physical education better role of youth improved examination system, etc.

The Teacher

The status of the teacher reflects the socio-cultural ethos of a society. It is said that no people can rise above the level of its teachers. Teachers should have the freedom to innovate, to devise appropriate methods of communication with activities relevant to the needs and capabilities of and the concerns of the community. The methods of recruiting teachers will be reorganized to ensure merit objectively and conformity with spatial and functional requirements. The pay and service conditions of the teachers have to be commensurate with their social and professional responsibilities and with the need to attract talent to the profession.

Apart from that the policy includes provisions for the reorientation of the existing administration at all the levels, better resources for education and review of the implementation of the policy after every five years.

The new policy was much needed. But it seems that it is neither very much different nor a new document, there is a need for certain basic changes and minor changes here and there will not do. However, it can achieve a lot if it is implemented in true spirit. Only time will answer the following questions:

   (a) Whether the heavy budget needs would be met?

   (b) Whether it would improve the quality of education without which the task of national reconstruction can never be completed?

   (c) Whether it would develop employment oriented vocational skills without the needed resources?

   (d) Will it be able to reform the examination system thoroughly?

   (e) Will it develop among the people such habits, attitudes and qualities of character as will enable them to bear worthily the responsibilities of democratic citizenship?

Administration of Education

The union and state governments are responsible for all matters relating to education, except medical, agricultural and legal education. Before 1976 education was exclusively a state subject the Central Government being concerned directly with certain areas like co-ordination and determination of the standards in technical and higher education, etc. In 1976 by a constitutional amendment, education was made the joint responsibility of the Central and State Governments. However, the primary responsibility continues to be that of the states. Apart from this the union government continues to administer the central universities institutions of national importance and other scientific and technical institutions. It has also the responsibility for the promotion of the education of the weaker sections, particularly the scheduled castes and the scheduled tribes.

At the Union level, the responsibility of administration of education lies with the Department of Education which functions with the help of numerous bodies including the UGC and the NCERT.

Origin[12]

For the first time, an Education Branch was created in the Home Department in 1857 while the Department of Public Instruction was created in the provinces in 1854. In 1882, a Commission was appointed and in 1901, a conference was convened to discuss all matters pertaining to education. To strengthen the machinery at the Centre, a Director-General of Education was appointed in 1901 who was primarily responsible for advising the Government of India on subjects pertaining to education. In 1910 a separate department of education was created. The shape and size of the department went on changing from time to time. After 1947, Scientific research received due recognition and the subject was declared as a portfolio directly under the Prime Minister. Later the Department of Scientific Research was created in 1948, and in 1957 the two subjects Education and Scientific Research came under one ministry. In 1958, these two subjects were bifurcated but again combined into one Ministry in 1963. In June, 1964 the social security subjects were transferred from the Ministry of Education to the newly created department of social security. In February 1969, the Ministry was renamed as the Ministry of Education and Youth Services. In May 1971, the subjects relating to culture science and Technology were transferred to the newly created departments and the Ministry was redesignated as the Ministry of Education and Social Welfare having two departments, viz. department of education and department of social welfare. After a few year the ministry was renamed as the Ministry of Education and Culture. In the year 1985, the department of education was made a part of the newly constituted Ministry of Human Resource Development.

Ministry of Human Resource Development

This ministry was created on 26 September 1985, and was constituted by five departments namely, department of education, department of culture, department of arts, department of youth affairs and sports and department of women's welfare. The conceptual framework of this ministry consists in building up the all-round personality of human beings, and to this end integrating under one umbrella as many relevant activities as possible with a view to evolve a package of inputs. The process is not merely one of coordination, but real integration so that all the components are woven into a single continuous harmonious programme.[13] The Ministry of Human Resource Development is constituted by the following four departments (as on 1 January 2000):

(a) Department of Education

(b) Department of Youth Affairs and Sports

(c) Department of Culture

(d) Department of Women and Child Development

Department of Education

Organizational set-up.[14]

The department of education one of the constituent parts of the Ministry of Human Resources Development is under the charge of a Ministry of State under the overall charge of the Ministry for Human Resource development. The secretarial of the department is headed by the secretary who is assisted by one special secretary (higher education), Additional Secretary and Educational Adviser (Technical). The department is organized into bureaux, divisions desks, sections and units. Each bureau is under the charge of a Joint Secretary/Joint Educational Adviser assisted by divisional heads.

The work of the department is carried out through the following Divisions/Units:

1. Book promotion division and copyright
2. National scholarship division
3. Hindi translation unit and Hindi publication unit
4. Sanskrit
5. Languages
6. University and higher education unit
7. Parliament unit
8. UNESCO
9. Publication unit
10. Adult education
11. Planning monitoring division and statistics division
12. Pay and accounts office
13. Finance
14. Administrative
15. Physical education division
16. Union territories and school education
17. Technical education bureau
18. School division
19. National commission on teachers
20. External scholarship division

Over the years a number of subordinate offices and organizations have come up under the department. For the co-ordination and determination of standards in higher education, the University Grants Commission was set up in 1956 by an Act of the Parliament. Besides, a number of organizations have been set up to discharge specific responsibilities. Among them is the National Council of Education Research and Training which strives to promote the qualitative aspects of school education throughout the country. The other important organizations are:

(a) National Institute of Educational Planning and Administration, New Delhi

(b) Indian Institute of Advanced Studies, Shimla

(c) Indian Council of Social Science Research, New Delhi

(d) Indian Council of Historical Research, New Delhi

(e) Indian Council of Philosophical Research, New Delhi

(f) Kendriya Vidyalaya Sangathan, New Delhi

(g) Central Board of Secondary Education, New Delhi

(h) Kendriya Hindi Sansthan, Agra

(i) Central Institute of Indian Languages, Mysore

(j) Central Institute of English and Foreign Languages, Hyderabad

(k) Central Hindi Directorate, New Delhi

(l) Commission for Scientific and Technical Terminology, New Delhi

(m) Rashtriya Sanskrit Sansthan, New Delhi

(n) National Book Trust, New Delhi

(o) Navodaya Vidyalaya Samiti, New Delhi

(p) Indira Gandhi National Open University, New Delhi

In the field of technical education there are the Indian Institute of Science, Bangalore; Indian School of Mines. Dhanbad; National Institute of Training in Industrial Engineering, Bombay; National Institute of Foundry and Forge Technology, Ranchi; School of Planning and Architecture, New Delhi; Administrative Staff College of India, Hyderabad; Indian Institutes of Management at Ahmedabad (IIM's), Bangalore, Calcutta and Lucknow; Technical Teachers Training Institutes at Bhopal, Kolkata, Chandigarh and Madras; Indian Institutes of Technology (IIT) Bombay, Delhi, Kanpur, Kharagpur and Madras and arround is Regional Engineering Colleges spread all over the country. Approval had been accorded for setting up two more Regional Engineering Colleges at Hamirpur (HP) and Jalandhar (Punjab).[15]

The other technical Institutes are as follows:

(a) National Council for Women Education

(b) Central Advisory Board of Education

(c) National Council for Rural Higher Education

(d) Central Advisory Board of Museums

(e) Art Purchase Committee

(f) Central Advisory Board of Archaeology

(g) All-India Council of Sports

(h) All-India Council for Technical Education

(i) National Book Development Board

(j) Central Sanskrit Board

(k) Hindi Siksha Samiti, etc.

Functions[16]

Important functions of the department of education are to evolve educational policy in all aspects and to co-ordinate and determine the standards of higher education and technical education and to administer various Acts plans and programmes for the promotion of education in the country. Its major functions are as follows:

Formulation of educational policies and plans

The department of education plays a vital role in the formulation of educational policies and plans. As stated earlier, the department has played a dominant role in evolving the new education policy (1986). In fact, the role of the Central Government has become more important after the transfer of education from the State list to the concurrent list. Similarly, it plays a key role in the formulation of Five Year Plans.

Elementary education

Under the constitutional provision regarding free and compulsory education for children upto the age of 14 years, elementary education has become a regular part of the programmes of the department. The programme of universalization of education is being pursued by the department. Some of the important steps taken in this regard are listed as follows:

(a) Meeting of the National Committee on point 16 of the 20-point programme as a part of the conference of education secretaries to review the progress of universalization in the nine educationally backward States in particular.

(b) Meetings of the State task force on elementary education in the 9 educationally backward states were held to review the progress of efforts made by the State governments for the implementation of UEE and NFE programmes.

(c) Mounting of a national campaign on the universalization of elementary education for intensifying efforts to increase enrolment and retention at the elementary stage.

Non-formal education

Special emphasis is also being laid on reducing the rate of drop-outs. The non-formal education programme forms the second major component of the strategy employed to achieve universalization of education since a large number of children are either not able or unwilling to attend school. The number of children to be covered by the NFE programme during the Seventh Plan is estimated at 2.5 crore. The programme has acquired good momentum in 9 educationally backward States and by the end of 1985–86, the coverage of the programme would be of the order of 41.41 lakhs in about 1.65 lakh centres.

Higher education

The department of education through the UGC, pursues the policy of the improvement of standards and quality of education and removal of disparities and regional imbalances in higher education. Science education and promotion of Gandhian and Nehru studies received special attention under UGC programme of quality improvement. The UGC has taken steps to develop facilities at the national level for the use of university scientists in the field of Nuclear Science, Materials-Research, Laser and Fibre Optics. Astro-physics, Astronomy, Biotechnology, Mass Communication, Educational Technology, and Higher Education among the Scheduled Castes/ Scheduled Tribes has continued to receive emphasis with the financial assistance provided by the UGC for special programmes for these groups. The Indira Gandhi National Open University (IGNOU) was established in Delhi in September 1985, to disseminate and advance knowledge by providing instructional and research facilities. It will lay stress on continuing vocational education with a view to improve knowledge and skills and to promote educational opportunities for the community in general and the disadvantaged groups in particular. Another Central University, namely Pondicherry University has been established at Pondicherry on 16 October 1985 to serve the needs of the Union Territory of Pondcherry.

Physical education and sports

Physical education and sports are today accepted as an integral part of education and sports new National Sports Policy, covering inter-alia physical education and yoga has since been placed before the Parliament as a government resolution which makes it the duty of the Central and State Governments to accord a very high priority to the promotion of sports and physical education in the process of all round development. The policy also recognizes the need of every citizen irrespective of age and sex to participate and enjoy sports and recreational activities.

Technical education

The socio-economic progress of a country is intimately connected with the availability of properly trained technical manpower. Our country, therefore, accorded top priority to developing extensive facilities for technical education in the country since the attainment of her independence. A number of steps taken in this regard include amongst others modernization and removal of obsolescence in the engineering colleges and polytechnics, application of science and technology for rural development, establishment of linkages between the technical education system and the development sectors and providing computing facilities in technical institutions.

Adult education

Considering that adult education is an important component of the socio-economic development and also a crucial element in the family welfare programme, the Government has accorded high priority to the adult education programme by including it in the Minimum Needs Programme and the 20-point programme. A look at the major thrust areas like the development of a programme of continuing education motivation, launching of mass programmes, effective linkages with various developmental programmes of rural development and family welfare, larger involvement of voluntary agencies. NYKs NSS shows that the government was keen to cover all illiterate adults in the shortest possible time.

Administration of scholarships

The Government of India has been offering a large number of scholarships for enabling students to prosecute further studies both in India and abroad. Scholarships are generally awarded to meritorious students without adequate means. These include National Merit Scholarships given to children belonging to the rural areas. SCs/STs and poor families. The Ministry has also been providing scholarships to Indian students for study abroad so that they may be able to undertake research in newly emerging specializations.

Book promotion and copyright

The programmes of this Ministry in the field of book promotion are aimed at facilitating the production of good literature at moderate prices, encouraging Indian authorship and publishing industry formulating a book import policy, promoting the export of Indian books and fostering reading habits among the people. The National Book Trust organizes and participates in Book Fairs/Exhibitions at the international, national and regional levels. The government also administers the Copyright Act and protects the interests of the authors and composers.

Cooperation with UNESCO

India plays a leading role in matters relating to the UNESCO (United Nations Educational Scientific and Cultural Organization) and participates in many important international conferences/meetings organized under the auspices of the UNESCO. In this regard, there is a special UNESCO Division in the department of education.

Propagation and development of languages

The policy of the government is to encourage the development of all Indian languages including classical modern and tribal languages. In this regard, the department of education deals with the training of teachers for facilitation the implementation of the three languages formula and the production of University level textbooks with a view to facilitate the switch over from English to regional languages as the media of instruction.

Administration of certain institutions

The department of education looks after the administration of some educational institutions of national importance. These are financed by the Union government wholly or partially and declared by the Parliament by law to be institutions of national importance. Besides, it finances and administers the Central Universities.

Some other functions of the department of education include administration direction and control of education in the UTs: publications information and statistics relating to educations recruitment of teachers for foreign countries admission of foreign students in Indian Universities, grants-in-aid to state government institutions non-government institutions professional bodies and technical institutions of UTs for technical education.

Criticism

Despite a big machinery with a long list of activities and the aid of innumerous other agencies and institutions throughout the country, the department of education has failed on a number of fronts. A list of the shortcomings has already been given. Some broad failures are:

(a) Failure to implement the education policies in their true spirit

(b) Poor implementation of Five Year Plans

(c) Mushroom growth of institutions

(d) Poor evaluation of the activities

(e) Too much bureaucratization

(f) No guarantee of objectives dealing with persons of merit

(g) Lack of effective co-ordination between different agencies/levels of administration

(h) Regional imbalances in educational development.

It is therefore emphasized that a good administrative machinery is required in order to implement the new educational policy which otherwise is of no use.

The new educational policy document suggested the following additional is of no use.

The Central Advisory Board of Education will play a pivotal role in reviewing educational development determining the changes required to improve the system and monitoring implementation. It will function through appropriate committees and other mechanisms created to ensure contact with and co-ordination among the various areas of Human Resource Department. The departments of education at the Center and in the states will be strengthened through the involvement of professionals.

Non-government and voluntary efforts including social activist groups will be encouraged subject to the provision of proper management and financial assistance. At the same time steps will be taken to prevent the establishment of institution set up to commercialize education.

University Grants Commission (UGC)

The UGC was set up initially as an advisory committee in 1945. At that time no funds were placed at its disposal. Its function was merely to make recommendations to the Ministry of Education for grants to the Central Universities. The full commission was set up in 1953, and it became a statutory body under the University Grants Commission Act, 1956 of the Parliament.[18] It comprises one Chairman one Deputy Chairman and ten other members. It has a large organization headed by a Secretary.

Functions

(a) To act as an expert body to advise the Central Government on problems connected with the co-ordination of facilities and the maintenance of standards in the Universities and to take such executive actions as may be necessary on their behalf.

(b) To enquire into the functional needs of universities and to advise the Central Government on the allocation of funds for grants-in-aid to them.

(c) To take all necessary executive actions in the matter of deciding on the grants to be made to the universities and in disbursing them out of the funds placed at the disposal of the commission.

(d) To advise any authority if such advice is asked for on the establishment of a new university or on the proposals connected with the expansion of the activities of any university.

(e) To advise the Central Government or any university on any question which may be referred to the commission by the Central Government or the university, as the case may be.

(f) To advise the Central Government or a State government in regard to the recognition of any degree conferred or granted by a university for the purpose of employment under the Central Government or a State Government or for any other purpose.

(g) To advise the universities on measures necessary for the reform and improvement of university education.

(h) To undertake such other duties and functions as may be prescribed or deemed necessary by the Government of India for advancing the cause of education in India or as may be incidental or/and conducive to the attainment of the above functions.

(i) To present a report to the Government of India on the working of the commission during the financial year.

The UGC tries to promote and co-ordinate university education and determines and maintains standards of teaching examination and research in the universities. It has the authority to enquire into the financial universities. As on 1 January 1982, higher education was imparted through 116 universities and a number of arts, science, commerce and professional colleges affiliated to them. Besides, there were 13 research institutions which were deemed to be universities under the University Grants Commission Act.[19]

With the passage of time, it has been seen that the Commission has not been successful in achieving its objectives. It is not covering up all the fields of education and has neglected the teacher's training.

The Estimates Committee (1965–66) of the Third Lok Sabha reviewed in its report of 306 pages practically all the aspects of the working of the University Grants Commission. It must be recorded at the outset that the committee formed a favourable impression of the commission for it concluded its report by recording appreciation of the fact that the University Grants Commission. Within its limited resources and limited authority had been trying to perform a very difficult task", that "it has been able to a certain extent, to co-ordinate the efforts of different States and universities and also to maintain some standard of education.

The committee urged the commission to exercise its legitimate powers effectively improve its methods of determination and co-ordination of standards, quicken the pace of development in the universities and prevent discontinuation of by the universities after the assistance is withdrawn in accordance with agreed conditions take follow-up action on the recommendations of its own committees, take effective action against wastage and stagnation and unequal standard in the universities and particularly in the colleges and to prevent institutions of higher education from directly and indirectly encouraging social and class disparities in the academic life of the country.[20]

National Council of Educational Research and Training (NCERT)

Set up as an autonomous organization, the NCERT acts as the principal agency of academic advice to the Union Ministry of Education on matters pertaining to qualitative improvement of social education. The Council works in cooperation with the state education departments and universities and other institutions for promoting school education. It also maintains close collaboration with international organizations.

It has a general body which is the policy-making body of the council. The Union Education Minister is its President and Education Ministers of all the States and UTs are among its members. In addition, the Chairman UGC Secretary (education), four VCs of universities (one from each region), all members of the Executive Committee and 12 other members are its members.

The Council conducts and sponsors research, undertakes teachers training programmes at the national and international levels, develops instructional material and offers consultative services on various facets of school education. The functions of the NCERT may be summarized under the following headings:[21]

(a) To promote aid and co-ordinate educational research

(b) To provide extension service

(c) To organize pre-service and in-service training

(d) To disseminate information on the latest educational techniques and practices

(e) To sponsor or organize surveys of national importance

(f) To emphasize the investigation of immediate problems in Indian Education

Among its major programmes is included the implementation of the 10 + 2 + 3 pattern of education in the states. Besides the formation of a new curricular framework, the Council has been producing model textbooks in all the subjects for the entire school stage. These books are adopted by the states for use in their schools.

The NCERT is also engaged in the implementation of the five UNICEF assisted projects related to elementary education, community education and nutrition education.[22]

The Council has a centre for education technology which is engaged in undertaking research and development in the effective utilization of media in education and for the development of appropriate technology and delivery system.[23]

The education commission pin-pointed that the principal function of the NCERT is extension work with the State Education Departments centering around the improvement of school education. It is uniquely suited for this purpose because the Union Education Minister is its President and all the State Education Ministers are its members. The objective of the policy should be to develop the NCERT as the principal technical agency functioning at the national level for the improvement of school education.

The Council has the Union Education Minister as its President and the State Education Ministers as its members. It has a governing body which has an All India character. The Kothari Commission has recommended that the governing body should have a majority of non-officials. It is considered desirable to have at least one outstanding teacher from the secondary schools and a person specializing in primary education preferably a primary teacher, among its members. Then, the NCERT has the Secretary to the Ministry of Education as the Joint Director. The Kothari Commission found fault within this system and made a suggestion that the Council should have a whole-time Director of its own who should be an eminent educationist in the field. The status of the Director should be that of a Vice-Chancellor of a University and his term of office should be five years only, which should be renewable for not more than one term. The Joint Director may be an officer lent by the Ministry and his functions should be mainly to assist the Director and to relieve him of routine administrative matters.

ADMINISTRATION OF EDUCATION AT THE STATE LEVEL

As regards the constitutional provisions, the administration of education is primarily a state responsibility. Its development however, is a concurrent responsibility.

In most of the states the pattern of administration is similar. There is generally a separate Ministry of Education under the charge of a Minister of cabinet rank. The Minister is aided by a Secretary who is assisted by one or more Directors of Public Instruction (DPIs). All the decisions of Directorate level are taken by the Director.

The Education Minister is the overall incharge of the education department who lays down the policies and controls of the entire administration through the Financial Commissioner and the Secretary to the government. Punjab Education Department who is assisted by a team of senior officers of, viz. 2-Joint Secretaries, 1-Deputy Secretary and 1-Under Secretary. The Education Secretary carries out the work of the Department in collaboration with the following Directorates:

1. Primary
2. School
3. College and
4. State Council of Educational Research and Ttraining

Primary Directorate

The Primary Directorate was set up in February 1978 to ensure top priority to the primary education which is the basis of overall education and also to meet the long-standing demand of the primary school teachers. Earlier it was a part of the School Directorate. The task before the Directorate is to strengthen the machinery from the supervision and inspection of Primary Schools.

The Primary Directorate is headed by a Director of public instruction (primary), who is assisted by a Deputy Director (Examinations) an Administrative Officer three Assistant Directors (Primary Education—I, II and III) an Accounts Officer, an Evaluation Officer, an Assistant Registrar. The Directorate has the following branches:

(a) Services

(b) Examinations

(c) Establishment–I and Planning.

(d) Establishment–II and Care

(e) Budget and Primary School Education

(f) Teacher's training

School Directorate

The Directorate is headed by the Director of Public Instruction (schools), who is assisted by the four Deputy Directors, viz. Deputy Director (school administration). Deputy Director (secondary education), Deputy Director (vocationalization) and Deputy Director (books). The Deputy Directors are further assisted by three Assistant Directors and two officers on special duty, one Assistant Accounts Officer and some subject specialists.

In regard to the youth welfare functions, the DPIs are assisted by an Additional Director (Youth Programmes), a Youth Welfare Officer, a Sports Organizer and a Statistical Officer.

In regard to the general administration of the Directorate the DPI is assisted by an Administrative Officer, who looks after the general administration at the Directorate and filed levels and all matters relating to the Punjab Education Service class I and II (schools and inspection) cadre officers and also advises the DPI on financial matters. He is assisted by a Registrar and an Assistant Director (Secondary Education).

The Directorate looks after the administrative control of schools, academic matters, implementation of various schemes of expansion of education in all spheres of secondary education, vocationalization sanctioning of grants-in-aid to denominational institutions. The functions of the Directoraterate relate to the following items:

(a) School education

(b) Social (adult) education

(c) Women's education

(d) Vocational education

(e) Practical arts education

(f) School administration

(g) Educational planning

(h) Educational reforms

(i) Miscellaneous.

Agricultural education, scholarships, school buildings, grants-in-aid, purchase of books, school sports, national fitness corps scheme.

College Directorate

The Directorate of Public Instruction (Colleges) is headed by a Director who is assisted by a Joint Director (Administration), a Deputy Director (Colleges and Planning), an Advisor Reforms Committee, Five Assistant Directors and one Accounts Officers. The Joint Director (Administration) deals with the establishment matters of the headquarters and the principles/lecturers in the government colleges and the record section.

The Deputy Director (colleges and planning) deals with educational and university matters and planning works, establishment of ministerial/miscellaneous staff in the government colleges and libraries. The five Assistant Directors deal with all matters relating to private colleges, grants including UGC grants all types of scholarships, cultural activities, youth programmes in colleges, etc.

State Council of Educational Research and Training (SCERT)

The SCERT was established in July 1981 in order to achieve the following objectives:

    (a) To bring about qualitative improvement in the existing educational system of the state

    (b) To develop the syllable and curriculum of various school subjects

    (c) To undertake and promote investigations, surveys, studies and researches in various fields or sectors of education

    (d) To provide pre- and in-service education for teachers and educational supervisors

    (e) To formulate and implement pilot projects for bringing about qualitative improvement in different fields of school education

    (f) To develop new techniques and methodologies in the field of school education

    (g) To evaluate, monitor and develop educational programmes

The Council is headed by a Director, who is assisted by about six Deputy Directors, a Survey Officer, a librarian (film library) and a team of administrative and technical staff. The Council comprises the following units:

    (a) State Institute of Science Education

    (b) Evaluation

    (c) Survey (10 + 2)

    (d) Vocational guidance

    (e) Technology Cell including the Film Library

    (f) In-service training institutes (three)

Some major activities of the SCERT include the following:

Science fairs/exhibitions, in-service teachers training, science demonstration kits and apparatus, periodic inspections, national talent search examination, evaluation of on going schemes or programmes, loading of Audio Visual Education Films to various educational institutions, evolving new techniques of sample surveys, etc.

The new educational policy has recommended the following additional machinery at the State and local levels.[25]

The state governments may establish State Advisory Boards of Education on the lines of CABE. Effective measures should be taken to integrate mechanisms in various state departments concerned with Human Resource Department.

Special attention will be paid to the training of educational planners, administrators and heads of institutions, institutional arrangements for this purpose should be set up in stages.

District boards of education will be created to manage education upto the higher secondary level, State governments will prepare a framework of Educational Development, Central State District and local level agencies will participate in planning co-ordination monitoring and evaluation.

A very important role must be assigned to the head of an educational institution. The heads will be specially selected and trained. School complexes will be promoted on a flexible pattern so as to serve as networks of institutions and synergic alliances to encourage professionalism among teachers, to ensure observance of norms of conduct and to enable the sharing of experiences of facilities. It is expected that a developed system of school complexes will take over much of the inspection functions in due course. Local communities, through appropriate bodies will be assigned a major role in the programmes of school improvement.

The constitution admits that all minorities, whether based on religion or language, shall have the right to establish and administer educational institutions of their choice. They have the right to admit student to their institutions, to have their own governing bodies and to adopt their respective systems of instructions. The State universities cannot impose a particular medium of instructions on the minority institutions. Further, the State while providing grants-in-aid to educational institutions cannot discriminate against such minority institutions. The minority character of such institutions cannot be destroyed by the state and Right to Education has also been made as a fundamental right.

EXERCISES

1. Discuss educational administration in India.
2. Critically examine new education policy.
3. Examine administration of education at the state level.
4. Write short notes on the following:
   (a) University Grants Commission (UGC).
   (b) NCERT

REFERENCES

[1] Myrdal, Gunnar, _Asian Drama_, Penguin Books, London, 1972, pp. 313–314.

[2] Ali, Mansoor, _Missing Links in Indian Planning_, Life and Light Publishers, 1978, New Delhi, p. 157.

[3] Myint, H., "The Universities of South East Asia and Economic Development," _Pacific Affairs_, Summer 1962 in Ali, Mansoor, pp. 157–158.

[4] The Sixth Five Year Plan, _op. cit.,_ pp. 252–253.

[5] _Ibid.,_ pp. 121–122.

[6] _Ibid.,_ p. 166.

[7] The Seventh Five Year Plan, _op. cit.,_ The Eight Five Year Plan, 1992–97, p. 252.

[8] Shamsuddin, "New Education Policy—A View Point", _Yojana_, Vol. 29, No. 20, November 1–15, 1985, p. 9.

[9] _Ibid.,_ p. 178.

[10] Annual Report, Ministry of Human Resource Development, Department of Education, Government of India, 1986, p. iii.

[11] National Policy on Education, Government of India, New Delhi, May 1986, Revised in 1992.

[12] Indian Institute of Public Administration, Organization, Government of India, Somaiya Publications, New Delhi, 1971, pp. 930–933.

[13] Annual Report, _op. cit.,_ p. 1.

[14] _Ibid.,_ p. 183.

[15] _Ibid.,_ pp. 187–188.

[16] _India 1997 and 2000_, Publication Division GOI, New Delhi and Annual Report, _op. cit,_ pp. i–v.

[17] National Policy on Education 1986, pp. 25–26.

[18] Mathur, S.S., _Educational Administration Principles and Practices,_ Krishna Brothers, 1975, pp. 138–139.

[19] India–1999, 2000.

[20] Estimates Committee (1965–66), 102nd Report, Lok Sabha Secretariat, New Delhi, p. 305.

[21] Annual Report–1984, 95, NCERT, New Delhi, 1985, p. 5.

[22] India–2000, _op. cit._

[23] _Ibid.,_ p. 192.

[24] Based on the reports released by education department (Punjab) including Annual Progress Reports.

[25] National Policy on Education–1986, _op. cit.,_ pp. 26–27.

Chapter

12

Role of Voluntary Agencies in Social Welfare

Most of the developing countries engaged in large-scale socio-economic reconstruction are faced with the choice of instrumentalities for organization and action. One important strand in development administration has been to move away from bureaucratic organization and search for decentralized and debureaucratized social efforts. One such instrument may be the voluntary agencies. Milton Esman attaches special importance to the role of voluntary agencies in development, as he observes : "…..deliberate social change may be greatly facilitated by community organization. In the performance of many service and control functions, governments cannot deal effectively with unorganized individuals. It is thus important that the community be organized in order to relate it effectively to the administrative institutions performing services associated with nation-building and development programmes".[1]

One of the core areas of voluntary action has been social welfare. The role and realities of voluntary action in social welfare however, differ from generation to generation and place to place. In India, traditionally, the major areas of needs in the field of social welfare were covered by voluntary welfare agencies, who with their long history have been playing an important role in providing services for the under privileged while the governments devoted only a minimal fraction of their resources to social welfare programmes.

It would be appropriate here to understand the meaning of a few terms. The term voluntarism is derived from the Latin word voluntas which means will. The assumes various forms like impulses passions appetites or desires. It is prior to or superior to the intellect or reason. It is the will that may produce miracles, and thereby, some of the social evils of which the unfortunate sections of the society are the victims, can be eradicated.

Voluntary efforts refer to those acts of individuals groups which though motivated by different considerations are spontaneous and aim at providing services to the needy the destitute and the handicapped. The nature of voluntary efforts has been undergoing changes from time to time. In the olden days, social service was rendered generally on individual basis by wealthy or philanthropic persons by giving their time and money for serving the needy. Even today, there is a certain amount of individual efforts put in volunteers working with the welfare organizations for specific jobs assigned to them by these agencies. These persons are neither on the Board, nor on the committees of the voluntary agencies nor their employees but they utilize their leisure in assisting the voluntary agencies in their day-to-day work.[2]

A *voluntary organization* on the other hand, is an organization which whether its workers are paid or unpaid is initiated and governed by its own members without any external control; voluntary action is by its very nature local. In many cases, the source of voluntary efforts is one individual, but in this age of democracy, this effort is being channelized through agencies and institutions. Apart from the benefit of group thinking, an agency system helps in pooling the resources and efforts of many individuals for the utilization of the community's resources on democratic basis. Voluntary organizations as have been mentioned earlier, have always played a very important role in the development of social welfare services. Apart from providing relief at the time of emergency—fire, floods, famine, etc. they have always played a pioneering role in helping the needy, the destitute and the handicapped sections of the society. They did not wait for the government to undertake work, but on their own initiative and with their own resources and community's participation, they organized the needed services. Voluntary agencies provide human touch and flexibility of approach, which though essential in the field of social welfare, is missing in government institutions.[3]

Apart from voluntary agencies, there are some other organizations which may be termed non-official *agencies*. Whereas, voluntary agencies are spontaneous in their origin, non-official agencies may be sponsored by the government. Such agencies have been setup to organize welfare services in areas where these do not exist. The examples of such agencies are—All India Women's Conference, Indian Red Cross Society, etc. Project Implementation Committees appointed by the Central Social Welfare Board to run Welfare Extension Projects. Committees for running after-care homes appointed by the State governments. Though constituted primarily of voluntary workers, they are not voluntary agencies, but are known as non-official agencies, since they do not come into existence voluntarily but are sponsored by the government.[4]

Characteristics of a Voluntary Agency

The following are the characteristics of a voluntary agency for social welfare:[5]

(a) It is the results of voluntary effort, which though motivated by different factors, is spontaneous in nature.

(b) It is an organization initiated and governed by its own members on democratic principles without external control.

(c) It is registered under an appropriated Act to give a corporate status to a group of individuals, so that it may get a legal personality and individual liability may give place to group liability.

(d) It has a general body and a regularly constituted Managing Committee, representing all interests—men, women, professionals, policemen, etc.

(e) It has definite aims and objects and a programme for the fulfillment of these objectives.

(f) It is known and accepted by the community in which it is formed.

The Essential Requirements

A voluntary organization must have the following:[6]

(a) An ideal/ideology/inspiration

(b) A written constitution corporate and organizational structure and legal status

(c) Autonomy in functioning within constitutional limits

(d) Flexibility in approach within the limits of announced objectives

(e) Freedom of action in the best interest of the people served

(f) A clearly defined programme of action adjusted to local needs and available resources

(g) A dedicated and committed band of workers

(h) Ability to mobilize resources locally or from outside

(i) A well-organized accounting system duly audited by a firm of Chartered Accountants

(j) A continuous system of evaluation of performance in relation to the set objectives

According to the Seventh Five Year Plan, voluntary agencies are essentially non-profit making and non-partisan organizations. The criteria for identifying voluntary agencies for enlisting help in relation to the rural development programmes can be as follows:[7]

(a) The organization should be a legal entity.

(b) It should be based in a rural area and be working for a minimum period of 3 years.

(c) It should have broad objectives serving the social and economic needs of the community as a whole and mainly of the weaker sections. It must not work for profit, but on no profit and no loss basis.

(d) Its activities should be open to all the citizens of India irrespective of religion, caste, creed, sex, or race.

(e) It should have the necessary flexibility, professional competence and organizational skills to implement its programmes.

(f) Its office bearers should not be elected members of any political party.

(g) It declares that it will adopt constitutional and non-violent means for rural development purposes.

(h) It is committed to secular and democratic concepts and methods of functioning.

Finances

Almost all the agencies receive government subsidies either in the form of direct grants-in-aid from the national budget for welfare, or from special lotteries and charity sweeps takes or as payment for the purchase of services on a per capita basis. The greatest advantage of getting the grants is that it has enabled the organization to plan and regulate their proposals and services. In the absence of such grants a voluntary organization would face a certain amount of uncertainly regarding the availability of resources. Raising of funds from the public demands, time and energy of the organizations. Apart from other things these grants provide a good point of contact between voluntary organizations and the state.[8]

State Control

There is always a need to control the voluntary agencies even though they are for the general well-being of the community. The state has the responsibility to see that they do not misuse public trust and there is some minimum standard of social welfare services. The control is being exercised through:[9]

(a) Registration of voluntary agencies under the appropriate acts

(b) Regulating conditions of grants

(c) Publication and enforcement of minimum standards

(d) Inspection by grant-giving departments

(e) Guidance and supervision of branches

(f) Control over fund raising campaigns

Voluntary agencies viz-a-viz CSWB. As stated earlier, voluntary organizations depend on grants for their financial requirements. The Central Social Welfare Board having launched a large programme of financial assistance to the voluntary welfare organizations provides guidance and advice to regulate their working and even to set a certain minimum standard of services.

Role of Voluntary Agencies

Voluntary agencies have played an important role in providing welfare services to the vulnerable sections of the society—the poor, the wretched, the unprivileged and the deprived. The Reformation Movement of the 19th century created in its trail quite a number of voluntary organizations particularly for the welfare of women, children and also of the downtrodden. Even today organizations working for the welfare of women and children form a sizeable portion of the total number of organizations in social welfare. While in 1953, the agencies working for women and children formed a little over 50 per cent of the total number of agencies in the field of social welfare, in 1980 they accounted for about 70 per cent of the total number of agencies. The First Five Year Plan stated, "A major responsibility for organizing activities in different fields of social welfare like the welfare of women and children social education community development, etc. falls naturally on private voluntary agencies." Similar dependence on voluntary organizations was indicated by later plans. Therefore, in the first two decades after independence, the government adopted a policy of working with voluntary organizations for promoting the welfare of the people. These organizations were considered more appropriate instruments for carrying out the task of reaching the people because of their characteristics of flexibility speed, humaneness and innovativeness. In particular the role of the voluntary agencies can be analyzed into the following points:

People's participation

The most important role of voluntary agencies is to stimulate active participation of the citizens in matters that concern them and their community. The importance of people's participation as the key to all anti-poverty and social welfare programmes has been accepted officially but it is questionable whether the official system is capable of it. Voluntary agencies are generally capable of providing linkage between the official programmes and the beneficiaries. Voluntary agencies try to involve the beneficiaries in decision making implementation monitoring and evaluation of the programmes.[10]

Development of the masses

The voluntary agencies, through their specific activities come close to the beneficiaries and educate and train them in regard to their problems, the ways to solve these problems and the obstacles in the way of solving these problems. These agencies create the necessary awareness and develop a positive outlook among the beneficiaries. In this way, they play the important role of consciousness raising, awakening conscientising educating and development of human beings.

Organizing the beneficiaries

Apart from awakening and mobilizing the community, voluntary organizations play an important role in organizing the beneficiaries. There have been repeated calls that the poor and the exploited should organize themselves and fight to ensure their rights particularly their legitimate share of the national cake. This, in effect is a call to break the unjust status quo, to promote revolutionary change in the rural countryside and in the growing urban slums. The poor on their own are not capable of this. It is the voluntary agencies which try to mobilize and organize the poor so that they, by applying pressure, can improve the quality of the service and the attitude of the government functionaries.[11]

Development of socio-economic environment

A voluntary action may also be directed towards the socio-economic transformation on an area basis covering all the people in a given area or concentration only or a particular group of people normally neglected and in need of help. In this regard, voluntary agencies mobilize financial resources from the community and promote self-reliance. The role could also be to show how local resources could be used for self-development and to remove gross under-utilization of human and other resources in the villages/localities.

Providing of services

The voluntary agencies also play an important role in socio-economic development by way of providing certain services such as building up of infrastructure in depressed or backward areas, providing tractor hiring services providing or facilitating credit, supply of seeds fertilizers technical know-how, etc.

Professional and vocational training

A number of voluntary agencies are playing an important role in training a cadre of grass root village workers with the induction of professional expertise and scientific knowledge so that the poor (particularly the rural poor) may learn to depend on themselves and not depend on intermediaries. In this regard, a variety of vocational training programmes have been introduced even for the newly skilled and semi-skilled workers.[12]

To supplement government efforts

As stated earlier, traditionally it is the voluntary agencies in India which have been doing a lot in the field of social welfare in one or the other way. Even after forty years of planned development, the government looks up to these agencies for help in the implementation of various programmes of social welfare, rural development, etc. However, to expect the voluntary organizations to replace even partly, the official machinery engaged in development is expecting too much from them. Still there is no doubt that they play a supportive and complementary role.[13]

Experimentation

Though voluntary agencies supplement government efforts, they do so without compromising on strategies, policies and methods adopted by the government. They are independent enough to devise their own strategies and methods. They may set an example in the field of flexibility, initiative low cost techniques simple or effective methods and the ability to improvise.[14]

SOCIAL LEGISLATION

Voluntary agencies have a very important function in highlighting the legislative loop holes in social legislation and in ensuring that legislations like the Minimum Wages Act, the Abolition of Bonded Labour Act, the Protection of Civil Rights Act, land ceiling legislation, etc. are being properly adhered to however, only uncommitted and freely operating voluntary agencies can perform this function as repeated studies indicate.[15] They have highlighted the legislative loop holes built into the land ceiling legislation through which a whole troop of party functionaries got their ownership/tenancy rights registered and helped the informal tenants in getting their tenancies regularized in village records and by the *tehsildars* by identifying the name transfers of surplus lands and publishing such violations of ceiling laws in the villages and blocks with the name of the land owners involved and other details of the violators being made public. Thus, voluntary agencies have an important function of over-seeing the implementation of the legislations.[16]

LEADERSHIP ROLE

On the basis of above discussion, one can very conveniently conclude that voluntary agencies are playing a leadership role in a number of areas. These agencies are the real organizers which mobilizes and change agents for the poor. They are the eyes and ears of the people in certain areas and give reliable feedback and reach the voice of the people to the planners and policy makers. They activate the system and make it move and respond to the felt needs of the people.

Problems and Limitations

In discharging their functions, voluntary agencies face a number of limitations and problems. Some major problems are discussed as follows.

Financial problems

One of the top most problems of the voluntary agencies is the lack of financial resources. They depend on grants and contributions but most of them find it difficult to get regular grants from the government and to raise funds from the business community. Also related with this is the problem of misuse of funds. The money meant for welfare activities generally doesn't reach the beneficiaries fully. This is mainly due to the mismanagement and embezzlement of funds.

Improper network

There has been a mushroom growth of voluntary organizations but none of them has a nation wide outreach or network reaching out to every state and UT and certainly not to every district block or village in the country. This poses a problem for the government in depending upon these agencies.

Mostly urban based

Another weakness of these agencies is their improper concentration. The number of agencies which are located in the rural areas where the major job has to be done is very limited. A study of the comprehensive list of voluntary agencies maintained by the Union Ministry of Social Welfare and the CSWB shows that most of them are head quartered in urban locales and go out to work in the cities which brings in an appearance of 'Good Samaritan' like charity to their work in the rural areas.

Problem of co-ordination

Co-ordination and cooperation involve mutual consent of the agencies. Although co-ordination between voluntary agencies and state agencies is easy, co-ordination among the voluntary agencies themselves presents some problems. These problems are as follows:[17]

(a) There is overlapping of efforts in certain areas

(b) Because of the mushroom growth of voluntary agencies and the political patronage to some. It is often difficult to bring them on a common forum.

(c) Each voluntary agency has its own sources of funds. It does not like to pool or share its resources with other agencies.

(d) There is jealousy amongst the voluntary agencies which make co-ordination still more difficult.

Apart from this, it has been found that except for the co-ordination between voluntary agencies and the ministry of social welfare, there is mutual distrust between these agencies and other ministries/departments—which makes joint planning and delivery of goods and services impossible. The health, education, at rural development departments, both at the union and state levels, regard the voluntary agencies as unwelcome intruders into their terrain.

Governmental interference

Whereas, it is difficult to achieve proper co-ordination between voluntary agencies and some governmental agencies, on the other hand, a number of governmental agencies resent the governmental grants, which are accompanied by controls and interference. Some of the governmental agencies even join the dominant political party in the state in obstructing the work of the voluntary agencies.

Bureaucratic hurdles

The bureaucracy is generally hostile to the voluntary agencies. In the words of Professor Raj Krishna, a former member of the Planning Commission, "The condition for the growth of a large healthy voluntary sector will not in fact be allowed to be created by the power hungry and money hungry bureaucrats and dadas. Therefore, it can be safely predicted that a truly voluntary sector is not likely to emerge and grow in India. The sector would consist of the so called voluntary agencies which are simply agents of the local oligarchy and/or the bureaucracy and remains another channel for the misappropriation of funds".[18]

Shortage of trained and dedicated workers

Shortage of trained and committed workers has been the paramount problem of all the countries. In the words of Durgabai Deshmukh. "Several organizations have built up huge structures, many of them are laying unused for the purposes for which they were built. Many of them have developed cracks. It is not the funds which are most essential, what is needed is honest devoted workers....High principles of service must be retained by men and women with a zeal for service, empathy for the needy."[19] Low salaries, inadequate security, poor personnel practices and competing job opportunities in industry and business for the people with social work skills and low prestige and cited as the major causes for the shortage of trained and committed workers.

Domination by the elite

The pattern of administration of major voluntary organizations shows that the governing board members have high social, economic and political status. This is often so because the agency depends on them for the financial support that they can give, or get from the community and from government subsidies. Conspicuous by their absence are the representatives of the client systems who are the beneficiaries and consumers of the services.[20] The interpretation of needs and problems is more often than not done by the staff, whose values and competence can, at times, be questioned especially when they are untrained or semi-trained. For the agency to serve its purpose, there is a need to bridge the social distance between the elite board members and the clients.

Apart from the above discussed problems, there are numerous other problems which the voluntary agencies face. Another weakness in the working of the voluntary agencies is the absence of proper planning and strategies on their part to tackle the social problems. Moreover, the expansion of their own organizations is not properly planned. This leads to uncontrolled and unregulated growth of voluntary agencies and overlapping of their activities with other agencies and with governmental activities. Besides, there is no proper arrangement for the training of workers and organizers of the voluntary agencies. Some of these problems and the problems discussed earlier can also be related to the deterioration of overall moral standards in general and among those involved in these agencies in particular.[21]

The present day voluntary agencies in the country can be divided into two broad categories: the first are organized by such socially spirited individuals as group themselves and go out to work. They are well-educated and well-informed people. The other kind of agencies are those that help people chalk out and run their own development programmes. Most of the agencies fit into the first category, but most of them are prone to communal, political and to some extent even exploitative pressures which ultimately defeat the ideals they are wedded to.[22] What the country really needs is the latter kind of voluntary agencies that are free from any kind of pressures. Unfortunately, their number is small.

Properly organized voluntary effort may go far towards augmenting the facilities available to the community for helping the weakest and the most needy to a somewhat better life. It is because of the flexibility of the voluntary agencies that they can also go in search of new needs, new areas, bring to light the hitherto suppressed social evils, and give attention to the unprivileged and unattended. They can be fore-runners of change, and anticipate and take action to make the transition a little less painful. In the present situation, no regional voluntary agency can, however hope to succeed unless it comprises the depressed classes, the SC's and the ST's and also the people belonging to other sections of the society. There should be small committees at the apex which should sit together and review the programmes affecting the entire area of their work. Besides, there should be broad based people's participation.[23]

Co-ordination in the field of social welfare is as difficult as it is important. If larger numbers of people are to take advantage of social welfare programmes with less cost, since our resources are limited. It has to be ensured that any possible overlapping or duplication is avoided and gaps in services are filled through proper co-ordination among voluntary and public agencies at various levels—national, state and local. Such co-ordination among the voluntary agencies can be achieved by constituting co-ordinating councils at the city/district/State level. These co-ordinating councils should have the following functions:[24]

(a) Research in joint programme planning which should include research facilities and monitoring services with a view to decide what new services should be developed

(b) Rendering services to other agencies

(c) Co-ordinating programmes of various agencies with a view to bring about harmony and improvement in the standard of services of the agencies affiliated to a co-ordinating council, etc. avoiding administrative difficulties and overlapping. This would include:[25]

1. Working out the minimum standard of services in special fields.

2. A co-ordinated forum for arranging meetings and conferences with experts:

3. Starting model/pilot projects in new areas

4. Joint training and orientation course for the workers of the agencies

5. Providing the services of experts like nutritionists, accountants, social scientists, legal experts, engineers, etc. which otherwise the agencies cannot afford

6. Development of literature, information services and recruitment of staff

7. Joint fund raising through community chests

8. Maintenance and audit of accounts through a pool of accountants and auditors

9. Working on social legislation

10. Discussing common problems trying to solve them and bringing these to the notice of the Government for joint efforts to solve them[26]

Tasks assigned to voluntary organizations under the Recent Five Year Plans:

The Seventh Plan document states, "At present, the effort by voluntary agencies is rather uneven, and is mostly concentrated in urban areas. These agencies have to be stimulated to extend their programmes to rural hilly and backward areas. They would be encouraged to create public opinion against social evils like child marriage, dowry, illiteracy and atrocities on women. Sustained efforts would be made for increasing the age at marriage of girls and for improving the adverse sex ratio. There is lack of awareness about the existing social legislation to protect the interest of women. Voluntary agencies would be supported to undertake their rights and privileges. They would also be associated in extension activities."[27]

"The voluntary organizations would be involved in delivering the Message on preventive and promotive health and social and nutritive care for women and children."

"There has been inadequate recognition of their role in accelerating the process of social and economic development. These agencies have been known to play an important role by providing a basis for innovation with new models and approaches, ensuring feedback and securing the involvement of families living below the poverty line. Therefore, during the Seventh Plan, serious efforts were to be made to involve voluntary agencies in various development programmes, particularly in the planning and implementation of programmes of rural development."[28]

The Eighth Five Year Plan too has relied on the voluntary organizations working in the areas of women welfare, child development, nutrition and welfare of the SC's/ST's/OBC's and the handicapped. "Voluntary organizations will be encouraged and assisted to work in partnership with stage agencies. Increasing emphasis will be laid on the streamlining of voluntary action for the development of welfare services. The existing grant-in-aid procedures will be reviewed, streamlined and decentralized so as to minimize delays in the sanction and release of funds. The procedures will be simplified without sacrificing the principle of accountability."[29] Towards women welfare the plan pointed out to identify where the voluntary sector was weak, and stressed that "efforts will be made to promote and stimulate agencies to work in such areas". Similar strategy has been stressed in the areas of welfare of SC's and ST's.[30]

EXERCISES

1. Discuss characteristics of voluntary agencies.

2. Critically examine the role of voluntary agencies in Social Welfare.

3. Examine problems and limitations of voluntary agencies.

4. Write short notes on the following:
   (a) State control over voluntary agencies.
   (b) Voluntary agencies and people participation.

REFERENCES

[1] Chandra, Kailash, *Central Social Welfare Board—Proposal for a New Set Up*, Popular Prakashan, Bombay, 1974, p. 424 in Chatterjee, B. and Gokhale, S.D. (Eds.), Social Welfare—Legend and Legacy". and The Seventh Five Year Plan, Planning Commission, GOI, 1985, p. 317.

[2] Gopalan, Sarla, "The Central Social Welfare Board—An Experiment in Cooperation of Government and Voluntary Organizations for Welfare and Development of Women," in Chaturvedi, T.N. and Shanta Kohli Chandra (Eds.), Social Administration-Development of Change, Indian Institute of Public Administration, New Delhi, 1980, p. 269.

[3] *Ibid.,* pp. 271–272.

[4] Puri, R.B., "Central Social Welfare Board", in Chaturvedi, T.N., *op. cit.,* pp. 287–291.

[5] Gopalan, *op. cit.,* p. 272.

[6] *Ibid.,* pp. 272–273.

[7] Social Welfare, Spl. No. on the Silver Jubilee of the Central Social Welfare Board, Vol. XXV, No. 5–6, Aug–Sept. 1978, CSWB, N. Delhi.

[8] *Ibid.,* p. 293.

[9] Compendium–Second Training Programme for the Welfare Officers of the SCWB. Tata Institute of Social Sciences, Bombay, March 22–May 3, 1982 and Social Welfare –Spl. No. *op. cit.,* 1948.

[10] Kulkarni, P.D., "The Central Social Welfare Board—Promise and Performance", in *Compendium, op. cit.,* p. 71.

[11] *Ibid.,* p. 284.

[12] Kulkarni, P.D., "The Central Social Welfare Board–Promise and Performance", in Compendium, *op. cit.,* p. 80.

[13] The Seventh Five Year Plan, *op. cit.,* p. 306.

[14] Kulkarni, "The Central Social Welfare Board", *op. cit.,* p. 44.

[15] *Ibid.,* p. 298.

[16] Puri, *op. cit.,* p. 291.

[17] *Ibid.,* p. 292.

[18] Kulkarni, *op. cit.,* p. 80.

[19] Luthra, P.N., "Central Social Welfare Board—Its Role and Challenges", in Chatterjee and Gokhale, *op. cit.,* p. 422 and the Seventh Five Year Plan, *op. cit.,* p. 308.

[20] Rohatagi Shushila, "Role of Central Social Welfare Board", in Compendium, *op. cit.,* p. 308.

[21] Chowdhry, D. Paul, *Voluntary Social Welfare in India,* Sterling Publishers, New Delhi, 1971, p. 3.

[22] *Ibid.,* p. 35.

[23] *Ibid.,* pp. 35–36.

[24] *Ibid.,* p. 36.

[25] Excerpts from "The Role of Voluntary Agencies in Social Welfare Programmes in ECAFE Region—Bangkok, Thailand, October 1970.

[26] Singh, J.B., "Let's First Understand Them," *Yojana*—Spl. Number, Testing Voluntary Agencies, Vol. 28, No. 20 and 21, November, 1984. p. 47.

[27] The Seventh Five Year Plan, *op. cit.,* pp. 306–317.

[28] *Ibid.,* p. 42.

[29] The Eighth Five Year Plan, GOI, Planning Commission, New Delhi, pp. 395.

[30] *Ibid.,* p. 89.

13

Administrative Capability for Development

Most of the developing countries are involved in major societal changes. They want to achieve a secure place in the international community, to protect themselves against outside aggression. To preserve domestic order, to increase the rate of economic growth and to provide both psychological and material security. To meet these demands, the administration has to play a key role in the modernizing process.[1] Administration has to play a key role in the modernizing success or failure of development effort. There was time not long ago. When development planning gave no place to the administrative factor or when proposals for new development projects and programmes were considered only in terms of technical and economical feasibility, with no recognition being given to the importance of administrative feasibility.[2] Since the end the World War II. Administrative modernization has been increasingly recognized as an integral part of the development process. The ability to assume new tasks to cope with complexity, to solve novel problems. The modernization of resources depends on the administrative capacity based on increased professionalization, bureaucratization, modernization and administrative talent.

The developing countries require an administrative revolution in support of revolutionary changes in the economic and social fields. Public administrations must be recreated, renewed and revitalized to produce the changes and achievements required in the transformation of societies. This necessitates different kind and magnitude of administrative capability. The challenge and the task ahead is to devise and install administrative systems that can actually accelerate development and enable developing countries to make effective use of their resources. Dysfunctional and incapable administrative structures, Systems and practices must be replaced. Nothing less than dynamic organizations, resourceful management and streamlined administrative process will suffice. A new concentration on achieving goals and the ability to solve complex operational problems becomes indispensable. The administration for development thus requires a commitment and capability of implementing plans, programmes and projects. It must remove obstacles to action, mobilize manpower, materials and equipment, for example, erect a new facility, deliver a service, operate a programmer and it must do all these effectively with speed.[3]

As the past experience shows, no great achievement could have been attained without substantial administrative capacity. Even in the most favorable conditions. Rich resources, Self-sufficiency, austerity and self-sacrifice for investment, high literacy and so on, a number of societies failed to achieve their full potential or even make substantial success towards that because they lacked the necessary administrative capacity, Whether it is the building of large cities, buildings and public works or balanced exploitation of natural resources and producing and distributing other resources, a well-developed administrative system is essential.

ADMINISTRATIVE CAPABILITY DEFINED

In simple words, administrative capability means the ability of the organizations to carry out the required tasks in order to achieve the desired goals.

In a UN publication, administrative capability is defined as the management capacity of government or of the public sector as a whole, or the administrative capability of specific organizations or sets of organization, or the administrative feasibility of specific development projects or programmes. In any of these categories, administrative capacity is major and crucial factor in the success or failure of development efforts.[4]

According to Katz, "Administrative capability for development involves the ability to mobilize, allocate and combine the actions that are technically needed to achieve development objectives."[5]

Administrative capability is scarce as it involves programmes of training, civil service reform, reorganization and procedural changes in addition to activities, which necessarily divert the time energy of high quality personnel from other activities.

Public administration must be recreated, revitalized to produce the change and achievements in the transformation of societies. This necessitates a different kind and magnitude of administrative capability. It must show adequate capacity to set the major objectives of government, to ensure their consistency, to define the constraints within which the objectives are to be sought and determined and the basic organizational framework operate. Such is a policy-making machinery and part to be played by each of the major components of the government.

Measuring Administrative Capability

According to the orthodox school of economic development and public administration, both the concepts, that of development and that of administrative capacity for development may be defined in concrete terms. To them, development means economic development, and economic development means increase in national product per capita. The classical model of economic development may be expressed as O, I, and O/I in which O designates output (gross national production), I inputs and O/I productivity or efficiency, Economic development means increase in O (especially increase in O per capita). This is mainly achieved through productively (O/I) and through inputs (I). Administrative capability means the ability to mobilize inputs and increase their productivity or efficiency. All this can be measured in quantitative terms. For the country as a whole, the administrative capability, for development is measured by the performance of the administrative arm of the government in achieving maximum output, or the highest possible national product or national product per capita through mobilization and the most efficient (or most productive) use of inputs (or resources). For an individual organization or project, the administrative capacity is similarly measured by the mobilization and utilization of inputs to produce output.[6]

The above concept explained by the orthodox school is not sufficient and must be supplemented by other concepts. One of the most significant changes that has occurred since the World War II is the broadening of scope of both development and public administration. Development has become far broader than economic growth. The function of public administration goes far beyond the implementation of policy, Among the additional functions of the administrative arm of the government are its participation in decision-making at the policy level (i.e., policy-making) and its active role in forecasting, projecting and planning especially in the field of economic development.[7]

In the light of the above changes in the concepts of administrative capability and performance, the gross national product can no longer be treated as synonymous with output. The performance of an organizational system or unit must be linked with objectives. The administrative capability has to be examined from the perspective of management by objectives. In other words, it is necessary to use another indicator of performance effectiveness. By effectiveness is meant the degree of objective achievement or goal-achievement. Using effectiveness as an indicator, one treats administrative capability as the ability to achieve goals or objectives. Now combining all the aspects of performance, it can be said that administrative capability can be measured in terms of productivity, efficiency, effectiveness and profitability. In this sense, administrative capability means the ability to mobilize inputs and increase productivity or efficiency.

According to Norman Uphoff[8] administrative capability involves efficiency related to the conversion of inputs and outputs, with special attention as to how the inputs are used. Effectiveness relates to the production as to how the inputs are intended to yield certain desired outcomes. Innovation can relate to the whole process, but its key function is to get more outputs that achieve the desired outcomes. Efficiency deals with their achievement, but in extra-bureaucratic ways, especially involving inputs from the public so that the output of administration indeed matches-up with public needs.

The principal values or objectives associated respectively with these four performances are—rationalization, impact, adaptation and responsiveness, while the respective activities associated with them are: organization within the bureaucracy, bureaucratic linkages to the environment, planning activities to alter the administrative process itself and mechanism for providing feedback from the public.

These four kinds of performances can be viewed with respect to two dimensions (as shown in Figure 13.1):

1. The locus of administrative activity—whether activity occurs primarily internally within the bureaucracy or externally outside its confines and instead in interaction with the public.

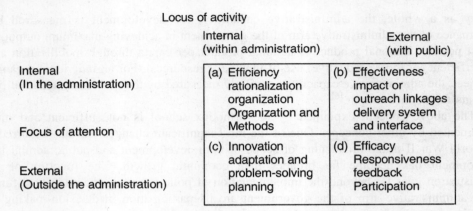

Figure 13.1　Four kinds of performances.

2. The focus of administrative attention—whether the concern is primarily with the bureaucracy internally and how it functions, or externally with regard to the impact achieved in public realm.

These four performances relate to the process of transforming inputs into outcomes as shown in Figure 13.2.

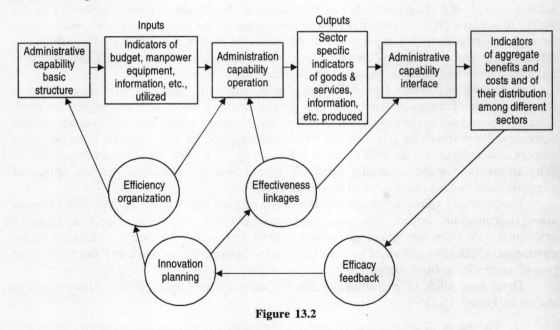

Figure 13.2

In the above sense, performance includes the following things:

(a) The acquisition of inputs by an organization or a system from its environment and the costs involved;

(b) The ways in which work is organized, the methods that are used and the costs involved in transforming inputs into outputs;

(c) The quantity and quality of the output, which must be appraised in relation to the goals and objects of the system or organization;

(d) The various effects, both beneficial and harmful, of the output, as well as the use of the inputs; and

(e) The side effects and the ultimate outcome of the activities involved.

The measurement or appraisal of performance is, therefore, a multi-dimensional and highly complicated problem. It is often not possible to deal with efficiency and effectiveness in precise and quantitative terms. But one can still determine, in general terms, whether an administrative system is actually performing well in the sense of what it is supposed to be doing effectively and efficiently, and whether it has the capability to perform. Still the appraisal is considered to be an integral part of the larger effort change, motivate and improve the administration of the development system. The appraisal should be a continuing activity, that is, a part of a system improvement strategy of successive approximations, the first approximation involving appraisal based on the best activity, that is, a part of a system. The appraisal should be a continuing activity, that is, part of system improvement strategy of successive approximations, the first approximation involving appraisal based on the best available information and knowledge and using to design immediate improvement action within existing environmental constraints, at the same time, taking steps to improve appraisal and design and modify constraints; the second approximation. Following from the first, and using new information and knowledge to improve appraisals and to design better action within the new somewhat modified environment, correcting mistakes made in the first approximation and so on.[10]

The performance of the administration in the above-discussed manner relates to the implementation of policies. As indicated earlier, public administration is today much broader than the above classical concept. Public administration has an increasingly important advisory role to play in policy making, and since the public administration system in the government provides such technical advice of specialists and on the experience of generalists, their advice has been given more and more weight by the political leaders. In fact, the way in which public administrators collect the data necessary for policy decisions, analyse the problems involved and present the pros and cons of selected policy alternatives, has a significant influence on the final policy decisions. Also public policies are implemented by public administrators. The way in which they put a policy into operation and the interpretation which they give to specific provisions in a policy may have far reaching policy implications. An appraisal of administrative capability under the prevailing condition of uncertainty and rapid change should definitely include an evaluation of the capability to render appropriate advice on major polices, make projections and undertake development planning.

Enhancing Administrative Capability

The work and the responsibilities of the Civil Service have changed profoundly during the 20th century, especially during and since the Second World War. First, much more sophisticated techniques are currently needed to match the increasingly complex problems with which government are faced. Hence, the Civil Service must draw on a widening range of professional skills. Secondly, the increasingly rapid pace of change has brought an unprecedented urgency into public administration, resulting in stresses and stresses and strains within the service, to which the younger Civil Servants have adopted better than their older colleagues. Thirdly, the work of the Civil Service is changing in kind; a far higher proportion of the duties have come to be run things or to be responsible for preserving the public interest in running things as a result, the qualities, sometimes called the managerial ones have become more necessary to supplement and sometimes to supersede, those associated with the other tasks and methods.[11]

To enhance the above capacity of public administration, the following functions must be performed by the administrators:

(a) The administrators must clearly know the basic values in the form of goal. They should assist policy makers in avoiding ambiguities and unclear points as far as possible. They should know who is to give interpretations of the executive or the unclear elements—the court, the legislature, the executive or the government servants. They should know what objectives are well within the achievement.

(b) Administrators must adopt a scientific approach and utilize a rationality model as far as possible. Social costs and social benefits must be taken into account while evaluating the overall performance. This can be done by the latest sociological parameters of measurement and through cost benefit analysis. At the same time, the administrators must recognize that for certain policies, cost and benefit do not enter into the picture. In other words, public administrators must recognize the political nature of policy making.

(c) Constant monitoring and examination of administrative performance must be carried out.

(d) Planning, in the sense of foresight, is essential to the improvement of government machinery. Ultimately, the goal any administrative reform programmer is the actual adoption of new mode of operation and of new agricultural structure. Forecasting of the future setting of public administration includes the political, economic and social environment and the probable availability of resources available to administration, as well as to its reforms or improvements.

(e) Development of alternative plans for innovations and reforms.

(f) Decision to proceed on the best feasible plan.

(g) In view of the multiplicity and complexity of both the organizations and objectives special attention should be paid to the co-ordination of objectives, policies and implementation. Inconsistencies of contradictions, wherever existing, should be checked.

(h) The human element is no less important. All training programmes for improving managerial competence.

(i) The element is no less important. All developing countries which are facing the challenge of accelerating socio-economic development depend critically on the capability, motivation and performance of the personnel in the public services. Thus, there should be a streamlined personnel system.

(j) Finally, there should be constant attempts at administrative reforms. An important factor influencing the efficiency and effectiveness of a public administrative system is organization (usually in the form of administrative machinery), and methods (management technology and procedures), commonly known as O&M. In every country, whether it is new or long-established, whether it is underdeveloped or highly developed, any programme can only succeed if it is supported by machinery and methods established under sound principles of public administration and adapted to the circumstances of the country concerned.

Requirements of New Bureaucracies

Hahn-Been Lee[12], in a study of Asian bureaucracies finds them inadequate for the new task of managing the great transformation, which the Asian countries are undertaking. He suggests some requirements of the new bureaucracies needed in Asia.

First, the new bureaucracies must quickly absorb at all echelons new indigenous talents who espouse more positive attitudes and actions regarding the country's modernization. Asian bureaucracies have the tendency to overrate their expertise and underrate the quality of their peers in their institutions such as industry, the military, the universities and the press. Adequate and timely injection of talents and energies from these organizations at all levels of the bureaucracy, high, middle and low, may avert some unexpected wholesale breakdowns of the bureaucracy at moments of violent social upheavals.

Second, recruitment procedures must be radically changed to facilitate the lateral entry of more broadly-oriented new blood from other sectors of the society. The monolithic method of recruiting candidates for the higher civil service at very young ages on the basis of some outmoded examination system, and then closing the channels of later inflow is at one obsolete and inappropriate to the conditions and requirements of the Asian countries under transformation.

Third, bureaucratic roles and initiatives in technical and developmental fields such as agriculture, health, education, and industrial promotion, urban and regional development should enjoy greater priority and regard than those in the traditional order maintenance fields such as internal security, financial and personnel management and ceremonious activities of the state. It must be recognized that such a shifting of priority and regard has delicate but far-reaching implications on the deep-rooted structure like bureaucracy requires some cumulative snow-ball effect of subtle, but concrete shifts and changers.

Fourth, organizations promoting special developmental programmer should be encouraged to emerge and grow. In some cases, some units might be created in addition to, and deliberate overlap with more conventional bureaucratic structures. This may sound unorthodox, but is often necessary. The conventional doctrine of economy and efficiency has too often been used as pretext for discouraging innovation and retaining existing bureaucratic privileges. There are many examples demonstrating the effectiveness of new organization becoming the initial haven of the much needed outside talents and serving as the launching pad for key developmental projects. The apparent diseconomy of overlap at the initial period would be more than compensated by the beneficial injection of new bureaucracy in response to social demand. Often such drastic steps are justified for the internal transformation and ultimately the very survival of the bureaucracy.

To conclude, it can be said the task of socio-economic development and of reform and reconstruction is of great magnitudes and requires large scale organizational efforts in all countries. It necessitates continuous attempts to improve the administrative capability of the vast administrative system. Harnessing the administration for the task of societal transformation has not been successfully accomplished in various new and developing countries. This is an enterprise yet to be undertaken with success. It requires a dedicated political and administrative leadership, streamlined administrative machinery; constant reforms, appraisal and feedback.

The multipurpose and multifunctional programmes and projects are the most important fields of development and performance in them provides the touchstone of administrative capabilities.

EXERCISES

1. Explain in brief meaning of administrative capability.
2. Write an essay on measuring of administrative capability.
3. Examine enhancing the administrative capability.

REFERENCES

[1]   Sharma, S.K., *Development Administration in India*, p. 3.

[2]   United Nations, Development Administration: Current Approaches and Trends in Public Administration for National Development, Dept. of Economic and Social Affairs, New York, 1975, p. 32..

[3]   United Nations, Public Administration in the Second United Nations Development Decade-Report of the Second Meeting of the Experts, 16–26 January, 1971, Public Administration Division, Dept. of Economic and Social Affairs, New York, 1971, p. 4.

[4]   Development Administration: Current Approaches and Trends in Public Administration National Development, *op. cit.*, p. 32.

[5]   Katz, Saul M., "A Methodological Note on Appraising Administrative Capability of Development," in United Nations, Appraising Administration for Division, New York, 1960, pp. 99–100.

[6]   Development Administration: Current Approaches and Trends in Public Administration for National Development, *op. cit.*, p. 32.

[7] *Ibid.,* p. 35.

[8] Uphoff, Norman, "An Analytical Model of Process and Performance for Developing Indicators of Administrative Capability", *Philippine Journal of Public Administration,* Vol. XVII, No. 3, July, 1973, p. 378.

[9] *Ibid.,* p. 373.

[10] Katz, *op. cit.,* p. 115.

[11] United Nations, Dept. of Economic and Social Affairs, International Seminar on Major Administrative Reforms in Development Countries, Flamer, Brighton, U.K., New York, 1973, p. 5.

[12] Lee, Hahn Been, 'The Development Role of Bureaucracy in Societal Transformation," S.K. Sharma (Ed.), *Dynamics of Development,* Concept Publishing Co., Delhi, 1978, p. 307.

Chapter
14

Citizens Participation and Development

In a democratic system of government, the citizens and the public servants are not two separate entities. Much of the success of public administration depends on its capacity to enlist public participation in the administrative process. Many of our developmental programmes like family planning, community development and social welfare have failed due to the lack of citizens' participation in them. Once of the main reasons for the failure of municipal administration to provide adequate civic amenities to the people is its failure to enlist people's cooperation. The fifth plan, having recognized the need for the people's participation in planning, states, "The involvement of the people and their elected representatives is a pre-requisite for effective planning. A plan which does not take into account the people's aspirations and preferences can have no operational validity, especially since its successful implementation can be ensured only if the majority of citizens, functioning as entrepreneur decision-makers in relation to consumption, savings, investments, etc. endorse the envisaged policies and programmes by their whole-hearted participation".[1] Thus, both democratic administration and development administration call forth people's participation in order to successfully achieve the goals of democratic socialism enshrined in the Constitution of India. It may be pointed out that democratic political system does not necessarily ensure democratic administration.

Popular participation in government and development is emphasized in the ideals of the United Nations. Article 21 of the Universal Declaration of Human Rights stipulates that "Everyone has the right to take part in the government of his country, directly or through freely chosen representatives. The will of the people shall be the basis of the authority of government".

The development process in a developing economy will acquire a fuller meaning if the citizens not only associate themselves with planning development programmes but also participate fully in their implementation. The Eighth Five Year Plan document asserts: "... it is necessary to make development a people's movements. People's initiative and participation must become the key element in the whole process of development".[2] Citizen participation, therefore, seems to be much significance for proper development administration, particularly in relation to measures, which require structural changes, It tends to bring the government closer to the people.

MEANING AND IMPORTANCE

Citizens participation has come to mean the direct involvement of citizens in the process of administrative decision-making, policy formulation, and policy implementation. In relation to development, it embraces all forms of action by which they participate in the operation of development administration. It refers to the role of citizen as distinguished from that of public servants (in their official capacity) in exerting influence on the developmental activities of government. People's Participation, says the Report of the Team for the Study of Community Projects and National Extension Service, "is not merely their providing a certain proportion of the cost of a particular work in cash, kind or manual labour. It is their full realization that all aspects of community development are their concern and that the Governments participation is only to assist them where such assistance is necessary. It co-operative action in solving their local problems."[3]

The UNRISD promotes the concept of people's participation as the organized efforts to increase control over the resources and regulative institutions in given social situations on the part of groups and movements of those hitherto excluded from such control. Economic and Social Council of the United Nations in its Resolution 1929 (LVIII) defines it in terms of involvement of people in contributing to the development effort, sharing equitably in the benefits derived therefrom and in decision-making in respect of setting goals, formulating policies and planning and implementing economic and social development programmes.

In practice, different countries attribute different meaning to people or popular participation depending on their socio-political system and policy choices concerning the importance of economic growth, use of scarce resources and the role of planning and market. These range from popular participation as a strategy to mobilize national human resources for development to genuine transfer of matters affecting their welfare.

Citizen participation is often used in conjunction with the term participatory democracy. It may range from the village level (construction of rural roads) to the national level (defence). It may involve only decision-making or extend to actual execution. Again, the participation may be direct (as in community projects) or indirect (through electoral representatives). Direct citizen participation is distinguished from indirect citizen participation, a means of getting things done. On the other hand, when it arises from the point of view of the groups able to participate, of obtaining a larger immediate share of the fruits of development.

Thus, participation covers every kind of action by which citizens take part in development administration. In a real sense, participation can only be explained when the citizens who take part in the development effort are fully conscious of owning responsibility. In a narrow sense, participation consists in a convergent action by which the citizen take part in the accomplishment of administrative services without, however, belonging to the governing or managing organs.[4] However, in a broader sense, participation comprises all forms of action in the form of decision making, implementation and evaluation. In the right setting, it implies greater decentralization of government power and resources.

Citizen's association with or intervention in the development effort of a democratic country like India has several advantages. First, it kindles the interest of local people in imparting a new thrust to programmes of which they are beneficiaries. In other words participation is a means of showing, by behaviour and action, that they are capable of assuming responsibility, Secondly, it is a means of ventilating their feelings and thoughts. Third, it offers them an opportunity to demonstrate their willingness to do constructive work and show that they are good citizens. Fourth, it is cure for the unresponsiveness and repressiveness of traditional decision-making mechanisms. It is a remedy to check corrupt practices. Another advantage of community-based programmes is that they be less of a financial burden on governments since they can be managed by volunteers or community-based workers. Moreover, citizen participation ensures that the accruing benefits of education, health and family planning programmes, for example, reach the residents of remote and rural areas.[5]

Participation of citizens in development efforts is gaining ground both through voluntary agencies and through non-governmental organizations. Perhaps this is an indication of the importance that issues of development have drawn attention to the perception of the citizens. Citizen participation differs from country to country, depending on their political, social and economic systems. In developed countries, participation is due to the citizens' having become conscious of their responsibility and wanting to be associated in some way or the other with the process of governmental decision-making and action. In developing countries, however, participation has not gained much momentum. The governments of these countries feel the need of prompt people's participation, because it helps them achieve their objectives. They initiate measures in this direction. Participation in both developed and developing countries has grown for three reasons.

The first is the expansion of government responsibilities. Governments have assumed increasing responsibilities in regulating the economies, planning for financial resources for accelerating development and exploitation of natural resources. In the social sphere they have the responsibilities in regulating the economies, planning for financial resources for accelerating development and exploitation of natural resources. In the social sphere, they have the responsibility of improving the well-being of the people and decreasing the level of unemployment and poverty and disease. Political development relating to the building of the nation state, modernization of development of law, strengthening of the judiciary, the legislature and the executive and other democratic institutions as well as many other broad aspects of development are among their other responsibilities. The government is today directly and indirectly a trader, industrialist, financier, and entrepreneur. To gain acceptance for its objectives and policies, particularly in the economic and social spheres, it has to rely on the citizens' willingness and understanding. As a result of the increasing function of the state and government's desire to seek the cooperation of the people for its new policies and decisions, opportunities for contact between government and the people have multiplied. Citizens have become very much active and asserted their right of being heard and of voicing their opinions at various levels of administrative action.

The second reason which has led to the growth of citizen participation is the explosion of knowledge and communication. More new knowledge in science and technology and education has been developed in the last thirty years than in the previous history of mankind. Today people have received an education which has made them better able to understand the problems of life in society and a training which has made them responsible to carry out constructive public work. With the explosion of communications, the means of information have become diversified. These help the citizens of a modern state to exercise critical control over its activities. They feel that if they wish to exert pressure on governmental authorities, they can be better heard through collective action. The pressure will be all the more effective if the group, which exerts it, represents a large number of citizens.

The third contributing factor in the citizen participation is the perceived failure of the bureaucracy to meet the growing demands of the citizens at the local level. A continuing struggle is called for against the biases to bureaucracy and technocracy, which are among the most widespread and persistent impediments to effective state support of participation. Against these tendencies, it is desirable that the people, through their own participatory organizations, acquire the capacity to control public officials and they themselves undertake many of the present responsibilities of the state.

These three factors—expansion in the functions of the state, explosion of knowledge and communication, and the failure of the bureaucracy to meet the growing demands the growth of citizen participation in the development effort all the more effective and challenging. In most development societies, democratic or otherwise, citizens seek representation of their interests beyond electoral participation: as tax payers, as users of public services, and increasingly as consumers or members of NGOs and voluntary organizations. Against a backdrop of competing social demands, rising expectations, and variable government performance, these expressions of voice and participation are mounting.

METHODS OF PARTICIPATION

The intensity of people participation is attributed to differing endowments of social capital, the informal rules and effective partnerships.

Social Mechanisms

The social mechanisms that constitute social capital (defined in terms of the degree of participation in village-level social organizations) and myriad forms of more formal non-governmental activity directly reflect the heterogeneity of demands and preferences in society. However, these non-governmental organizations (NGOs) provide services of high quality, but some suffer from serious inadequacies including poor in community participation, weak accountability and paucity of funds. In several developing countries including India, NGOs provide sixty per cent of primary healthcare services, and most agricultural services, low-cost housing schemes, and micro-credit. Similarly, in Cambodia, around fifty NGOs provide micro-credit to rural and urban entrepreneurs in the absence of alternative government programmes for poverty alleviation.

Some NGOs are created opportunistically to advance the interests of narrow and privileged constancies. Many others are civic education groups, advocacy organizations (Chip Movement), and professional and business associations (FICCI) that represent particular interests of seek to educate the public about issues in their collective interest. Similarly, locally based organizations, such as rotating credit associations, associations, farmers' associations, worker cooperatives, parent-teacher associations, and even religious congregations, are valuable not only for the role they play in building public trust. Associations and organizations that seek to work in public interest or promote the cause of their own members are:

(a) Employer organizations, trade unions, professional associations, etc.

(b) Non-governmental organizations, cooperatives

(c) Private voluntary organizations

Yet despite the fact that associations suffer from serious problems in articulating and pressing their members' interests or peoples' demands, these play a vital role in channelsing their voice and in creating capacity for participation in public service.[6]

Ingredients of effective institutions

Various models of people's institutions have the following ingredients:

(a) They are owned and managed by the users/stakeholders, producers or beneficiaries themselves

(b) They are accountable to the community

(c) They have the capacity to become self-reliant over a period of time

(d) They have the capacity to diagnose the areas, interact with governmental agencies in order to draw need-based local level plans, and to implement them in close cooperation with the administration

(e) They tend to bring about integration of various segments of the society for the achievement of common goals of development.[7]

Informal Rules and Norms

The presence of rules conducive to social organizations can improve people participation, but the absence of such rules do not necessarily mean a permanent condition. These can be generated by participation itself, and here public authorities and other formal organizations such as professional associations can play a contributory role.

Effective Partnerships

Encouraging wide participation in the design and delivery of public goods and services through partnerships among government, business, and social organizations can enhance their supply. For example, public officials in West Bengal and Tamil Nadu achieved a substantial improvement in management of irrigation systems through co-management of water resources by farmers. In several social programmes, many governments are searching for new institutional arrangements for public goods, which involve both the private sector and voluntary organizations.

However, it is observed that effective citizen participation does not come easily. It requires enlightened government intervention; including improving the institutional environment where in social human capital is created and strengthened.

PARTICIPATORY MECHANISMS

Mechanisms for Informing and Consulting

Informing and consulting mechanisms are widely used in areas of public decision-making. Public-private deliberation is not just desirable in such areas as health and agricultural production, but in fact critical to success. In many developing countries, such as India, Botswana, Mexico, and Uganda, by institutionalizing public-private deliberation councils (e.g., Standing Labour Committee of the Indian Labour Conference) comprising representatives of labour unions, industry and government, policy makers were able to get broad agreements on economic policy issues. Yet these mechanisms may not enable the government to be effective in the long run if its policies appear unresponsive to crucial societal demands. There is, however, a possibility that adoption of specific public services. For example, in Bangalore report cards administered by the Public Affairs Centre can provide valuable information about a public agency's quality of services citizens. Besides providing valuable information to public officials, for citizen and consumer consultation can introduce more transparency into the system.

Mechanisms for Design and Implementation

There is considerable scope for involving people in the design and implementation of public services and programmes. In education sector, for example, inadequate monitoring and supervision of local schools lead to poor return. There is compelling evidence to suggest that by increasing the involvement of parents and communities in school management it can improve its functioning. With the enactment of a statute in 1993 school development boards have been established in Sri Lanka to promote community participation in school management. However, effective involvement of parents in school management does not come easily. In Uganda, community training for parent-teacher association is being provided in several districts to ensure proper school management.

In the management of common property and natural resources, such as forests and wildlife, water sources and other environmental resources, citizen participation is of critical importance. Evidence also suggests that bureaucratic control over such resources has not only proved to be inadequate in many different institutional settings, but also in some public officials entrusted with the job of managing them. Recognizing the importance of sustainable development, NGOs and local communities are being extensively involved. The National Forest Policy (1988) in India embraces increased participation of local people in managing forests.

Similarly, to promote scientific use of land and water resources, farmers and labour are being associated in each command, watershed and catchments area in the development and management of soil, recovery of wastelands, minor irrigation and water resources in India. Government efforts are also directed towards securing people participation in the family planning, health, nutrition, education and community-based health programmes. Government also seeks the cooperation of the people in rural development and poverty alleviation programmes. For weaker sections and rural poor, development of women and children, social defence and welfare of the aged, etc., help of voluntary organizations and communities must sought.

And across Africa, Asia and Latin America, high levels of beneficiary participation in the design and management of rural water supply projects have found to be highly correlated with project success.

Nature of Administrative Action

From the point of view of contacts between the citizen and administrators, P.R. Dubhashi classifies administrative activities as the following:

    (a) Citizen contacting administration in order to pay dues to Government

    (b) Citizen contacting administration to obtain dues or money from Government

    (c) Citizen contacting administration for obtaining licenses and permits or getting legal sanction to his activity where required

    (d) Citizen contacting administration in order get property rights registered

    (e) Citizen contacting administration agencies for obtaining specific services

    (f) Citizen contacting administration for obtaining general services

    (g) Citizen contacting administration for obtaining specific individual assistance

    (h) Citizen contacting administration for getting general support and guidace.[8]

Thus, the nature of administrative action itself is of great importance to the relationship between the citizen and the administrator.

PARTICIPATION OF WOMEN IN DEVELOPMENT

"Women's participation in economic, political and public life was given special attention. Reflecting the different experiences and the best methods to promote it range widely. In practice, approaches and solutions to problems must be sensitive to local cultural traditions and patterns. Among the important issues with regard to participation of women are the following:

Women are increasingly becoming more economically active in many parts of the world and they contribute significantly to the family, community and nation in this way. In many parts of the world, there remain patterns of discrimination against women. Their exclusion from decision-making and many aspects of life is an issue, which must be addressed. A number of circumstances contribute to this problem. They were primarily caused by the under-estimation of the value of labour, particularly women's labour, including that based on sex, created quite unfavourable conditions for treatment of women as a worker and as a human and social subject. The exploitative economic structures and systems have consistently benefited from the abuse of women's labour being manifested particularly in such aspects as unequal pay, unacceptable work conditions. These activates resisted change even under the conditions of economic life and division of labour in modern societies.

The effect of such relationships manifests itself in several prejudices. Social traditions and customs in some areas have relegated women to an inferior position legally, socially and economically. A stereotype has arisen that women's biological role is a personal function rather than a social function. In economic relations, there has been a pattern of economic dependence of women on men. The exploitative economic policies and practices of multinational corporations in many cases have had a special effect on women. Women have also suffered from lack of education and skills for functioning in a larger society and economy than the home. In some instances, there is unwillingness to recognize the rights and freedoms of people to participate in public life, including women, as equal and some women also prefer to be passive object of a man's care rather than a responsible and self-reliant member of society.

The majority of countries nowadays have full guarantees of the equality and protection of men and women before the law. Many have constitutional guarantees of equality in their basic national documents. However, in many countries there is a gap between the provisions of these legal structures and the experience of women in daily life.

The process of eliminating material obstacles and of learning to practice equality can be slow and difficult and needs attention from men and women, from governments and communities. Action programmes, especially those adopted by the two world conferences of United Nations Decade for Women,[9] should be more rapidly implemented through legal codes and national policy reviews intensification of education of men and women; and enforcement of relevant laws. However, the legal protection of women's position and equality in society is to a large extent conditioned by the recognition of women's rights as worker, producers and social subjects. This relates particularly to women in agriculture who may not have such recognition in many countries. This may require changes in existing forms of social and economic organization.

Frequently, and particularly in developing countries, women are active in such informal sectors as self-employment, small industry, small-scale marketing, casual employment. However, they are often persistently excluded from equal participation in, and access to, the management and politics. These practices are wasteful and work to the disadvantage of not only women, but society as a whole.

Economic participation of women in national life is being repeatedly stressed as an important factor for overall social development, It should be consciously planned and included in systems of planning of national economies, as well as in long-term programmes of economic and social development. Action must also be taken in the educational field, information activities and cultural life to facilitate a broad women's participation in socio-economic activities.

Action is also needed with regard to economic institutions, government and international agencies, as employers, must set the example for equal and appropriate policy and practice with regard to employment and career advancement of men and women. The special and important role of trade unions should be fostered for achieving the necessary results.

Of critical importance to the whole issue of economic activity of women is the question of childcare. As a general rule, childcare must be recognized as a community responsibility, as well as a shared responsibility of both parents and institutions, and institutions, and facilities provided accordingly. Childcare institutions and their large-scale operation, in developing countries in particular, are a necessary precondition for the betterment of women, parents and families as subjects of social and community life. The promotion of a broad, deficient, socialized and participative system of childcare, is therefore, an essential factor of development.

Attention is also called to the phenomenon, which has been observed in more than one country. At the time of struggle for independence and nationhood, women are often actively involved and gain with the passage of time, however, there is often a tendency to return women to the home. This tendency should be guarded against by continuing campaigns to institutionalize and facilitate the full and equal participation of women in all aspects of life. The same is true of recessions and economic crises that deteriorate the position of, and lead to unemployment among women.

Education and training have a major role to play in facilitating the participation of women. Three kinds of education are needed education for all boys and girls up to a level of basic literacy which will enable them to be active and informed citizens, parents, husbands and wives, on-going education and motivation for both men and women with regard to the importance of full participation for both in social, economic and political life, and specific training for skills appropriate to women.

As to women's organizations, historically, these have been of two kinds: those where the membership was general policy matters, independence or national development, including the effort for equality of women; and those where focus of concern was women's issues, for example, marriage law, legal protection of women, and the right to political participation. On view is that if the equality of women is guaranteed in law, it is inappropriate to have separate organizations for men and women. The other view is that women's organizations or women' sections within mass organizations can serve some important purposes—mobilization of women on issues of importance, education of women in their roles and responsibilities to society, advocacy for women on issues already formally resolved, but not yet effectively practiced—such issues also can provide women important opportunities to participate in societies in which women traditionally have had little exposure.

Caution is needed in connection with this issue since diversity of interests and need among women can often be at least as wide-ranging as between men and women. The existence of women's organizations, therefore, should not be seen as a substitute to fuller participation in society. Although the conditions for the creation and activities of women' organizations differ from country to country, it is essential that these organizations enable and promote women's direct involvement in economic, social and political life, and that the organize and facilitate their broad engagement in self-management and other forms of popular participation.

REQUIREMENTS FOR EFFECTIVE CITIZEN PARTICIPATION

Effective citizen participation in development administration does not come easily. Several conditions have been laid down with a view to making citizen participation more effective Below are some of them:

First, and the foremost, participation requires that citizens who take part in the development process must be knowledgeable and competent. They should be able to express their opinions freely and frankly. Secondly, care should be taken to keep the citizens adequately informed of the matters in which they will participate, the nature of their action, the level on which it will occur, and so on. The information required or taking decisions has to be clear and precise and adjusted to suit the citizens for whom it is intended. Third, participation requires a well-organized communication network, which is adjusted to the question involved. Fourth, both sides, namely, the authority and the citizens, must demonstrate willingness to take on responsibility. Working closely with people often requires redefining tasks and responsibilities reallocating staff resources and developing new mechanisms for learning. Fifth, the state has an important role to play in enhancing the people participation. The World Development Report (1977) maintains: "Capable states are therefore likely to be those that strengthen and increase their efficiency of local organizations and associations rather than replace them.... To get users or clients to become partners, public agencies often must invest considerable time and energy in building ties with communities, in building commitment among their own staff, and in ensuring that minimum standards of quality and equity are maintained."

The role of government should be to facilitate the process of people's participation in development programmes and projects by creating the right type of institutional infrastructure—Panchayati Raj Institutions particularly in rural areas. Government can also support participation by safeguarding the right of people to organize, to again access to information, to engage in contracts, and to own and manage assets.

Finally, for participation to be defective, an important prerequisite is to make a practical survey of the environment for which it is intended to specify its proposed objective carefully, and to ensure that representatives of the administrative authorities who come into contact with the citizens have received a training which enables them to discuss matters with the latter. Striking the right balance between participatory mechanisms and enlightened government control is critical success.

In conclusion it can be said that citizen's participation indicates that there is a big gap between theory and practice. The notion of involvement of the people in the development process has by and large remained a myth. This is so in spite of several pronouncements made in the successive plan documents as well as in the policies and programmes putforth by the central and state governments from time with regard to involving people in developmental activities. Speaking of his experience. C. Ashokvardhan writes in an article: "While the bureaucracy, barring exceptions, tends to be autocratic, swayed by found notions to intellectual excellence and a certain broadness of vision, the political element castigates it as being too wooden, mechanical and stereotyped to respond to the needs and aspirations of the common man, much less to the vote bank which demands special cares and cajolery".[10]

On the contrary, in many developed and a few developing countries, the benefits of citizen participation show up in improvements in the process of public policy-making, in the delivery of qualitative services, and, in some instances, in improved rates of return. On the whole, one can say that the effective citizen participation requires enlightened government intervention, including improving the institutional environment.

EXERCISES

1. Explain meaning and importance of citizens participation.
2. Discuss methods of participation.
3. Critically examine participation of women in development.
4. Explain requirements for effective citizens participation.

REFERENCES

[1]   Planning Commission, *Fifth Five Year Plan* 1974–79, New Delhi, p. 131.

[2]   Planning Commission, *Eighth Five Year Plan* 1992–97, New Delhi: Planning Commission, 1992, Vol. I, p. 17.

[3]   *Report of the Team for the Study of Community Projects and National Extension Service*, Vol. I, November 1957, p. 3.

[4]   B. Dillon and M. Stiefel, "Making the Concept Concrete: United Nations Research Institute for Social Development Participation Programme", in Reading "Rural Development Communications, Bulletin 21 (University of Reading), 1987.

[5]   Geoffrey Mc.Nicoll, "Community-Level Population Policy: An Exploration", *Populations and Development Review,* Vol. I. No.1. September 1975, pp. 1–21.

[6]   Some examples of forms of institutionalized action in India are the Jamkhed Project in Child and Healthcare in Maharashrta, Bharat Agro Industries Foundation Programme in animal husbandry and social forestry, and Self-employed Women's Association of Ahmedabad.

[7]   *Planning Commission, op. cit.,* p. 17.

[8]   Dubhashi, P.R., "Administrator and Citizen: Some General Reflections and their Relevance to the Field of Cooperation", *The Indian Journal of Public Administration*, Vol. XXI, No. 3, July 1975, p. 329.

       *United Nations, Popular Participation in Economic and Social Development (New York: UN DTCD, 1986), pp. 32–35.

[9]   *Planning Commission, op. cit.,* p. 17.

[10]   C. Ashokvardhan, "People's Participation in Planning", *Indian Journal of Public Administration*, Vol. XXXVI, No. 1, January–March 1990, p. 92.

Bibliography

Almond, Gabrical A. and James, S. Coleman (Eds.), *The Politics of Developing Areas,* Princeton University, 1960.

Bansal, J.C. and B. Ghosh, *Project Management of Process Plants,* Chandigarh, Punjab University, 1985.

Bansal, Prem Latha, *Administrative Development in India,* Sterling, New Delhi, 1974.

Bartelmus, P., *Environment and Development,* Allen and Unwin, London, 1986.

Barthwal, C.P. (Ed.), *Public Administration in India: Retrospects and Prospects*, Ashish Publishers, New Delhi, 1993.

Basu, Ashok Ranjan and Nijhawan, Satish (Eds.), *Tribal Development Administration in India,* Mittal Publishers, New Delhi, 1994.

Basu, Prahlad Kumar, *The Policy, Performance and Professionalisation in Public Enterprises,* Allied Publishers, New Delhi, 1982.

Bennis, Warren, *Organisation Development,* Addison-Wesley, London, 1969.

Bhambri, C.P., *The Indian State: Fifty Years,* Shipra Publishers, Delhi, 1997.

Bhaskar Rao, V. and Arvind K. Sharma, *Public Administration: Quest for Identity*, Vikas, New Delhi, 1996.

Bhattacharya, Mohit, *Development Administration,* World Press, Kolkata, 1997.

Braibanti, Ralph (Ed.), *Political and Administrative Development,* Duke University Press, Durham 1969.

Chandler, Ralph C., and Jack, C. Plano (Eds.), *The Public Administration Dictionary,* John Wiley, New York, 1982.

Chapman, Brian, *The Profession of Government,* Allen and Unwin, London, 1959.

Chaturvedi, T.N. (Ed.), *Ethics in Public Life,* IIPA, New Delhi, 1996.

Chaturvedi, T.N., *Politics, Bureaucracy and Development,* Uppal, New Delhi, 1998.

Clark, W.C., and R.E. Munn (Eds.), *Sustainable Development of the Biosphere,* Cambridge University Press, Cambridge, 1986.

Cohen, John, and Norman Uphoff, *Rural Development Participation,* Cornell University, Ithaca, 1977.

Dey, Bata K., Bureaucracy, *Development and Public Management in India* (New Delhi: Uppal, 1978).

Dwivedi, O.P., *Development Administration: From Underdevelopment to Sustainable Development,* Macmillan Press, London, 1994.

Dwivedi, Onkar P.R.B. Jain and Dhirendra K. Vajpeyi, *Governing India*: *Issues Concerning Public Policy*, Institutions and Administration (Delhi: BRPC, 1998).

Edari, R.S., *Social Change*, W.C. Brown, New York, 1976.

Edmunds, Stahri, and John Letey, *Environmental Administration,* New York, McGraw-Hill, 1973.

Farazmand, Ali (Ed.), *Handbook of Comparative and Development Public Administration,* Marcel Dekker, New York, 1991.

———, *Modern System of Governance, Exploring the Role of Bureaucrats and Politicians,* Sage Publishers, Thousand Oaks, CA, 1997.

Frank, Andre G., *Latin America: Underdevelopment or Revolution, Monthly Review Press,* New York, 1969.

Gant, G.F., *Development Administration: Concepts, Goals, Methods,* University of Wisconsin Press, Madison, 1979.

Gastil, Raymond, *Freedom in the World,* Freedoms House, New York, 1989.

Hagen, Evertt, *On the Theory of Social Change,* Dorsey, Chicago, 1962.

Hanson, A.H., *Public Enterprise and Economic Development*, Routledge, London, 1972.

Harrison, David, *The Sociology of Modernization and Development*, Allen and Unwin, London, 1988.

——— , *The Third World Tomorrow*, Harmondsworth, Penguin Publishers, 1980.

Heady, Ferrel, *Public Administration: A Comparative Perspective,* 5th ed. Marcel Dekker, New York, 1996.

Hope, K.R., *The Dynamics of Development and Development Administration,* Greenwood, Westport, 1984.

Hoshiar Singh, *Administration of Rural Development in India,* Sterling, New Delhi, 1995.

Independent Commission on International Development Issues, *North-South: A Programme for Surival,* Pan Books, London, 1980.

India, Planning Commission, *Eighth Five Year Plan 1992–97,* Planning Commission, New Delhi, 1992, 2 Volumes.

Jain, B., and P.N. Chaudhuri, *Bureaucratic Values in Development,* Centre for Policy Research, New Delhi, 1982.

Kaul, Mohan, *Managing the Public Service, Strategies for Improvement,* Commonwealth Secretariat, London, 1995.

Kriesberg, M. (Ed.), *Public Administration in Developing Countries,* The Brooking Institution, Washington, 1965.

LaPalombara, Joseph (Ed.), *Bureaucracy and Political Development,* Princeton University Press, Princeton, 1963.

Lin, Wuu-Long, and M.G. Ottobiani-Carra, *A Systems Simulation Approach to Integrated Population and Economic Planning,* FAO, Rome, 1975.

Maheswari, Shriman, *Indian Administrative System,* Jawahar, New Delhi, 1994.

Marthe, Sharad, *Regulation and Development: The Indian Policy Experience of Controls over Industry,* Sage, New Delhi, 1986.

Mathur, Kuldeep, *Bureaucratic Response to Development,* National, Delhi, 1973.

———— (Ed.), *Development Policy and Administration,* Sage, New Delhi, 1996.

Mattoo, P.K., *Project Formulation in Developing Countries,* Macmillan, Delhi, 1978.

Mridula Krishna, *Project Planning in India,* IIPA, New Delhi, 1983.

Myrdal, Gunnar, *The Challenge of World Poverty,* Pantheon, New York, 1970.

Pai Panandikar, V.A. (Ed.), *Development Administration in India,* Macmillan, New Delhi, 1974.

Potter, David C., *India's Political Administrators,* 2nd ed., Clarendon Press, Oxford, 1996.

Rabin, Jack, W. Bartley, Hinldreth, and Gerald J. Miller (Eds.), *Handbook of Public Administration,* Marcel Dekker, New York, 1998.

Raksasataya, Amara, and Heinrich Siedentopf (Eds.), *Asian Civil Services: Developments and Trends,* Asian and Pacific Development and Administrative Centre, Kuala Lumpur, 1980.

Ray, Jayant Kumar, *Administrators in Mixed Polity,* Macmillan, Delhi, 1981.

Riggs, Fred W., *Administration in Developing Countries: The Theory of Prismatic Society,* Houghton, Boston, 1964.

———— (Ed.), *Frontiers of Development Administration,* Duke University Press, Durham, 1970.

Rogers, Everett, *Diffusion of Innovations,* Free Press, New York, 1983.

Sapru, R.K., *Civil Service Administration in India,* Deep and Deep Publications, New Delhi, 1985.

Sapru, R.K., *Development Administration,* Deep and Deep Publications, New Delhi, 1986.

———— (Ed.), *Environment Management in India,* Ashish Publishing House, New Delhi, 1987, 2 Volumes.

———— (Ed.), *Management of Public Sector Enterprises in India,* Ashish Publishing House, New Delhi, 1987, 2 Volumes.

Sapru, R.K., *Managing Projects and Public Enterprises,* Sterling, New Delhi, 1998.

————, *Public Policy: Formulation, Implementation and Evaluation,* Sterling, New Delhi, 1994.

————, *Indian Administration,* Kalyani Publishers, Ludhiana, 2001.

Sharma, S.L. (Ed.), *Development: Socio-Cultural Dimensions*, Rawat, Jaipur, 1986.

Sharma, Udesh Kumar (Ed.), *Dynamics of Development: An International Perspective*, Concept, Delhi, 1980, 2 Volumes.

Swerdlow, Irving, *Development Administration: Concepts and Problems*, Syracuse University, Syracuse, 1963.

Todaro, Michael P., *Economics for a Developing World*, Longman Group, London, 1977.

Tummals, Krishna, K., *Public Administration in India*, Vikas Publisher, Delhi, 1996.

United Nations, *Administration of Development Programmes and Projects*: *Some Major Issues*, United Nations, Geneva, 1971.

————, *Appraising Administrative Capability for Development*, New York: United Nations, 1968.

————, *Development Administration: Current Approaches and Trends in Public Administration for National Development*, United Nations, New York, 1975.

————, *Economic Performance of Public Enterprises: Major Issues and Strategies for Actions*, United Nations, New York, 1986.

————, *Enhancing Capabilities for Administrative Reform in Developing Counties*, United Nations, New York, 1983.

————, Organization, *Management and Supervision of Public Enterprises in Developing Countries*, United Nations, New York, 1974.

————, *Priority Areas for Action in Public Administration and Finance in the 1980s*, United Nations, New York, 1981.

————, *Role and Extent of Competition in Improving the Performance of Public Enterprises*, United Nations, New York, 1989.

Waldo, Dwight (Ed.), *Temporal Dimensions of Development Administration*, Duke University Press, Durham, 1970.

Waterson, Albert, *Development Planning—Lessons of Experience*, Johns Hopkins University, Maryland, 1965.

Weber, Max, *The Protestant Ethic and the Spirit of Capitalism, translated by Talcott Parsons*, Oxford University Press, New York, 1947.

————, The Theory of Social and Economic Organization, *translated by A.M. Henderson and Talcott Parsons*, Oxford University Press, New York, 1947.

Weldner, Edward W. (Ed.), *Development Administration in Asia*, Duke University Press, Durham, 1970.

World Bank, *World Development Report*, Oxford University Press, New York, Various years.

World Commission on Environment and Development, *Our Common Future*, Oxford University Press, New York, 1987.

Zartman, William (Ed.), *Collapsed States: The Disintegration and Restoration of Legitimate Authority*, Lyone Rienner, Boulder, London, 1995.

Author Index

Subject Index

Absolute nationalism, 20
Activity, 32
Administration of development, 2, 6, 8, 10
   capability, 5, 177, 178, 179, 184
   capacity, 177
   coherence, 27
   planning, 65
   process, 186
Agrarian
   economy, 28
   societies, 41
ARC, 91, 92, 97, 100
Area development, 9
Ascription, 19

Biosphere, 53
Brundtland report, 46

CAG, 39
Capital deficiency, 24
Capitalist economy, 114
Change-oriented, 140
Client-oriented, 136
Collegiate decision-making, 140
Cost-conscious, 62
CPM, 58

Debureaucratized, 165
Democratic administration, 186
Derision OLIM, 38
Desultory, 37

Developed
   countries, 19, 20, 27, 49, 50
   societies, 14
   world, 18, 21
Developing countries, 11, 48, 133, 137, 177, 191
Development of administration, 2, 8
Development planning, 123
Disguised unemployment, 23
Drop-outs, 154

Ecological balance, 51
Economic
   dualism, 21
   environments, 28
   planning, 69
EIA, 52
Environment administration, 46
ENVIS, 52
Excessive formalism, 138

Functional analysis, 36
Fused model, 43

Gandhian plan, 72
General administration, 136
Global warming, 49
Good programme, 34

Interference complex, 28